Voices Carry

ASIAN VOICES
A Subseries of Asian/Pacific/Perspectives
Series Editor: Mark Selden

Tales of Tibet: Sky Burials, Prayer Wheels, and Wind Horses
edited and translated by Herbert Batt, foreword by Tsering Shakya
The Subject of Gender: Daughters and Mothers in Urban China
by Harriet Evans
Peasants, Rebels, Women, and Outcastes: The Underside of Modern Japan
by Mikiso Hane
Comfort Woman: A Filipina's Story of Prostitution and Slavery under the Japanese Military
by Maria Rosa Henson, introduction by Yuki Tanaka
Japan's Past, Japan's Future: One Historian's Odyssey
by Ienaga Saburō, translated and introduced by Richard H. Minear
I'm Married to Your Company! Everyday Voices of Japanese Women
by Masako Itoh, edited by Nobuko Adachi and James Stanlaw
Queer Japan from the Pacific War to the Internet Age
by Mark McLelland
Behind the Silence: Chinese Voices on Abortion
by Nie Jing-Bao
Rowing the Eternal Sea: The Life of a Minamata Fisherman
by Oiwa Keibo, narrated by Ogata Masato, translated by Karen Colligan-Taylor
The Scars of War: Tokyo during World War II: Writings of Takeyama Michio
edited and translated by Richard H. Minear
Growing Up Untouchable in India: A Dalit Autobiography
by Vasant Moon, translated by Gail Omvedt, introduction by Eleanor Zelliot
Exodus to North Korea: Shadows from Japan's Cold War
by Tessa Morris-Suzuki
China Ink: The Changing Face of Chinese Journalism
by Judy Polumbaum
*Red Is Not the Only Color: Contemporary Chinese Fiction on Love and Sex between Women,
Collected Stories*
edited by Patricia Sieber
Sweet and Sour: Life-Worlds of Taipei Women Entrepreneurs
by Scott Simon
Dear General MacArthur: Letters from the Japanese during the American Occupation
by Sodei Rinjirō, edited by John Junkerman, translated by Shizue Matsuda,
foreword by John W. Dower
Unbroken Spirits: Nineteen Years in South Korea's Gulag
by Suh Sung, translated by Jean Inglis, foreword by James Palais
A Thousand Miles of Dreams: The Journeys of Two Chinese Sisters
by Sasha Su-Ling Welland
Dancing in Shadows: Sihanouk, the Khmer Rouge, and the United Nations in Cambodia
by Benny Widyono

For more books in this series, go to www.rowmanlittlefield.com/series

Voices Carry

Behind Bars and Backstage
during China's Revolution and Reform

Ying Ruocheng
and
Claire Conceison

ROWMAN & LITTLEFIELD PUBLISHERS, INC.
Lanham • Boulder • New York • Toronto • Plymouth, UK

ROWMAN & LITTLEFIELD PUBLISHERS, INC.

Published in the United States of America
by Rowman & Littlefield Publishers, Inc.
A wholly owned subsidiary of The Rowman & Littlefield Publishing Group, Inc.
4501 Forbes Boulevard, Suite 200, Lanham, Maryland 20706
www.rowmanlittlefield.com

Estover Road, Plymouth PL6 7PY, United Kingdom

British Library Cataloguing in Publication Information Available

Library of Congress Cataloging-in-Publication Data
Ying, Ruocheng.
   Voices carry : behind bars and backstage during China's Revolution and reform /
Ying Ruocheng and Claire Conceison.
      p. cm. — (Asian voices)
   Includes bibliographical references and index.
   ISBN-13: 978-0-7425-5554-9 (cloth : alk. paper)
   ISBN-10: 0-7425-5554-2 (cloth : alk. paper)
   ISBN-13: 978-0-7425-5555-6 (paper : alk. paper)
   ISBN-10: 0-7425-5555-0 (paper : alk. paper)
   ISBN-13: 978-0-7425-5746-8 (electronic)
   ISBN-10: 0-7425-5746-4 (electronic)
   1. Ying, Ruocheng. 2. Actors—China—Biography. 3. Theatrical producers and
directors—China—Biography. 4. Translators—China—Biography. 5. Motion picture
actors and actresses—Biography. 6. College teachers—United States—Biography. 7.
Beijing (China)—Biography. 8. China. Wen hua bu—Officials and employees—
Biography. 9. China—History—1912–1949—Biography. 10. China—History—1949–
—Biography. I. Conceison, Claire, 1965– II. Title.
   CT1828.Y55A3 2009
   951.04092—dc22
   [B]

                             2008023410

Printed in the United States of America

In loving memory of Wu Shiliang

In loving hope to Bayan

Contents

Acknowledgments

It is ironic that the kindness, wisdom, and assistance of so many was necessary to produce the life narrative of one single individual in his own words, but Ying Ruocheng's story could not have been told the way he wanted it to be without the contributions of the following people. I have been humbled by their enthusiasm for the project and I am deeply grateful.

Above all, of course, I must thank Ying Ruocheng, a great man who became my good friend. It is an understatement to say that it was an honor, privilege, and pleasure to sit by his side and listen to his remarkable story in his remarkable prose. Our partnership, which I discuss in the introduction, was a unique experience in my life. It is my sincere wish that the pages that follow represent his voice, life, and legacy the way he intended.

Ying Ruocheng had many significant partnerships in his life. The greatest, of course, was with his wife Wu Shiliang, who, as you will read, was missed by her husband every day after her death in January 1987. One of Ying's pleasures in narrating his life experiences in English was that it brought back fond memories of speaking English with her.

Another great partnership in Ying's life was with Arthur Miller—together they collaborated on a Chinese production of *Death of a Salesman* in Beijing in 1983. Mr. Miller had kindly agreed to author the foreword to this book, but he passed away in February 2005 before writing it. I am grateful to him for his four years of correspondence with me and his support of the project, as well as his deep affection for Ying Ruocheng. In the absence of his foreword, I have selected excerpts from his published book *"Salesman" in Beijing* to share in the introduction. I also wish to thank Julia Bolus and the late Inge Morath for their kindness, as well as John Jacob and Emma Winter of the Inge Morath Foundation in New York.

My deepest gratitude lies with the Ying family, especially Ying Ruocheng's daughter Xiaole (Felicia King) and son-in-law Jin Yijian (John King); his son Ying Da and daughter-in-law Liang Huan; his brothers Ying Ruocong, Ying Ruoshi, and Ying Ruozhi; his nephews Ying Zhuang and Ying Ning; and his sister Ying Ruoxian. They opened their homes—and their memories—to me, and trusted me with their contents (including fragile photographs and precious moments in their lives), for which I am forever grateful. Ying Ruocheng's "adopted sister" Stella Shen (Han Gongchen) provided a rich archive of documents and photographs pertaining to both Ying Qianli and Ying Ruocheng that were immensely valuable to the book. Chen Yanni (Jenny Ma) likewise offered materials and her friendship.

Many of the hours I spent with Ying Ruocheng at his home and in the hospital were also spent with his faithful nurse, Shao Derong. She took wonderful care of him, and her laughter eased his pain on countless occasions.

Several of Ying Ruocheng's colleagues at the Beijing People's Art Theatre contributed to this project by sharing their reminiscences and assisting me in locating relevant archival material. Most helpful of all was my "big brother" Yang Lixin, whose love and respect for his mentor—and protective care for me—solidified my friendship with Ying before our collaboration began and sustained me throughout every stage, even after his death. Pu Cunxin and Lin Zhaohua also extended kind support, as did Meng He, Fu Yunjun, Liu Zhangchun, Bai Yan, Su Dexin, Yu Wenping, Chen Qiuhuai, Ma Xin, Feng Liping, Qi Jihua, Yin Wenzhen, Xia Meng, and Wu Jianhua. Gao Xingjian, Ying's former colleague from both the theatre and the Foreign Languages Press, spoke to me about their experiences together during our conversations at his home in Paris in June 2006.

The staff of the Foreign Affairs Office at Beijing's Central Academy of Drama welcomed me back "home" every year, allowing me to maintain an affiliation with the institution while I continued the project. I am especially grateful to Gao Haiyun, Zhou Shaoyu, and Bian Baorui. My dear mentor Shen Lin offered lively encouragement. Special acknowledgment is due Han Yonggang, a stranger who befriended me and tried to help me gain entrance to the former Prince Qing's palace on Dingfu Road (Ying Ruocheng's childhood home, now a government office that is off limits to the public) and also led me through the grounds of the adjacent former site of Furen University and Furen Middle School. Delightful Yu Rongjun and his staff looked after me during my brief stays in Shanghai.

My annual residences in China would not have been possible without substantial financial support. The seed money for the first phase of the project in 2001 was provided by the Asian Cultural Council—I am grateful to Ralph Samuelson for his many years of encouragement, which go above and beyond the financial. Colleagues and administrators at Tufts University helped to fund the final phase of the project after Ying's death through small but significant Faculty Research Awards in 2006 and 2007, a Faculty Research Summer Grant in 2005, and ample time to write and conduct research during two Junior Faculty Research leaves. Much of my collaboration with Ying Ruocheng was facilitated by a generous Pacific Rim Research Grant from the University of California, Santa Barbara, administered by Tim Schmidt and the wonderful staff at ISBER in 2003–2004. Their funding also allowed me to hire several outstanding students to assist in transcribing audio and videotape. Graduate students Jason Scott and Adrienne MacIain and undergraduate Mandi Muehlbauer helped at UCSB, and my faithful team of undergraduate superwomen at the University of Michigan consisted of Katie Gleason, Su Panetta, Justine Silver, Elizabeth Bovair, Kristina Sepe, and Yiting Liu. Beth, Kristina, and Yiting continued with the project long after their official commitment, with Yiting taking on the particularly challenging task of translating Ying Ruocheng's prison notes scrawled in miniscule characters that had faded with time. Ying was delighted when I presented him with a group photograph of "his girls."

Sidonie Smith and Peter Ho Davies at the University of Michigan offered advice as I entered the new territory of autobiography. David Rolston and his fabulous family provided me with a second home in Ann Arbor—while Ena Schlorff provided the actual roof over my head—and Margaret Baker provided prayer and care. Tom Weisskopf and everyone at the Residential College made academic life a pleasure, and Coach Lloyd Carr and his entire staff at Michigan Football provided frequent smiles and hugs that helped me more than they ever knew.

At UCSB, President Henry Yang and his wife Dilling cheered me on, along with my dean, David Marshall, my department chair, W. Davies King, and my cherished friends in Asian studies, Ron and Susan Egan and Michael Berry. Among my wonderful current colleagues at Tufts University, I would especially like to thank Barbara Grossman, Laurence Senelick, Xueping Zhong, Francie Chew, and Jay Shimshack; my deans Susan Ernst, Kevin Dunn, Andrew McClellan, and Robert Sternberg; Provost Jamshed Bharucha; and President Lawrence Bacow. I am also indebted to the students in my graduate seminar on modern and contemporary Chinese theatre during spring 2006 and fall 2007, who read early drafts of chapters and offered helpful comments.

At Harvard University, Sophia Huang assisted with scanning photographs, while Tony Saich kindly examined Ying's prison notebook with me. Julian Chang kept the notebook safe for several years, and donated more time, effort, and advice to this project than I can ever properly thank him for.

Many acquaintances from near and far tolerated my creative questions during the course of my research, responding cheerfully with priceless insights and citations. These people include Robert Chi, Yomi Braester, Jeffrey Wasserstrom, John Weinstein, Carsey Yee, Siyuan Liu, Timothy Wong, Colin Mackerras, Daniel Abramson (via Robin Visser), Wang Ke-wen (via Ronald Suleski), Wen-ling Lin, Dassia Possner, Sharon Pei, Rosa Tsai, Fr. Jeremy Clarke, SJ, and Fr. Donald Glover, MM. I am grateful to all of them, and their efforts are reflected in many of the rich endnotes that enhance the reading experience of Ying Ruocheng's narrative. Particularly generous with her time and resources was reference librarian Chao Chen at Tufts University's Tisch Library. A special thank-you is also due Jonathan Spence and Calvin Chen, who carefully reviewed the final draft of the manuscript.

During a fleeting moment as I completed my graduate work at Cornell University, Joseph Roach (perhaps unknowingly) helped convince me that Ying Ruocheng's story needed to be told in the West. Pete and Amy Mangurian and Susan Sullivan offered immense support during the eight years of the project, along with my parents, siblings, and their families. As I entered the home stretch, Colleen Rua and Rebeca Plantier provided priceless friendship and advice—and Christopher Masters came along and suited up late in the game, leading in unexpected ways to the successful completion of this book. I hope they will be among the first to read it, and I extend to them my sincere gratitude and deep affection.

There are a few people I wish to thank most of all. Motivated by her own friendship and collaboration with Ying Ruocheng, Felicia Londré consistently wished for this book to materialize and did everything within her power to help make that happen. In 2001, Mark Selden accepted a long e-mail from me with documents attached, and graciously became my editor and advisor, sticking by me ever since. The fabulous Susan McEachern from Rowman & Littlefield joined him in 2006 and together they, assisted by Jessica Gribble, Janice Braunstein, Carrie Broadwell-Tkach, and Brooke Bascietto, saw me through the final stages of this book with patience, kindness, wisdom, and good humor. Zhang Fang jumped on board to translate the book into Chinese, and Liu Zhangchun helped facilitate a contract in China, making Ying's autobiography available to those who knew him best and loved him most. Finally, the very busy Ying Da provided immeasurable assistance, including polishing the Chinese translation to make it sound as much as possible like his father's voice. The title of the Chinese version of this book is *Shuiliu yunzai* 水流云在 .

My father, Manuel Conceison, viewed every transcript and videotape over the years, was the first to read the final manuscript, and listened to almost every detail of my experience with Ying Ruocheng. How I wish these two men who have had such a profound impact on me could have met.

—C.C.

Introduction

Claire Conceison

Occasionally in our lives, we encounter human beings who are so unique and compelling that we wish we could introduce them to everyone we know. We revel in the moments we are blessed to enjoy alone with them, and at the same time are eager to share their presence with others. I am sure there is someone in your life that fits this description.

For me, this person was Ying Ruocheng. It was not only because he was a hugely important figure in twentieth-century Chinese theatre and politics that I wanted others to know him—though he was. In an obituary, Tony Rayns described Ying as "a highly cosmopolitan intellectual and an exceptionally gifted actor-director . . . the last of the cultural movers and shakers produced by China in the early decades of the twentieth century."[1] As you will read below, Ying hailed from an important family and carried on that legacy, making crucial contributions to Chinese society during a century of political, intellectual, and social upheaval. He also made a name for himself on the stage and screen, and as a cultural diplomat.

At the same time, he was incredibly down to earth and a master of the English language, his adopted second tongue. A gifted storyteller with irresistible charm and a brilliant sense of humor, he was warm, unassuming, and slightly—delightfully—mischievous. His colleagues at the Beijing People's Art Theatre remembered him after his death in 2003 as a life-giving force; a kind-hearted magnanimous person with incomparable gifts of resourcefulness and creativity; a level-headed gentleman who never lost his temper; an eternal optimist in the face of bitter life struggles and a debilitating terminal illness; a rare renaissance man with innovative vision who could relate to people of any generation; a truly noble intellectual who nevertheless considered no task to be below him; and an extraordinary individual who could never be replaced.[2]

Foreigners as well as Chinese found it impossible not to fall under the spell of his charisma and authenticity. Professor Felicia Londré said it best when, after a long conversation with Ying about Eastern and Western theatre, she wrote in her diary: "What a wonderful man and brilliant mind he is . . . [he] hobnobs with royalty, heads of state, and international arts celebrities, yet it was like having a fireside chat with a best friend."[3]

Ying Ruocheng joined forces with some of the most impressive individuals in his various fields. As an actor, he is best known for his roles in Bernardo Bertolucci's films *The Last Emperor* and *Little Buddha*. He is also widely recognized for his performance as Willy Loman when Arthur Miller directed *Death of a Salesman* in Beijing in 1983. The following year, Miller introduced him to Dustin Hoffman at the Broadway performance of the play and the two actors compared notes about playing Willy on opposite sides of the globe, and a decade later Ying directed *Salesman* at the College of William and Mary. As China's vice minister of culture from 1986 to 1990, his feats included bringing Charlton Heston to Beijing in 1988 to direct Herman Wouk's *The Caine Mutiny Court-martial*. Ying was known as "one of China's most famous actors and a brilliant translator," fondly remembered for his savvy interpreting for Bob Hope in 1979 as well as his numerous literary renderings of classic plays from English into Chinese and vice versa. He made his mark as a director in projects like his partnership with England's Toby Robertson on *Measure for Measure* in 1982, a production that "achieved a level of excellence worthy of admiration and emulation anywhere in the world."[4] *Salesman*, *Mutiny*, and *Measure* all reached the Chinese public because Ying translated them.

Ying Ruocheng was not the only gifted member of the Ying family, though he was considered exceptional even in the eyes of his talented siblings, each of whom excelled in some form of academics, art, or athletics. His brother Ruoshi is a renowned painter, whose twin Ruozhi is a successful engineer. Another brother, Ruocong, is an accomplished architect; Ruocai excelled in women's basketball; and sister Ruoxian, the only sibling to settle outside of China, is a physicist at Columbia University. Ying Ruocheng's daughter Xiaole is an artist in Chicago, while son Ying Da has become one of China's most prominent celebrities as a film and television actor, television director-producer and talk show host.

I met Ying Ruocheng in 1991 when he was directing his translation of George Bernard Shaw's *Major Barbara* at the Beijing People's Art Theatre and I was a graduate student from Harvard University conducting field work for my master's thesis. I had the good fortune to spend time with him again in 1994 when he appeared as a guest star in Ying Da's wildly popular sitcom *I Love My Family* (*Wo ai wo jia*). After visiting him at his home during his illness in 1996 and 2000, I subsequently enjoyed the unique privilege of sitting by his bedside during the summers of 2001, 2002, and 2003 as he recounted to me his rich life experiences in order to publish this autobiography in English for Western readers. Each of these conversations over the course of a decade was indeed like having a fireside chat with a best friend.

An Uncommon Everyman

Ying Ruocheng was born into an elite family—his grandmother was a descendant of China's last imperial family and his grandfather was a high intellectual. But he hailed from a Manchu clan that was illiterate and disenfranchised; his grandfather was a convert to Catholicism; and he had eight siblings, two of whom died in their youth from tuberculosis. His humility, morality, and charity were the products of this Manchu Catholic upbringing. He spoke of his fellow prisoners from the Cultural Revolution—many of whom were poor peasants—with the same esteem and affection with which he spoke of great playwrights like Cao Yu or Arthur Miller, because he felt equally fortunate to have earned their respect and friendship. One of the most touching passages of Ying's autobiography is his separation from a rural childhood playmate at his family's summer home in Wenquan after her feet were bound. As a young boy, Ying did not fully comprehend the class difference between his family with the mansion on the hill and the children in the small dwellings below. And as an old man dying in his hospital room, he remained nostalgic for a time and place that transcended such divisions, a world in which a prince's palace could be the home where educators' children like himself romped and played.

Perhaps it is this simultaneity of greatness and simplicity—of intellectual acumen and dyed-in-the-wool common sense—that made Ying Ruocheng and Arthur Miller kindred spirits when they met in 1978 and collaborated on *Death of a Salesman* in 1983. In China, Miller directed his own play for the first time, and Ying appropriately played the role of Willy Loman, that iconic figure in American drama through which Miller reinvented the tragic hero as the common man. Miller regarded Ying as a genius because of his skills in translation, diplomacy, and acting, but also felt that Ying was able to embody Willy Loman in a way no other actor had before him, because he relinquished his "superiority" over the character and "gave up his own invulnerability . . . [thereby] acknowledg[ing] his affinities with the character and in the bargain transcend[ing] himself." Miller called Ying "a real pro, yet a man full of intelligent feeling who is ready to try anything" and observed that he "has a kind of absolute control that brings Olivier to mind—he simply does what is called for, easily, directly, effortlessly." Miller marveled at Ying's facility in translation as well as stage acting, saying, "I am spoiled by Ying's instantaneous and colloquial renderings. . . . [W]ith him beside me I forget altogether that I am not understanding the Chinese; he is but a breath behind the speaker, with not a single hesitation."

This admiration was mutual, as exhibited in chapter 6 when Ying Ruocheng speaks at length about his partnership with Miller. It was Ying's wish that Miller would write the foreword for his autobiography, but Miller died before the words he graciously agreed to pen actually materialized. Thanks to his detailed journal documenting their collaboration—published as a book titled *"Salesman" in Beijing*—Miller's high esteem and personal fondness for Ying are nevertheless recorded for posterity. The day the play would open in Beijing (May 7, 1983), Miller visited Ying and his wife Wu Shiliang at their home, and reflected afterward:

> I have never had this kind of relationship with an actor—primarily, I think, because Ying is also a scholar and approaches concepts passionately; thus he can draw feeling from ideas as well as from sheer psychological experience. . . . Ying Ruocheng has been my rock, a man of double consciousness, Eastern and Western, literary and show business.[5]

In *Beijing Diary*, Charlton Heston's book detailing his 1988 experience, he recalled that "Ying Ruocheng put the full weight of his personal authority and his creative capacity into our undertaking. Without him, *Caine* would never have sailed."[6] As vice minister of culture (under Minister of Culture Wang Meng), Ying instituted sweeping reforms in the arts at considerable risk. A few months after *Caine* premiered, prodemocracy demonstrations began in nearby Tiananmen Square, triggered by the death of Hu Yaobang, the man who had hand-picked Ying for his government post.[7] It was a dark period for Ying—his beloved wife had died two years earlier and the pressure of serving as a high-ranking official in the midst of such political trauma was taking its toll. It was not unlike trials his own father had endured before him, and Ying remained ever-mindful of this family legacy.

The Ying Century

Ying Ruocheng's father, Ying Qianli, was born in 1900, at the dawn of a century that his father, Ying Lianzhi, had helped to shape. Born in 1866, Ying

Lianzhi had risen from a clan of illiterate Manchu warriors to become a prominent Catholic intellectual. Among his contributions were the founding of both a liberal newspaper in Tianjin during the twilight years of the Qing Dynasty and a Catholic university in Beijing in the midst of turmoil, when the Qing had given way to unequal treaties with Western powers, rule by warlords, and uneasy alliances and civil war between Nationalists and Communists. Amid this political upheaval, artists and intellectuals were calling for a "new culture," including the use of vernacular language to reach ordinary citizens for whom classical Chinese was inaccessible, and the exploration of pressing social issues of the day through literature and art. Intellectuals influenced by the May Fourth Movement imported Western-style spoken drama to China (via Japan, where it was already being absorbed) and Ying Ruocheng would eventually devote his life to developing modern theatre in China and using it to promote international dialogue and understanding.[8]

If during Ying Lianzhi's lifetime China's future was uncertain, during his son's lifetime it was uneasy. Ying Qianli aligned himself with the Nationalist Party (KMT) and worked underground against the Japanese; he was imprisoned twice during Japan's occupation of China from 1937 to 1945; and he was whisked off to Taiwan when Chiang Kai-shek retreated there in the wake of the Communist victory in 1949. Ying Ruocheng, a freshman in college, would never see his father again. Ying Qianli's contributions to education in Taiwan continued the legacy Ying Lianzhi had established on the mainland, but Ying Ruocheng would not learn of his father's accomplishments until more than a decade after his death, when a neighbor's daughter his father had helped raise in Taiwan tracked him down during his first visit to the United States in 1980. Stella Shen (Han Gongchen), who knew Ying Qianli as "Uncle," provided the Ying family with a missing chapter of their history and many precious photographs.

By the time the third generation of educated Yings was coming of age, the nation's future was not only uncertain and uneasy but downright unpredictable. As events in China created a political whirlwind around him, a young Ying Ruocheng rotated through a series of Chinese and foreign missionary school environments and survived a series of erratic government campaigns under Mao's leadership and beyond. In chapters 1 and 2 about his imprisonment from 1968 to 1971 and in chapter 5 when describing his early theatre career during the 1950s, Ying mentions political movements such as the Anti-Rightist Movement, the Great Leap Forward, the Four Cleanups Campaign, and the Cultural Revolution, conveying a personal insight into the policies and processes of each of these events and their effect on the ethos of a people and the individual lives of Chinese citizens. His autobiography is a lens through which to see and understand twentieth-century Beijing, including the unique life of a Manchu Catholic family, the first fifty years of China's premier theatre company, circumstances inside a Cultural Revolution prison, increasing cultural collaboration with the West, and tensions within the upper echelons of the central government during the critical moment of spring 1989.

Having held a high government post when tanks rolled into Tiananmen Square on June 4, Ying did not feel free to discuss the full extent of his experience at that moment or his subsequent disillusionment, but he does allow us to stand with him in panicked uncertainty and sense the depth of the danger he was in. He lived his entire life knowing his family background and personal activities could be praised by the state as priceless contributions at one moment only to be denounced as counterrevolutionary actions the next. In addition to June Fourth and the aforementioned movements, Ying lived through the Four Modernizations, anti–bourgeois liberalization and anti–spiritual pollution campaigns, Deng Xiaoping's economic reforms of 1992, the handover of Hong Kong in 1997, Beijing's successful Olympic bid of 2001, the SARS crisis of 2003, and countless other transitions. Throughout it all, he was an influential guide to senior officials, fostering increased awareness and understanding of foreigners through both his recruitment as a secret agent and his public activities as an internationally beloved cultural ambassador. Truly, there has never been another Chinese citizen like him.

What to Put In and What to Leave Out

Ying Ruocheng was reluctant to discuss his efforts as a government informant in his autobiography. People who knew him personally, as well as ordinary Chinese who only knew of him as a celebrity, sometimes referred to him as a spy in conversations with me, so I inevitably raised the subject with him. He expressed concern about endangering others by sharing this information publicly and feared that readers abroad would not understand how he could have been forming deep friendships with foreigners living in China while also submitting reports about them to the Chinese government behind their backs.[9]

"How would average Western readers understand the mentality of young Chinese living under the Japanese occupation for so many years?" he asked me. "How would they understand that I willingly rendered services to the new regime? I don't want to sound like a hypocrite." In struggling further with this dilemma, he said, "On the other hand, I think I should let them understand the young people of that age, of that time, especially during the Korean War."[10] As a result, in chapter 2, Ying explains how he was first approached as a young actor by Peng Zhen (then mayor of Beijing) and asked to relay information from conversations with foreign acquaintances. What Ying Ruocheng describes as occasional dinners during which he offered relatively harmless facts that Peng could have gleaned from reading English-language newspapers was actually far more extensive intelligence gathering conducted with his wife that continued for most of his life. It is not hard to understand why he did not want to divulge these details in his autobiography, particularly in light of the questions he poses above. In order to understand why Ying Ruocheng and Wu Shiliang would serve as informants for the new Communist government, one must grasp both the atmosphere of the times and the profound personal and national legacy Ying felt called to fulfill.

Ying and Wu were first approached in 1950 by public security agents in their dormitory at Qinghua University, where they had become good friends with American Fulbright scholar-lecturers Allyn and Adele Rickett. Warning them that the Ricketts were spies, the agents sought Ying and Wu's assistance in gathering evidence to arrest them. The foreign couple subsequently spent several years in a Chinese prison and published a book about their experience upon their return to the United States titled *Confessions of Two American Spies*.[11] As Ying Ruocheng recounts in chapter 5, he and his wife met as juniors at Qinghua, during the year that the Chinese Communist Party (CCP) would finally unify the nation after more than two decades of division caused by civil war against Chiang Kai-shek's KMT and the reign of warlords that preceded it. During his final conversation with his son, Ying Qianli had expressed sympathy with the Communist cause and an intention to cooperate. Ying Ruocheng, like most talented young students of his generation, greeted the CCP's victory with excitement, and his Qinghua drama group helped to spread the good news as the People's Liberation Army troops arrived and liberated Beijing. Soon after Ying and Wu joined the Beijing People's Art Theatre in 1950, spoken drama devoted itself to the "Resist America, Support Korea" (*kangMei yuanChao*) movement of the Korean War. Under these circumstances, Ying Ruocheng and Wu Shiliang were hardly alone in regarding it as not only their duty, but also an honor, to serve the new regime using their English-language skills and networks with foreigners. Many Chinese were called upon in such a way, and Ying and Wu had exceptional access to prominent foreign residents in Beijing, especially British and Americans.

Their habit of entertaining these guests in their home and then writing and submitting a long report at the end of the evening did not cease during subsequent years—even after their imprisonment during the Cultural Revolution at the hands of the same government they were serving. Why did Ying and Wu continue working for Section Two of the Public Security Bureau throughout their lives? And why did they never choose to leave China after the Cultural Revolution, when they easily could have? The simple answer is that Ying Ruocheng loved China, both the China his grandfather had helped to build and the China from which his father had been forcibly exiled. He saw it as his special talent and his duty to foster understanding between China and the West—through theatre, translation, and politics—by staying in China and not leaving when things got tough. The older he grew, the more he enjoyed traveling abroad for special projects, but he always returned.

It would have been hard for Ying to walk away from his responsibilities to the CCP anyway. Both he and Wu Shiliang had longed to join the party their whole lives, but they were denied entry because of their suspect family backgrounds (*chushen*). Labeled as having "reactionary" families (*fandong guanliao jiating*), it was imperative to gain the trust of the "organization" (as they most often called Section Two) in order to join the party ranks. They finally succeeded in 1979, and, according to their son, it was one of the happiest days of their lives.[12] Ying Ruocheng was disappointed when, upon his release from prison and his return to the theatre, he was temporarily forbidden to continue submitting intelligence reports. But when he transferred to the Foreign Languages Press in 1975, he resumed this work, and continued it after rejoining the Beijing People's Art Theatre in 1979. In addition to whatever influence Ying and Wu felt their reports on foreigners had on CCP policy— or in terms of helping China to better understand the West—their activity also brought tangible perks. "My parents would tell me that where I live is special," Ying Da recalls, "[because] we could always get food that regular citizens could not get in their weekly and monthly rations, in order to entertain the foreigners who would always come to our home—at a time when it was outrageous to have foreigners come to your home."

Their son remembers that before each picnic or dinner party, agents from Section Two would come to their home and meet with his parents, and he was always sent to his room to do homework so they could talk in private. After the party, Ying and Wu wrote reports that were subsequently submitted and later bound together with their reports from several other occasions in packets of approximately twenty to fifty pages, labeled with a simple brown cover page bearing two large red characters—*dang'an* (file)—in the center and black characters below identifying the Beijing Public Security Bureau. Written by hand on each cover were the title of the report, the date, and the cataloging information, including the number of pages. The reports, handwritten in Wu Shiliang's writing, are signed "Wu Ying"—a code name composed of a compound with a character Wu that sounds like (but does not look like) Wu's surname and the character Ying.[13]

A brief example of the reports they filed is a twenty-five-page document numbered "Internal 67-28"—identified on the cover as an early stage of informing on a certain Yi Wensi, dated February 1964. It turns out "Yi Wensi" is Sir Richard J. Evans, British ambassador to China from 1984 to 1988 (during the negotiation of the transfer of Hong Kong) and author of the 1993 book *Deng Xiaoping and the Making of Modern China*. He was first posted in Beijing in 1955–1957 and then again in 1964, the year this particular report by "Wu Ying" was filed. This is most likely when Ying and Wu first befriended Evans, and they remained good friends during Evans's term as ambassador— Evans even sold his car to Ying Da in 1987 when he returned from graduate school in the United States just before Wu Shiliang died. Striking an altogether different tone, the title of the report his parents submitted to public security officials was *Yi Wensi zhanyi* or "The Battle against Evans."[14]

While Ying Ruocheng's official work unit remained the Beijing People's Art Theatre throughout his life (except for his brief assignment at the Foreign Languages Press from 1975 to 1979), Wu Shiliang transferred her official affiliation to the Beijing Municipal Public Security Bureau in 1958, retaining a title as creative secretary (*chuangzuo mishu*) for playwright and theatre president Cao Yu, primarily as a cover for her real occupation (though she also continued to work on specific projects for Cao and the theatre).[15] Those closest to the couple—their children, siblings, and some colleagues at the theatre—knew of their work for the government, but never spoke of it. Even now, Ying Ruocheng's siblings will not discuss it with anyone outside the immediate family.[16]

The example of Ying Ruocheng's lifelong career as a "spy" raises the important question of—as Annie Dillard and Jill Kerr Conway both phrase it— "what to put in and what to leave out" when writing one's life narrative. Reflecting on their processes of constructing their memoirs, several renowned writers included in William Zinsser's collection *Inventing the Truth* address this dilemma, with which Ying Ruocheng clearly struggled. Conway echoes Ying in her consideration of the fact that sharing certain things could "hurt some people's feelings," while Dillard chose to leave out of her memoir "anything that might trouble" her family. She adds that she "didn't want to kiss and tell."[17] Likewise, Ying did not want to publish anything in print that might cause problems for anyone, so there are times when he narrated events and then asked me not to use names, or not to include the information at all. He didn't want to kiss and tell either. He loved his wife deeply, as is abundantly apparent in his story, but there had been other women in his life. Though he shared some of this information with me, we chose to exclude it from his memoir. Those who knew Ying Ruocheng personally were certainly aware of his charm, but they also knew that his devotion to his wife was remarkable and genuine.

Several of the writers in Zinsser's collection recommend sharing drafts of one's personal life writings with those discussed in its pages. Ying and I were unable to do this for two reasons. First, the manuscript is in English, a language that many of the people mentioned cannot read (the Chinese translation is being prepared after the final edits to the English version are completed). Second, due to the celebrity status of both Ying Ruocheng and his son Ying Da, there was a genuine danger that if any of the text left our hands, it could end up pirated in print or on the Internet, in either its original English or a Chinese translation that did not sound like its author. So Ying and I kept our work close to the vest. As Dillard points out, "literature is an art, but not a martial art"—and so Ying and I refrained from mounting any personal attacks (or defenses) in his autobiography, though at isolated moments, opinions about certain people he encountered during his life are candidly expressed, and there are still sure to be strong responses to some material Ying insisted on sharing with his readers.

Finally, there is one consideration that Ying faced that the writers in Zinsser's anthology did not—namely, political censorship. Even when preparing his story primarily for Western readers, Ying had to filter information through a long-ingrained habit of self-censorship to avoid repercussions from his own government. As the project progressed—particularly after his death and in light of the growing inevitability of the text reaching the Internet in China—I carried Ying's burden of self-censorship in compiling and editing the manuscript, particularly as an authorized translated print edition is already in preparation in Beijing.

I leave it to Ying Ruocheng's future biographers to dig up the dirt, or to otherwise expand on the work I have done here. As his "collaborative autobiographer," I followed his wishes throughout our partnership while he was alive and have used my best judgment since his death to write and edit according to his stated intentions.

Collaborative Autobiography

When I began to work on this project in 2000, I immediately conceived it as a process of collaborative autobiography, assuming that this term had already circulated and many articles and books had been written about it. I discovered that a genre specifically defined as collaborative autobiography did not exist, though plenty has been published on biography, autobiography, memoir, and oral history. It gradually became apparent that collaborative autobiography possesses a liminal identity somewhere in between these existing genres, while at the same time presenting its own unique constellation of conditions—particularly regarding the relationship between collaborators. In my reading on biography and particularly on oral history, scholars employed dyads such as "interviewer/interviewee," "interviewer/narrator," "historian/ source," "historian/subject," and "collector-editor/narrator" to define the relationship that develops when one person listens to another talk about his life and then develops that narrative into writing. That is precisely what Ying and I set out to do, and yet I did not see our relationship accurately reflected in any of these terms.

As Ying's collaborative autobiographer, I am neither invisible ghostwriter nor full coauthor, although my participation in our collaboration was rigorous and far-reaching. This book began with a conversation Ying and I had on January 22, 1996, and ended with compiling and editing transcripts of forty-one audio and video tapes totaling more than one hundred hours of material recorded between 2001 and 2003; it also embodies seven years of research that is reflected in endnotes and this introduction. Our mutual goal from the beginning was for Ying to tell his story in his own words, in English, for the benefit of a global readership. In addition to Ying's narrative of events in his life, we taped our discussions about the structure and purpose of the book, inclusion or exclusion of various material, and the publication process. I found that my role became quite complex, far from my initial naive assumption that I was merely a scribe or a conduit for what Ying would have done had he been healthy enough to write his autobiography unassisted. I was ultimately responsible for how his life would be presented to a reading public that might never have heard of him—or might know him well. And I was aware from the outset that the cross-cultural, cross-gender, cross-generational nature of our partnership made ours an unlikely yet dynamic collaboration.[18]

My goal—knowing what I knew then about his career, his legacy, and his ability to captivate a listener—was to ensure that Ying had a chance to tell his story before he died. His goal, on the other hand, was to finish a task he had begun several years earlier on his own (after our initial conversation, he showed me twenty pages of text he had written in English about his June 1968 arrest and his first day in prison, which he had intended to one day expand into his memoir—those pages are incorporated verbatim into chapter 1). But his motivation for agreeing to collaborate with me went beyond that impulse. As an American, I wanted international readers to hear his story.

We agreed he would narrate his story to me in English, a language he was eager to speak on a daily basis once again. At the same time, I was an established scholar of modern Chinese history, literature, and theatre who could absorb the complexity of his experiences and help organize them for an uninitiated readership. Finally, he would have my companionship every day for at least one month each summer while I was in Beijing for as long as we worked on the book—Ying was confined for the most part to his home and hospital room due to his illness, and I was the only consistent daily presence aside from his housemaids and nurses.

These benefits to Ying of agreeing to collaborate with me on his autobiography were of course benefits to me as well. Listening to his family's history and his own personal encounters during China's turbulent twentieth century added a rich context to my knowledge of the political events that inspired them, and the privilege of spending time daily with such an engaging person was one for which I will forever be grateful. Ying and I had a friendly acquaintance before we embarked on his autobiography project together, but by the time I last saw him in August 2003, we were close friends. I was ready for the hard work that writing the book would require, but I was not prepared for the difficulty of sitting by the bedside of a dying man. The hardest part of reading his narrative for me is recognizing the passages that contain his words during the final days I spent with him.

In the foreground of my collaboration with Ying was always the man himself and my desire to fulfill his wishes for the project—thus, I often asked him directly about his intentions and his anticipated audience. But in the background were pressures of another sort. Ying family members and Chinese and American colleagues urged me to change the project into a biography, which I did not have Ying Ruocheng's authorization to do—nor did either of us at any time seek to produce an account of his life as it had been lived in its entirety and perceived by others (which is the task of biography). As the project progressed—and particularly after Ying died in 2003—I became increasingly aware that in addition to being an engrossing narrative as told by a man who had lived an extraordinary life and had a way with words, the book would also stand as the authoritative publication in English about Ying Ruocheng as a historical figure. Furthermore, it was inevitable that the book would circulate in Chinese as well. This required that his son, Ying Da, agree to polish the Chinese translation so that it would sound as much as possible like his father.

Above all, I sought to honor my contracted agreement with Ying Ruocheng—to help him tell his story the way he wanted to tell it. I have maintained the integrity of autobiography throughout the first-person narrative in Ying's own words, while also providing important context for the reader in this introduction and the endnotes. In so doing, I have situated myself, Ying, and this text squarely between genres in the interstitial space of collaborative autobiography. While having employed oral history methodology, the book is neither pure autobiography nor a transformation of first-person life narrative into a third-person biography. In this sense, the introduction, acknowledgments, epilogue, appendices, and endnotes provide the biographer's touch; but as a narrative, chapters 1–6 are clearly autobiographical—they are self-reflexive, retrospective, narrated in the first person (by a person still living at the time they were narrated), based on memory as their primary source material, subjective, occasionally inaccurate, and incomplete.[19]

Ying's narrative straddles boundaries between genres even further. As a subcategory of autobiography, memoir records publicly a life that was witness to or participant in significant events, often limiting its material to a period in the author's life that was particularly vivid or influential. It is selective and piecemeal rather than comprehensive.[20] In narrating his life, Ying covers a vast terrain—ranging from his grandfather's childhood to his own experiences from youth through adulthood and up to his impending death—which is a characteristic of general autobiography as differentiated from memoir. Yet he expands on certain periods (describing his three years in prison in two full chapters) while condensing others (detailing a distinguished professional artistic career spanning half a century in one chapter), which is certainly the territory of memoir. Like the memoirist, Ying Ruocheng chooses not to "begin at the beginning," but rather to start his narrative with what he himself regarded as the most influential moment of his life—his incarceration during the Cultural Revolution—and, again resembling memoir, his prison account is anecdotal rather than exhaustive, and unexpectedly witty. However, Ying widens the lens beyond the scope of most memoirs in an effort to provide an overall understanding of his life as it was lived and the legacy it strove to uphold. Thus, this autobiography as a collaborative text combines the methodologies of autobiography, memoir, oral history, and biography in order to present Ying Ruocheng's life story as he chose to tell it in his own words, framed by cultural, historical, and sociopolitical context provided by his collaborator to enhance its reception for the general reader.

James Hoopes reminds us that "we can never know everything about anyone, living or dead—[t]he historical record is always incomplete." Challenging us to regard history as "a test of our ability imaginatively to place ourselves in the positions of other people," he urges the oral historian to endeavor to evaluate and share collected material according to its usefulness.[21] Completing this book is, for me, the fulfillment of a promise made to

Ying Ruocheng, and it is my hope that in that effort I have been useful—both to him, and to you, its reader.

When you turn the page, my introduction ends and Ying Ruocheng's narrative begins. He first takes you to the prisons where he spent three years at the height of the Cultural Revolution, and then on a journey to his grandfather's past, before describing his own childhood and subsequent adventures that his education, career in theatre and film, and service in cultural diplomacy entailed.

If Ying Ruocheng had one unique quality besides his keen memory, it was his cheery view of life. He chided despair and embraced hope, finding humor and dignity in even the most humorless and undignified circumstances—behind bars in a prison and backstage both literally and figuratively during the most turbulent moments of China's recent political history.

PART ONE

THE ADVENTURES OF
PRISON LIFE

CHAPTER ONE

~

My First Year Behind Bars

I've grown a bit tired of the kind of autobiography that begins at the beginning and ends at the end. So mine starts in the middle. The most interesting part of my life, I'm afraid, is when I was arrested in 1968 and imprisoned for three years.

The Cultural Revolution was the most destructive social upheaval modern China has endured. My wife and I were arrested and thrown into prison as suspected spies of this or that foreign power. Our home was broken up. My sixteen-year-old daughter was sent to the grasslands of Inner Mongolia, while my son, barely eight years old, had to be left behind with my mother, who lived on a meager pension. Our home was ransacked three times by different Red Guard factions. There was, however, one thing I was grateful for: the time I spent in prison taught me more about China's true state of affairs than I have learned during the rest of my life.

I was sent to several prisons during those three years, and I was quite naughty, appointing myself to try to help other prisoners because it was clear to me that at least ninety percent of them were people who were falsely accused and never should have been arrested in the first place. I watched many prisoners take their own lives or go insane, and I became determined that that would not happen to me. I decided I would use my time in prison to learn as much as I could from the other prisoners' backgrounds and experiences, and that I would survive by using my wits and my sense of humor. Prison became an exercise in anthropology, and a kind of intriguing and amusing game.

I think if there is a higher purpose in writing this memoir, it is this: to reveal that a life that might be considered full of misery or make others feel sorry for you is not at all what I experienced. People have a natural tendency to prefer something more pleasant. Even the caveman invented games to amuse himself. That's what I did, too. And if this autobiography is worth reading or writing, it is partially for that: to explain how to spend one's time pleasantly in prison during the Cultural Revolution . . . one of those how-to books.

Kites to Cuffs: My Arrest

My imprisonment began on the evening of April 28, 1968. By that time, we had been in the Cultural Revolution for two years. We actors at the Beijing People's Art Theatre had formed our own so-called combat groups, which seemed the best way to protect ourselves from the cascading attacks of the era. The one I was in was called Smiling Among the Flowers (*congzhong xiao*), a line taken from Mao Zedong's poem "Plum Blossom."[1] Our group consisted of a dozen seasoned actors. For one reason or another, these actors were never in the limelight or publicly acclaimed, though everyone in the theatre business knew that they were the backbone of the company, without whom none of the popular pieces in our repertoire could have been staged. One youngster had a questionable family background because his father was overseas in Japan. My own father was in an even more objectionable place, Taiwan, so we were both vulnerable to criticism that they were spies. Since the beginning of the Cultural Revolution, the question of family background or one's "roots" had been emphasized, so all of us were careful to keep a low profile. Little did we expect that such behavior would earn our group a new nickname, the Old Sportsmen.

This nickname did not have the humorous connotation it appears to have. The trouble is, the word "sport" (*yundong*) could also mean "movement" in modern Chinese political jargon. So Old Sportsmen actually meant we were a group of old-timers who were experienced in analyzing political trends and avoiding pitfalls with dexterity, even though we were inevitably at the wrong end of whatever "movement" was the rage at the time.

Now, in the spring of 1968, all of us Old Sportsmen were unanimous in our assessment of the current movement—the Cultural Revolution, which had begun in 1966. Judging by all the rules of the past, the movement should have been coming to an end. To us old-timers, all the signs of the movement's end were in sight. In fact, editorials from the few approved newspapers still in circulation during the past month or so were advocating the line that we should not regard every cadre (party official) as a confirmed "capitalist roader" (*zouzipai*)—some of them could be salvaged and made to serve the revolution in the future. Since capitalist roaders had been the main target of the Cultural Revolution, such a new rendering of the jargon could only mean that the light at the end of the tunnel was getting brighter. Little did we imagine the Cultural Revolution was going to last another eight years.

By some unforeseen turn of events, the seafood market was full of delicacies that year. Apparently, up until then, all the best catch had to be handed in to the state in order to be exported for much-sought-after foreign currency. After more than two years of the Cultural Revolution, the fishermen finally woke up to the fact that government inspectors had been stripped of their authority and it was up to the fishermen to decide how to dispose of their goods. The irony of the situation was that during a nationwide purge to stamp out capitalism we were actually enjoying some kind of a market economy. My wife, Wu Shiliang, was pleased, and we invited a couple of friends over to enjoy a feast.

The two friends belonged, of course, to the same "combat group" as I. We even made the pretense of drawing up another big character poster to justify the gathering.[2] I can't remember what the purpose of the poster was supposed to be—probably to denounce someone or some policy that was bringing the whole country back to all the evils of capitalism (something we hadn't had a taste of for decades). By this time in the Cultural Revolution, we had worked out a routine for our combat group that seemed to meet the demands of the situation, and we were feeling quite smug about it. Every week or so, we would produce some kind of poster commenting on the current events and the latest injunctions from the party center. No one paid the slightest attention to what we were trying to say. By this time, the entire theatre company, like every other institution, had organized itself into combat groups of various sizes, some with a membership of only two combatants. In order to survive, these little groups affiliated themselves with the two major groups, who were constantly at odds with each other, trying to prove their own superior revolutionary qualifications. The more radical of the two factions called itself "the rebels" and labeled the other faction "the loyalists." Since we did not wish to be mixed up with either faction, we always signed our big character posters with a name of our own—"The Amused"—which did not amuse either side and repeatedly exposed us to further attack.[3]

The question remained, however, of what to do with our idle time in a period when it was impossible to perform onstage and the theatre remained closed. It's all very well to stay aloof from the factional squabbles, but we still wanted to know what was happening in the world and how to cope with the new directives from the Central Cultural Revolution Group. Suddenly, one of us remembered that as kids we used to enjoy making and flying kites, a favorite pastime in Beijing. Since we would certainly not be missed in the theatre company, it seemed a brilliant idea to pick up our childhood hobby once again. We went about it in earnest, too. One was assigned the job of going out to buy the necessary raw materials: much to our delight, we discovered the ideal paper—tough but thin—for our purpose. (The paper was produced originally for more erudite uses, namely calligraphy and traditional Chinese painting.) We acquired stems of bamboo next, and prepared to splice them for making kite frames. Watercolors and painting brushes were easy to get: they were actually sold everywhere because everyone needed them for political posters. Our greatest discovery, however, was the nylon twine that was so much better than the cotton twine we had used as children. We chose one of the members of our group to design and direct the others. He proved to be a true connoisseur, and we made some of the best kites I've ever seen. Finally we were ready for our debut.

After much deliberation, we decided to launch them in Tiananmen Square, a vast space with no electrical wires to get in the way. The first outing was a great success, and soon we became a popular part of the milieu. Beijingers, easygoing and tolerant by nature, enjoyed watching the kites and we were even applauded one day for bringing new designs. Not long ago, I passed through Tiananmen Square to attend a meeting and saw the square full of kite flyers—so our tradition has continued to this day.

I remember that on that fateful evening, Wu Shiliang and I were dining with fellow actors from our theatre who belonged to our combat group, and we were eating conchs. We had been flying kites earlier that day and I remember we were all feeling content because the people watching us in Tiananmen Square seemed quite carefree. The conchs, moreover, tasted wonderful and we all felt more confident than ever that the Cultural Revolution was coming to an end. Just then the doorbell rang.

I told my friends about how the local children had unscrewed the bell button and taken it away as a free toy, forcing me to run all over town to find replacements until I discovered that a coin inserted in the right place worked just as well. We all had a good laugh. I assumed the visitor was another friend coming by to visit. I had had a few drinks with the conchs and felt warm enough to go answer the outer door in my shirt sleeves.

I was surprised to see two strangers smiling at me. Then I noticed that more than a dozen neighbors were sitting on tiny stools a few feet away. Some of them, those with unimpeachable family backgrounds, had new red armbands pinned to their sleeves. All of them looked rather stern. I did not give it much thought. Ever since some of the more zealous of the rebels from the theatre company had come and ransacked my house on the pretext of getting rid of remnant articles from the old society (which might include anything from old snapshots to old books and various bric-a-brac), my neighbors had dropped their former friendliness and tried to avoid me. If nobody else was around, most of them would still behave as usual, but as they were in a crowd now, I couldn't expect that from them. The two strangers asked for my name and then, quite courteously, invited me to go with them to the local police station as they had a few points to verify. Since I only had my shirt on, I asked to go and fetch a coat. They assured me that the station was just around the corner, and I would be back in no time. So, without telling my wife or any of our guests, I left with them.

As the evening air was getting to be a little brisk, I turned down my rolled-up sleeves. The two strangers were on either side of me, and I felt the cuff of each sleeve held by the tips of their fingers. This was the first moment I suspected something was wrong.

There was a car waiting for us. They managed to maneuver me into it, again one on either side. I blurted out, "Didn't you say it was just around the corner?"

Their noncommittal answer was, "It's so much easier by car."

"What is it you want to verify?" I asked.

"You'll know soon enough," was the reply, only this time their voices carried more authority.

In about five minutes we arrived, and I was told to get out of the car. By this time, the courteous smiles had totally disappeared. I was told to go forward, turn left, or turn right by the two men, who took care to stay behind me, out of my sight. In the years to come, this became the routine way to take me from place to place, and I became so used to it that I eventually felt positively uncomfortable when I walked with anyone side by side. We walked through a small courtyard and I was instructed to pass through a doorway. As soon as I entered, the room was suddenly ablaze with flood-lights. Momentarily the spotlights, flashes of cameras, and other sources of incandescence blinded me. Someone expertly handcuffed me and I was forced to sign my name on a document, on the dotted line. I was in a daze during all these proceedings. All I remembered was that there were a lot of flash photos taken and the thought that flitted across my mind was, "They really take me seriously . . . "

Next, I was unceremoniously hauled off and sandwiched between two new strangers in a different car. The strangers were in army uniforms this time. It was only months later that I learned these people were not really soldiers of the People's Liberation Army, but were former policemen who had themselves been politically disgraced and had lost whatever prestige they enjoyed before the Cultural Revolution, and thus took refuge in PLA uniforms. This was still a time when even a PLA cap or some discarded PLA uniform jacket carried a lot of weight. By this time I was already handcuffed and the two men in uniform each had a hand on the back of my head to keep it down. I had regained some of my wits and realized they did not want me to recognize our destination, but I sensed where we were going. I knew Beijing too well.

I could make out that we were heading south, far from the center of the city, past Tiananmen Square, past the usually bustling downtown Qianmen thoroughfare and then, turning west, into the southwest corner of Beijing, but still within the outer ancient city walls. Staring at the army boots on either side of me, I came to the conclusion this was not just a kidnapping by a rival faction, but the real thing—what we usually referred to as the "dictatorship of the proletariat." Old habits die hard: even in the predicament I was in, I could not help trying to figure out what kind of car I had been taken hostage in. I decided it was an old vintage Buick, something quite rare for Beijing in those days. Why did they use such a car? Was there some hidden significance in the choice? I never did find out.

Needless to say, one question above all occupied my thoughts: *Why was I being arrested?*

At the time, my mind was still full of the Cultural Revolution and the factional infighting at the theatre company. I had always known that the rebels never trusted me, and no matter how hard I tried to stay out of their controversy with the loyalists, they persisted in thinking that I was the loyalists' strategist behind the scenes. But the movement had been going on for two years now, and they had had plenty of time to do their mischief. So why wait until now?

As the car sped onward to the west, I suddenly remembered something that had happened about a year earlier. Three or four PLA servicemen were sent to the theatre company, calling themselves the Team for the Propagation of Mao Zedong Thought and claiming leadership of the company by authority of the newly formed Municipal Party Committee of Beijing. All members of the company were organized into "study groups" and leaders were appointed to each. Similar teams had been sent to the other professional theatre, opera, and song and dance companies as well. The "study sessions" they organized required that everyone sit together every day and air their views. As people had nothing better to say than how they welcomed the Cultural Revolution, or how it was high time all the "baddies" were uprooted from the ranks of the party, it soon became extremely boring. There was nothing we could do but endure it. So, more than two hundred people, including actors, directors, set designers, stagehands, box office workers, ushers, and even the bus drivers had to crowd themselves into a hall to hear the rigmarole repeated ad infinitum.

One day the leader of the team stood up and exhorted us: "The reason our study sessions have become dull and repetitive is because we have forgotten Comrade Lin Biao's teachings, 'In training for battle, I want to see your bayonet draw blood.'" Actually, the way the team leader put it was, "Your bayonet must see red!" It sounded pretty gruesome when applied to the battle-field, but he was talking about theoretical debates.

He expounded his doctrine further: "After the proletariat has seized power, its central mission is not to build up the country, but to continue class struggle. This mission is distorted and adulterated by a number of leaders in power. Our task is to unmask these leaders and crush them. The only ones to see through their diabolical conspiracy are the Great Helmsman and the 'leftist' leaders who support him. It is therefore our duty now to unearth these villains, not merely to repeat what is written in the newspaper editorials!" The purpose of his exhortations was quite clear: unmask these hidden ene-mies, even those who were not in power, because they at least constituted the social foundations of those who were.

It was quite successful, as exhortations went. The first ones to be attacked were the former leaders of the theatre company. Not only were decisions to mount productions of foreign classics by Molière and Chekhov condemned as efforts at subversion, but even modern Chinese writers like Cao Yu and Lao She were censured. Then the attacks broadened to those who had had incriminating evidence snatched during the ransacking a few months earlier. A picture of Chiang Kai-shek, so-called reactionary books, and even snap-shots with some objectionable person could be used as evidence.

One hot and stuffy afternoon, there was a lull in the meeting, mainly be-cause we actors were all being denied the Chinese custom of a two-hour nap following lunch. All of a sudden, a somewhat feeble and hesitant voice was heard saying, "May I reveal something? I heard Ying Ruocheng say that the slogan 'One Divides into Two' should be applied to Mao Zedong Thought as well." At this utterance, all sleepiness vanished from the meeting.

I felt my scalp tingle and my adrenaline rise. There was quite a commo-tion in the hall, and someone shouted, "Whoever is against Mao Zedong Thought shall be crushed!"

This was the first time a bona fide defiance of Mao Zedong Thought ap-peared in our midst. More slogans were shouted out, and the chairman of the meeting quickly conferred with some of the people near him. He then ordered me to come forward and face the crowd for their cross-examinations. I did what I was told, trying to walk to my appointed place with as much nonchalance as I could muster. My mind, however, was working at feverish speed thinking of a way to get out of my current predicament. I remembered clearly the occasion when I had made the comment and I also remembered the theoretical grounds I had for saying it. When I finally stopped and faced the crowd, the last of the slogans had died down, and there was absolute silence in the hall. One could literally hear a pin drop. A rather frivolous thought flitted across my mind: this must be what Stanislavsky meant when he advocated "solitude in front of the crowd."

Before I could think further, someone in the crowd jumped up and demanded, "Did you ever say those words?" Another commotion erupted in the meeting, probably because most people felt certain I would deny such a terrible accusation.

When the commotion died down, I said with composure, "Yes, I did." There was a shocked silence, then more slogans and more commotion.

The chairman of the meeting was a fellow actor who had been on more or less good terms with me. He managed to hush the crowd and instructed me to tell everyone where and how I had said these things. I looked at him and realized the PLA propaganda team trusted and favored him because he had a good family background, including some senior army officers.

"Not long ago," I started, "the PLA propaganda team organized a visit of the theatre company to Peking University to learn how to take part in the Cultural Revolution. During a period of rest, we talked about what was happening among the students. Someone said that one of the students was under criticism and was condemned because he said we should adhere to the law of 'One Divides into Two' in everything, including Mao Zedong Thought. That aroused public anger, and the other students criticized him. I said at the time that his mistake was not in applying the law of one into two, but the way he divided it. Because the Chairman himself declared unequivocally that everything under heaven should obey the law of 'One Divides into Two.'"

I was interrupted at this point by someone shouting in the audience, "When did the Chairman ever say that?"

I replied calmly, "At the Plenum of the Central Committee in Wuchang, Chairman Mao said, 'Everything under heaven must follow the law of One Divides into Two . . .'"

Another voice shouted, "Do we have to divide Chang Kai-shek into two as well?"

I was so happy to hear the question put that way. This was a lifesaver!

I seized the opportunity. "In 1947 the Chairman gave an interview with the famous U.S. journalist Anna Louise Strong and put forth his celebrated judgment that U.S. imperialism was nothing but a paper tiger," I said. "And in 1958 at the Wuchang Plenum, the Chairman further expounded his thesis, making it clear that we should adhere to the law of 'One Divides into Two' regarding U.S. imperialism and all reactionaries, Chang Kai-shek included. He said, 'There are true tigers and sham tigers, there are iron tigers and bean curd tigers.' Mao Zedong Thought is no exception to this law—the question is how to do the dividing: certainly not into what is right and what is wrong, but to understand that one thing can be used in two ways. To the people, Mao Zedong Thought is a beacon leading them forward, while to the enemy it is a weapon to be used against us."

At this moment the agitated young man couldn't help shouting back, but the more careful people sitting on either side of him quickly pulled him down, because they realized that I was quoting the Chairman, while he was indulging in outrageous, even treasonable, talk.

What followed was something I would never have expected. Two of the elder people, who as a rule never spoke up on such public occasions, now stood up to defend me, bearing witness that they were present when all this happened, and that it had happened just as I said.

Finally, the man with the feeble voice who was the first to reveal my reactionary words stood up and admitted that everything was just as I said. After another lull in the meeting, the acting chairman said to me, "You may go back to your seat now."

In retrospect, I had saved myself with a bit of twisted sophistry and illogical dialectics.

My New Home

I was still immersed in my memory of that event of the previous year when the car screeched to a stop.

We had arrived.

Having reached our destination so quickly, I realized that we were still within the confines of the ancient Beijing city walls, and for some reason that seemed to give me great consolation. When I was taken out of the car, I saw a colossal building in front of me, of indeterminate color in the darkness. The windows were all dimly lit in order to save electricity. I was taken to a narrow room with a counter. My handcuffs were removed, as were my watch, my fountain pen, some coins, and my keys. The uniformed man behind the counter meticulously jotted down every item on an official-looking form. Then the two men who had brought me in the car left and a younger man took over. The first thing he did was to ask me to hand over my belt, something I learned later was required of every prisoner on arrival as a deterrent against attempting escape. Before the introduction of Western-style trousers, people wore loose baggy pantaloons. Without a belt to tighten them at the waist, the whole caboodle would slip down to one's ankles, so the prisoner had to hold onto his trousers, making any attempted escape difficult, and generally compromising his decency and dignity—no right-minded Chinese would be seen running around holding his trousers. Luckily, I had worn the Western style that fastened in front.

After I was divested of my belt, the young man pointed to the door and gestured to me to go forward, with him following behind. We entered a huge building that was in semidarkness and I was ordered to go up the stairs, which I could hardly see. At the third floor, I was told to turn right, and the young man took out a set of keys. He opened the lock on the iron bolt, and gestured to me to enter. By this time I could make out the corridor ahead, with more doors on either side. We stopped in front of one of the doors and after it was opened up, I was pushed inside. The stench of human flesh hit me like a solid wall, and I was feeling quite cold in only my shirt sleeves.

"Don't you have any bedding with you?" the young man asked. I shook my head.

This was when I noticed that he was careful to keep himself outside the cell, because of the stench no doubt. He grunted, closed the door, bolted it from the outside, and left.

I looked around the room. It was more or less square, roughly five meters by five meters. Directly facing the door at the other end of the room was a window, under which there was a galvanized iron pail. On either side of the passage were raised low platforms, packed with people like sardines. Since they were all lying with their heads toward the center of the room, and there was an electric bulb hanging from the ceiling giving off some weak light, I could make a quick count. On one side, there were ten people, and on the other nine. I was obviously put into this cell to make the numbers balanced, ten on each side.

The young man returned with a shapeless dirty quilt, which he threw on the floor. Upon his entrance, everybody pretended to be asleep, so he had to prod two of them awake so they could make a little space for me to lie down. This was easier said than done, because even on the nine-person side, there was simply no room to spare. They each, in turn, had to push the next one over to make space, and the pushing went on in the manner of dominoes. Finally a small space was cleared for me.

The young man ordered me to lie down and left. After a lot of clumsy wiggling, I finally managed to lie down. I prodded the man sleeping beside me and asked if there were any pillows.

He didn't answer, pointing at the door. When my eyes adjusted to the darkness, I saw a small aperture, obviously put there for the guards to observe the room. I realized that the guard must still be there in case, as a newcomer, I was up to some mischief. My neighbor, still without a word, helped me take off my trousers and shoes, and rolled them up into a neat bundle to rest my head on. It wasn't very comfortable, but it did serve as my pillow for at least a week.

There was simply not enough space for me to lie on my back. Sleeping sideways was the only option, but I had to remember to keep my legs straight, which took a lot of training to do, because our legs naturally bend when we sleep sideways. Months later, I procured the supplies to make a graded ruler: a piece of paper, pen and ink, and a copy of *Quotations from Chairman Mao*, where on the flyleaf the publishers had very obligingly provided the exact measurements of the size of the book. According to my measurements and computing, the space allotted to each of us was thirty-six centimeters, equivalent to less than fifteen inches. To be fair, as my cellmates told me, it wasn't always this crowded. When they arrived at the end of the Four Cleanups Movement, each cell only had a dozen prisoners.[4] This crowd of twenty had been squeezed into the cells starting with the Cultural Revolution.

Inevitably my thoughts returned to myself. The big question remained, of course, why was I arrested? I rejected one idea after another, until my mind was numb. I remembered I had five brothers, and our names were all similar. Could I have been mistaken for one of them? I rejected the thought nearly as soon as it occurred. I had already enjoyed some reputation as an actor and my brothers were each doing well in their professions, so they couldn't have mixed us up.

At that moment, I did not worry too much about my wife and children. Wu Shiliang had a good job, and she was as a rule a rather quiet person. Certainly she and the children would be fine for the time being. I would not know until a year later that she had also been arrested and imprisoned that same evening.

Then a new thought struck me: I will need all my wits tomorrow, so I had better get some rest. The alcohol I had consumed with the conchs at dinner must have helped, for I soon fell asleep.

The next morning, I was awakened by the sound of a sharp whistle from the corridor. My neighbors, amid grunts and yawns, began to get up. There was, however, a discordant sound, something I had heard throughout the night—the sound of shackles and chains. Now that I was fully awake, I could make out who it was. He was younger than the others, in his thirties or so, though it was difficult to judge because none of the prisoners had had a haircut or a shave for ages. There was something strange about this man—he was smiling. At first I thought it was just a habitual expression on his face, but when one of the guards opened our door and gave orders for us to relieve ourselves, I could see his expression change into one of contempt and defiance—apparently it was his duty to carry the full pail to the lavatory. With his shackles and chains, and the full pail of urine, he made quite a racket in the otherwise silent corridor.

As we approached the end of the corridor where the lavatory was situated, the guard escorted out another dozen prisoners headed for the next door. Later I found out it was the room where water taps were provided. We were then told brusquely to enter, and the door locked again from the outside.

I looked around and I must admit I was surprised to find the area so clean and tidy. There were about ten places to squat and defecate, with water flushing automatically every few minutes. My neighbor squatting beside me whispered, "You're lucky to be put in here. This is a new prison, built less than two years ago.[5] They say the guy who designed it is locked up here as well. Serves him right." Apparently, the lavatory was the only safe place for a whispered conversation, the guards either feeling it was beneath their position to eavesdrop in such surroundings or being too busy getting the next group ready.

When we were herded into the room next door, everyone began to wash up using their towels and soap. I realized I had nothing with me, so I took out my hanky and tried to wet my face. Just then I discovered a sliver of yellow soap near my hand that could only have been put there by my neighbor moments ago. I gave him a look of gratitude, but received no acknowledgment. That sliver of soap meant a lot to me, and in a way restored my faith in human nature.

After our return to the cell, there was nothing for us to do but wait. I was still too much in a daze and busy with my own thoughts to notice anything.

Suddenly one of my cellmates whispered hoarsely, "They're here!"

Immediately the whole cell came alive with anticipation. A few moments later I realized what had caused the commotion—food.

A muffled voice from the corridor said, "Down with it!" followed by the sound of a heavy barrel being laid on the floor.

"Thin as usual," someone muttered. I supposed he was referring to the contents of the barrel, but how he could make such a judgment just from the sound of it touching the floor was beyond me.

Days passed before I became as adept as everyone else with my senses of hearing and smell. I discovered that with prolonged stretches of hunger, one's senses can be developed to an uncanny degree of sensitivity. This may be due to a survival instinct inherent in every human being. Little by little, I found myself pricking up my ears every time food was due in half an hour or so. I could always hear the prisoners coming up the stairs with their heavy burden, and the shuffling of their feet as they approached our corridor. Not only that, but I also learned to judge by hearing alone whether the soupy vegetable gruel given to us to wash down the coarse cornbread was thick or thin. By the time I could smell the saltiness or lack of it in the gruel, I considered myself a true graduate of prison life.

At any rate, we were soon served a meal.

One look at the fare was enough to take away whatever appetite I had. A glance at the cadaverous faces of my cellmates, however, changed my mind. I remembered that I still had to confront whoever it might be for my "case," and I needed all my wits and energy to see me through. I made up my mind then and there that I would consume everything offered, regardless of taste.

In later years, when I became used to the gnawing pains in my stomach owing to long periods of slow starvation, I often marveled at the potential of the human being for survival. By that time, I could not only smell out the saltiness and tastiness of what we were offered, but I could tell at a glance whether it met with the nutritional demands of our bodies.

As I finished my "meal," I looked around and discovered that most of the prisoners were watching me. After all, I was a newcomer and might bring them news from the outside. I was equally curious about them.

Who are these people, I wondered. Why are they here?

I scrutinized their faces: they all looked pretty old to me, people in their mid-sixties or at least their early fifties. From what I could deduce, their imprisonment had nothing to do with the Cultural Revolution. After all, the people's government had been in existence for less than twenty years when these people must have been in their prime. So I classified them as "historical counterrevolutionaries": perhaps singled out because they had fought on the wrong side of the civil war between Chiang Kai-shek's KMT and the Communists, or perhaps because they were designated as landlords (and hence class enemies) at the time of land reform. The curious fact remained that these "historical cases" looked down on us, the "active cases."

After puzzling over the problem for some days, I came to the conclusion that, as historical cases, they had been through God knows how many movements and had been punished time and time again. They were obviously leftovers from the most recent movement, the Four Cleanups, and the fact that they were still here in prison meant there was some catch in their cases and that no one could, within the confines of the legal system, reach a verdict and sentence them. With us, the active cases, it was a different question altogether. At any time, the masses could demand a "struggle session" against us.

Putting all that aside for the moment, I could not help thinking what a wonderful chance I had to learn about the true current social and economic conditions of China. As an actor, I had more chances to meet with odd and eccentric people than the average person, but I had long ago discovered that the juicy and interesting bits about life experienced firsthand hardly ever make it into a script.

Finally one of my cellmates plucked up enough courage to ask my name. Before I could give him a full answer, he made a gesture and pointed to a piece of official-looking paper on the back of the door. I walked up to the door to have a closer look while everybody else waited with bated breath (it was days later that I learned that we were not allowed to leave our places without permission). What I saw on the paper was a code of behavior for prisoners. We were not allowed to tell each other our names, only the word "number" followed by our surnames. So I became Number Ying to the rest of them. We were not allowed to discuss our cases either.

There go my grandiose plans for a bit of sociological study, I thought at the time.

In practice, no one paid any attention to this particular injunction, for a very simple reason: they were all anxious about the new political rules being practiced in the outside world and what kind of punishment they would receive once they went home, and the only way to assess the situation was to discuss their cases. There were other rules too, such as not allowing sharp or blunt instruments into the cell and walking single-file when supervised by a guard, with heads down, no idle ogling left or right, and no exchanging of whispers or gestures. These rules were obeyed.

"Call me Number Ying," I said.

Unexpectedly, that caused an argument, all conducted in whispers.

"What did I tell you? He knows the rules. He's an old-timer."

"How can you be sure?"

"From the way he slept last night. Didn't you hear him? He was even snoring."

Then another voice chimed in, "And the way he ate up all his food. Have you ever seen a newcomer do that?"

That seemed to have clinched the argument, until someone near the side of the door said, "Shut up all of you. Of course he's a newcomer. Remember what day it is?"

A brief pause ensued, while everyone tried to grasp what he was driving at. Then, one by one, they reached the same conclusion, nudged each other, and exchanged knowing glances.

I had been arrested on April 28, just three days before the national May First holiday. It was tradition for the authorities to make a number of arrests just before the first of May and the first of October (National Day). As far as I know, such measures are still being carried out. The purpose of these arrests was to put the fear of the dictatorship of the proletariat in the minds of would-be counterrevolutionaries, to deter them from subversive activities. Another purpose of these measures is to assure leaders that due attention is being paid to the suppression of undesirable elements in society. Some of them were released once the holidays were over—to be rounded up again during the next wave of arrests, no doubt.

Later I found out that the one nearest to the door—let's call him Number Wang—enjoyed privileges among the prisoners. As he told me in private, he had spent more time in prison since 1949 than out of it, so he knew the whole business backwards and forwards.

After our meal, the bowls and chopsticks were taken away. The man who asked me for my name said to me, "Number Ying, we have a system for the distribution of the food. Since you are a newcomer, we dispensed with it for today. From our next meal, we will resume it." When I showed my acquiescence with whatever system had been devised, he went on to say, "As you can see, the bowls are not exactly the same size, and neither is the corn bread. So in order to be fair to everybody, we have agreed that the soup and the vegetables are to be distributed by all of us in turns. Then, in order to avoid nepotism, while the distributing is going on, one of us, again by turns, faces the corner of the wall so that he cannot see what is going on. Finally he calls out a number—any number that comes to his mind at that moment—and the first portion will go to the person with that number. Now, do you agree?"

"I have no objections to any system," I said, "but is it necessary to go to such trouble?"

He looked at the others with an enigmatic smile and said, "Well, you are a newcomer after all. Now do you agree to the system?" Once more I nodded my acquiescence. At this moment, a voice from more or less directly opposite me said, "But I don't agree."

Everybody turned to him. Since the morning, I had noticed him muttering to himself with a strange light in his eyes. He did not speak to the others and nobody spoke to him. It was difficult to guess his age, since he badly needed a haircut, and it was obvious he had not shaved in ages. But his voice

sounded young enough. The man opposite Number Wang, the one who occupied the other favored position nearest the door, asked him nervously, "Do
you wish to say something, Number . . . ?"

"My name is none of your business. Yes, I have something to say."

"Please go ahead. After the morning meal, it is study time, and you are
welcome to say what you want."

"You are the study leader in this cell, aren't you? That's why you put on
airs all the time."

"I was appointed by . . . "

"And why were you appointed? Let me tell you. Because you are always
running to the guards and fabricating stories about everyone else in this cell."

"This is outrageous!" shouted the so-called study leader—let's call him
Number Wei. Later on I learned that he was not even a political prisoner, but
a self-appointed medical doctor who specialized in abortions. He had not attended medical school, had no degree and no license to practice medicine, so
was doing so illegally. He was arrested when one of his patients died, after paying him an exorbitant fee of course. Number Wei was a rather obnoxious person and what the younger man said about him was probably true. Again, it was
the Cultural Revolution that brought in such an influx of prisoners. Under
normal circumstances, he would not have been put together with the political
prisoners. As it was, he was not the only nonpolitical prisoner. On my right
side, for instance, was a kid of sixteen or so who was a professional pickpocket.

The argument between Number Wei the abortionist and Number what-
ever-his-name-was developed into a major quarrel. In the midst of it, my
neighbor on the left nudged me and whispered, "He is a newcomer too—
yesterday morning," indicating the guy who refused to give his name. At the
same time, we could hear hurried footsteps in the corridor and someone
shouting, "Stop it! Stop the disturbance!" In a moment the door was flung
open and several guards were standing there, panting.

With no change in his tempo or volume, the newcomer took up an entirely different subject: "Why did the government put us in here? Just for fun?
So we can have a nice time? No! Three times no! We should be here trying
our best to reform ourselves. To meditate and mend our ways. The government believes that people, even bad people, can be corrected and reformed!
But look at you! I felt so disgusted just now watching you eat your corn
bread!" He began mimicking how the food was consumed. "With one hand
you hold the bread, oh, ever so gingerly, with the other hand below it, ready
to scoop up any crumb or morsel that falls. What do you think you are doing? Enjoying an imperialist cream cake? How can you hope to be reformed
this way?"

He went on in the same vein until one of the guards stopped him and said, "That's enough!" Then he pointed at me and left.

My neighbor whispered to me, "Go! Go with him!"

Feeling somewhat dazed, I did as he said.

They took me to a room at the other end of the corridor. The door was carefully closed and two of them remained. I was told to sit on a stool and was asked, "What was that all about?"

I said, "I didn't understand it all. They were quarrelling about something else, but when the guards came in, the whole subject changed into what the guards heard."

There was a pause, and the two of them looked at each other. Then the guard who first spoke said, "All right, you may go back to your cell now." The other one stood up, ready to take me back. The senior guard said, as an afterthought, "Don't say anything to your cellmates."

At this point, I blurted out, "Can I ask a question?"

"Yes, what is it?"

"Why was I arrested?"

"Oh, that. You'll have to wait until your official interrogators meet with you."

"But I don't even have a toothbrush . . . "

"That will have to wait for your interrogators, too." So I was led back to the cell once more. I learned later that they were not trying to mislead me, but actually did not know why I was arrested either. They were forbidden to ask.

Once back at the cell, everyone was of course curious about what I had said to the guards, but a moment later, the guards reappeared, opened the door, and, without a word, pointed at the man who would not give his name. The guards gestured that he should get his things together and go with them. The man was bewildered and looked hard at me, but had to obey orders. After he was gone and the cell door once more was locked, I could hear a sigh of relief from all the occupants and felt like I should make a curtain call. The snag was that my big question remained unanswered. Why was I arrested? I would not get an answer to that question so easily.

I was surprised, however, at how quickly I became accustomed to the routine of the prison. We always got up at the same time, and after the business of the toilet and the morning wash (I took great care to use my sliver of yellow soap sparingly), we had our meal of corn bread and soupy vegetables. None of my cellmates was ever retrieved for questioning. The reason they were not asked to face what was known as pretrials was that they had already been through that time and again, and each of them must have had a file as thick as an encyclopedia. It must have been terrible to have the feeling that they had been forgotten by the rest of the world, including their own families. What lay in wait for most was to be sent to some farm specially reserved for ex-prisoners where, after they had served their sentence, they would be "rehabilitated" and earn a meager salary, but never be allowed to settle down in the big cities again. Life would be as boring as ever, but at least they would be breathing fresh air once more and, if lucky, have more food. In the meantime, they would just have to endure the boredom as best they could, so anything out of the routine— including a newcomer—was a welcome diversion.

Not long after my arrival, such diversion was provided, with a gruesome touch. A young man was led in and given the berth vacated by the prisoner who had scoffed at "Western imperialist cakes." This new arrival, dressed in rags, was taller than average. After the guard who brought him in had departed, he just stood there staring in front of him. He aroused a lot of interest, but refused to answer or even react to the whispered questions from the old-timers.

The prisoner beside me nudged me and whispered, "I think he's ga-ga."

True enough, he had that glassy-eyed look characteristic of the demented. I was still too preoccupied with my own troubles to give him much notice, and my cellmates soon lost interest in him as well. When bedtime came, he was finally persuaded and helped to lie down. In all that time he did not utter a sound.

In the middle of the night, we were suddenly awakened by wild shrieking. I couldn't make out where the noise came from or what it was all about. Gradually, I realized it came from the newcomer and that he was trying to say something, but he had a very heavy accent and I couldn't understand a word of it. By this time, the entire cell had been aroused, if not the entire corridor. Then we heard the running steps of the guards.

When they finally located the source of the noise, the door to our cell was thrown open, and several guards shouted, "Stop it! Stop the racket!"

Heedless of their orders, the newcomer raised his voice even higher and by this time I could make out that he was shouting, "Mother! Mother Jiang Qing! Come save me! They are torturing me!"

Several of the guards crowded into our cell, trying to stop his shouting by screaming at him and slapping him. One of them held his hands behind his back and handcuffed him, which made him holler his pleas to Mao's wife even louder. Finally one of the guards ran out and fetched a gas mask, which they buckled on his head. Apparently there was some kind of a contraption on the mask and by turning a knob the air flow could be controlled.

One of the more experienced guards took hold of it and threatened him, warning, "If you don't quiet down, I'll choke you!"

When the newcomer did not comply, he carried out his threat. Immediately, the shouting subsided, until we could only hear a gurgling sound from the man's throat and see him begin to writhe painfully, the veins on part of his neck visibly bulging. One of the younger guards seemed worried and pointed out the bulging veins to his superior, who shook his head reassuringly, until all movement ceased from the victim. After looking at his watch, the older guard finally released the knob on the mask.

After what seemed like a long time, we finally heard a drawn-out hissing sound from the man, indicating he had recovered his breath. The older guard gave him some final words of warning, peeling off the mask from his face, but he obviously had underestimated the demented energy of his antagonist because before he could take off the mask entirely, the man began to yell at the top of his lungs once more. It took two more guards to hold the man down so the choking process could be resumed. This went on three or four times until the man was so exhausted that he had to acquiesce.

All this rumpus took the better part of a night and none of us got much sleep. Finally, after our first meal the next day, the newcomer was taken away.

The elder guard came into our cell to talk to us, something that rarely happened. He closed the door carefully and leaned on it. Since nobody knew what to expect next, everyone kept silent and tried to look as innocent as possible. This was my first good look at him. He was much older than the other guards, and wore a PLA uniform that didn't seem to fit very well. It was too new, for one thing.

He began with a smile, something rarely seen in this place. "Quite a racket, last night, wasn't it?"

His air gave the impression that he was going to explain the young man's situation and his current fate, but instead he addressed us directly.

"You men can call yourselves lucky," he began. "You don't know what's happening outside the prison with the Red Guards. I myself don't know what's going to happen to me tomorrow." He continued, "You have been put inside a 'red safe,' and no Red Guard can touch you. The food, admittedly, isn't all that ideal, but I think most people would prefer to have less food and more peace." Finally he added, "And all we require you to do here is read Mao's works."

I had been telling the other prisoners a joke when the guard came in. Apparently, he had heard the tail end of it, because, as he left, he added the comment, "I think that's good, you know, to have some jokes."

He was a very old man, one of those left over from the pre–Cultural Revolution days. I don't know why he was kept on, because most of the other prison guards had either been put in prison themselves or at least had changed their jobs. But he was different. And to me, he looked quite experienced.

"I've come to warn some of you not to get ideas into your head," he said. "It doesn't pay to make trouble in this place. The man you saw last night started making trouble by trying to crash the entrance gate of Zhongnanhai, the party headquarters. He's out of his mind. That's the headquarters of the revolution! You know who he said he was? He claimed to be the long-lost son of our Great Leader himself! Well, he is in for some unpleasant surprises!"

None of us interrupted him, of course. We just kept our mouths shut, with no expression on our faces. He went on with his tirade for another twenty minutes until he felt he had made his point. "Now, you will go on with your political studies," he concluded, closing the door carefully as he exited.

After a prolonged silence, someone blurted out, "You know, there *was* a certain likeness . . . "

In terms of my own case, what surprised everyone was that since my arrest, no one came to question me or put me on trial for at least a month.

People began to whisper their suspicions: "Do you think his case is especially serious?"

And the experienced ones said, "Nah, if it was extra serious they would have come earlier, not later."

Nobody interrogated me. They just seemed to have forgotten that I existed.

After the young man who claimed to be the offspring of Chairman Mao and Jiang Qing was taken away, we in the tiny cell were reduced to eighteen again. I had only been there a little less than a week at that point, but one gets to be very impatient when put in such a position of not knowing why one is there and just being pushed around. I thought that at least once they started interrogating me, I might gain some idea of why I was there.

The day after the incident with the young man, two prisoners started quarreling. Apparently I was the neutral party in the cell, because I hadn't been there long enough to form allies and make enemies. And so the guards came and took me to a little room to question me, wanting to know what it was all about. I couldn't really tell because when people have been staying together for a number of years, not just days, they build up some kind of a relationship that is not mentioned openly but which goes very deep. As the newcomer, I was of no use to the guards in deciphering these relationships.

The guard who had made a big deal out of the argument between my two cellmates called me over. He got rid of his assistants, who were all older than he was. I could see that he was a type of junior-ranked officer from the army and not from the original organization that supervised arrests. Once he had removed his colleagues from the room, he asked me to sit down and tell him all about this quarrel. Explaining that I didn't understand what the quarrel was about, I replied that I only knew the matter was between two persons, but really didn't know whether or not there was long-term animosity.

And then he shrugged. "Okay," he said. "You can go back."

So I went back, led again by the older guards to my cell. Everyone pretended I didn't exist, but as soon as the guards left and locked the door, the prisoner closest to it listened to their receding steps and then gave the sign, upon which everyone came alive.

"What do they want with you? What did he say?" they asked, followed by various other questions.

I simply replied, "I don't really understand what he was driving at."

Such incidents, however disturbing, provided a break in our ordinary routine. But even daily prison rituals took on meanings very different from actions in the outside world.

I always loved food, good food. It took me only about three days to start feeling hungry, so you can imagine what the others felt—some of them had been there for at least three years.

Every day the food was brought up three floors to where we were located, and we could hear the two men responsible for carrying the food up. They had a thick pole, with a rope hanging on a ridge holding a big wooden tub with vegetables inside. In a very short time, I trained myself to hear like the others—and we could discern their steps because they were carrying this rather heavy load. There's this kind of walk they had, something between a regular gait and a shuffle with the soles of their shoes scraping against the floor. When they arrived at the appointed spot, one of them would say, "Put it down," and we could hear the tub being placed on the cement floor. They never could manage it so that the thing landed squarely on the floor—it always landed at a slight angle, so we could hear two sounds coming from the tub. By this time all the prisoners were full of attention, and all conversation had ceased. The one appointed to bring the food into the cell would go and carry back a pail with the watery vegetables inside. Before he returned, one of the prisoners—usually the most experienced one—would make a comment or give the verdict, saying, "As watery as ever" or "No salt."

And true enough, it always seemed to taste as predicted. I didn't know the nose had that function—prisoners could predict the texture and flavor of the food just from the sound and smell of it. The food was usually bland—prison authorities were afraid of causing swollen feet and other ailments due to malnutrition, so they added as little salt as possible.

During my years in prison, there were some memorable meals. One day everyone grew very excited because the smell was different.

"There's much more salt today," one prisoner said.

Then someone else said, "Sesame jam."

It wasn't simply water and vegetables that day—it had some flavor. We were not allowed to cheer, of course, but we were pretty near that state.

I remained with this same group of eighteen for about half a year. At the end of 1968, I was moved to another cell, and I thought that meant that they were ready to close my case.

The interrogations had finally begun about eight weeks after my arrest, and I was quite happy that I could at least learn why all this had occurred. The questioning was rather routine: my name, age, information about my family members, my scholastic record, and so on. And it was only at the end, when they asked me repeatedly, "Do you realize why you were arrested?" that I suppose I looked totally blank, and so they reminded me, "You have a number of foreign friends and acquaintances dating back to your middle school days through your years at Qinghua University." It was only then, after they reminded me, that I realized the connection.

I was told to think back. And when I did, like a big flashback, some of these acquaintances were brought back to mind, not only from my middle school days but also from my college days. When I graduated from Qinghua, I was asked after joining the Beijing People's Art Theatre to fill out a form that listed all my foreign contacts. It was my impression that this was a standard procedure, and I did not fear that it could be used in any negative way, because we were repeatedly told that nothing would happen to us and that this was just part of the routine: "If you want to join the revolution, you've got to make a clean breast of things."

I was twenty-two years old. I had just graduated from college, and was married with a baby daughter. The Korean War had broken out, and everyone of us was supposed to fill out a form and hand it in, telling our work unit what kinds of overseas associations we had. I looked at the other people's forms: some people had one or two pages—five would be quite impressive—but I filled up, God knows, quite a few pages, because I had been raised in missionary schools full of foreigners. At one school, out of more than two hundred students, there had been only four of us who were Chinese.

Now, in prison sixteen years later, I was discovering that these forms had all been carefully kept in my dossier. I was the inmate who not only had immediate family (my father) on the renegade island of Taiwan, but also had numerous friends and associates and classmates who were presumably counterrevolutionary elements. At the time of my arrest, it never occurred to me that this had anything to do with it.

After that first interrogation session was over, they said, "You can go back to your cell. Write it all out, again." And of course, I had to do it. But because I had so much to say about my one-time teachers, friends, and classmates, they gave me more paper and a small bottle of ink with a dip pen. My neighbors reminded me, "Don't use all that paper—store it away." I took their advice, because by that time I realized how valuable a piece of paper and ink were. Our watches and other belongings had been taken away from us, so these were now the most precious commodities. Paper and ink and pen were valuable because they could be used to pass messages.

When the guards gave them to me to write my self-criticisms, they said, "Honesty is the best policy. We know all about you—this is just to test your attitude. If you have a good attitude, you will be released early. Otherwise something drastic is going to happen to you." I used the pen and ink to compose my written confessions, but the guards never seemed satisfied. Every time I was taken into the questioning room, they'd say, "You've left out certain details."

Before long, I grew very impatient with this routine, and I learned that my reaction differed from that of the other prisoners. All around me, I saw people feeling guilty and powerless against the machine of the state. When the guards scolded other inmates, saying, "You think we were wrong to arrest you?" they would meekly reply, "No, no, no, of course the government is not wrong." But I still had a burning desire to understand what had really happened to me.

I decided to give it one last try and tell the guards the truth about how I was feeling. That was the moment I reached another level of consciousness and could actually feel a free sense of agency in making decisions and choices. Living is, after all, something one has to make a choice about. I decided I would do whatever my intelligence dictated to me that I should do, and I also came to the conclusion that I need not feel any guilt.

The next time the guards delivered their prize sentence—"You think we made a mistake by arresting you?"—I replied, "You could have. . . . Of all the people you arrest, don't you think there could be room for some mistakes?"

"We thought you were making good progress under our guidance," they said, disappointed.

Surprisingly, there were no repercussions, but they also ignored my appeals to their conscience about the possibility that mistakes had been made.

I came to the conclusion that the authorities had nothing on me, and I refused to go on feeling guilty. I decided to silence that part of my ego for good and to look at the world with a fair, level, sensible view instead of the warped perspective that my present fellow prisoners were trying to create around me.

"You think you've been wronged?" they would ask. "Well, you haven't been. The government doesn't arrest people for nothing!"

I got plenty of advice from these fellow inmates, who varied in nature and attitude, but were all alike in the way they acquiesced, admitting they were arrested because they had done something wrong.

In the end, we were all captive mice caught up in a cat-and-mouse game—but this mouse decided not to be willing prey.

I realized that the greatest danger I faced was that my senses would leave me, because the pressure was so great. I saw it happening to people around me and I made up my mind to keep my sanity by keeping myself busy. I had accumulated quite a supply of paper and ink, and on the rare days that we were allowed to walk from the cell block to the bath house, I'd be very careful to look on the ground for any broken pieces of glass. At every meal, we had chopsticks fashioned just for that meal, and then they were confiscated again. Somehow, I managed to keep a pair of chopsticks, and I knew that if I found a broken piece of glass, I could scrape the bamboo sticks to a very sharp point. It took more trouble than the goose feather pen, but it was worth the effort.

Once I had fashioned a writing instrument, I mainly drew pictures of my new cellmates. Some were poor peasants and had never had their photographs taken their whole lives, so they treasured those portraits. I was caught once because I was a little careless, but what I happened to be drawing was a portrait of Mao, so of course I was reprimanded, but the guard had to let it pass.

I was in that second cell for another six months before I was moved out of Beijing to a prison at Jixian. I had no idea what kind of fate awaited me at my next location, but I was glad to leave the prison in Beijing behind.

CHAPTER TWO

~

The Prison at Jixian

During the second year of my confinement I boarded a special train with the other prisoners and moved to Jixian, near Shijiazhuang, the capital of Hebei Province. Ostensibly, we were relocated from Beijing because we were important political prisoners. It was certainly a well-guarded train. We were assembled around midnight and herded onto the platform of an obscure railway station just outside Beijing, and could see that there were machine guns pointing at us just in case of trouble. This was in the second half of 1969, more than a year after my arrest.

The only nice thing about the trip was that they gave us buns, and we could eat as many as we wanted, so we had a full meal. Of course the machine guns bothered everybody, but after a while one gets used to just about anything. We arrived at a small city called Hengshui near Jixian and were loaded onto a few trucks. Altogether, there were sixty of us to be transported to the Jixian prison. Others stayed on the train, so their trip hadn't ended yet. Nobody was allowed to talk, so we never knew where those people ended up.

By the time our trucks arrived at Jixian, most of the prisoners were in a daze and didn't really know where they were. I knew better because when we left Beijing, the watches that had been temporarily confiscated upon our arrest were returned to us. Since we could wear our own wrist watches, I devised a system by looking at the time and judging from the direction of the sun to determine which direction we were going, and I calculated that we had turned south from Tianjin on the Beijing-Shandong line until we reached the border of Hebei, where we again turned right and traveled west

another hour or so. Thus, I could judge that we were on the railway somewhere between Shijiazhuang and Hengshui. Rather than sleeping, I kept my
eyes open, and eventually saw a road sign for Jixian, so I knew exactly where
we were. We arrived at the prison and we were told to get off the trucks and
walk single-file through a heavy gate into a courtyard. This was not our idea
of a prison at all—it was just a bunch of hovels, with PLA soldiers patrolling
the rooftops. We were called out by name and ordered to go to various
rooms—the one I was allotted was probably the largest and about twelve people were locked inside.

The room, of course, had bars on the windows and door so that the wardens could look inside, and there was also a small aperture that could slide
back and forth for the warden to look inside to see if the prisoners were
behaving.

Thus began a new phase of life. The next morning we had our first meal
since our arrival, which served as our breakfast. It was a kind of porridge of
ground-up maize, with carrots to give it some taste. At that time we were all
very hungry, but each of us could have only one bowl of this gruel. Suddenly
we heard a disturbance coming from the corner of the prison. There were still
about five or six old prisoners left over in that prison. They had the same
gruel as we did, but apparently for them it was a treat—not like us who had
been spoiled by the Beijing cuisine. A quarrel had started in that old prisoners' cell over the apportioning of the food.

Someone shouted for the warden. As in all the prisons at this time, the
wardens were called *duizhang*—I guess that was considered the highest rank
to flatter the wardens with—so there were shouts of "Duizhang! Duizhang!"
And the so-called duizhang came over and removed one prisoner whose head
was bleeding. We later learned that there were huge cast iron spoons used to
serve the gruel and someone must have snatched one and hit the poor man
on the head with it. It was messy with blood gushing out and so on. Then,
for the first time, we saw a female nurse who hurried in and bound his head
with bandages and took him out, presumably to a hospital. And we could
dimly hear other prisoners asking, "How did this happen? Why was this man
hit?"

The victim had apparently been a favorite of the warden, who entrusted
him with the job of keeping the prison in order. But this time, his fellow prisoners resented him for getting a spoonful more gruel than the others, and he
got hit on the head for it. By noon he returned, head bandaged, looking pale,
and the warden was very brusque with all of the prisoners, saying, "Shut up,
all of you, and go on with your studies!" So they started reading aloud from
Mao's Little Red Book.

This went on until late at night, at which point we were addressed by the warden. His speech generally described what kind of treatment we were going to receive: "Don't expect to be treated as you were in Beijing. There you had a soft life and here you're no longer going to enjoy that. You're not supposed to be living above the standard of the local peasants, so you're getting twenty-four catties, or twelve kilos of unground grain per person per month." That was far from enough for any adult.

The next day, news came that the poor man who got hit on the head had died during the night. It must have been from gangrene or some other infection, because the iron spoon was full of rust and dirt. Nobody wept for him— he was obviously detested for cheating his cellmates.

As his body was carried out of the courtyard, someone murmured, "Now there'll be trouble."

Another old-timer replied, "Naw, no trouble at all."

"How do you know there will be no trouble?" the other prisoners asked.

"Because, well, just use your brains and think—how are they going to report this? There was a fight in the cell? Are they going to report that? Then it is the prison's responsibility. So they will certainly try to bury the fact and pretend that nothing unusual happened—that this poor man was just ill and died."

And it turned out just as he predicted.

Merely as a survival strategy, I knew perfectly well that it was important at this juncture not to be led astray by any obsessions and that I should try to occupy myself, both mentally and physically, with something concrete. I had already seen that dazed look in the eyes of some of the other prisoners—they were obviously trying to cope with their situations, but having been indoctrinated for many years, they just couldn't. If one was not careful, one would have all sorts of wild ideas about oneself.

For instance, there was a young man who, when he was still a free citizen, was quite a good singer in a professional opera troupe, and suddenly in prison he went berserk. One morning, we all discovered that there was something different than usual about him and he kept muttering to himself.

"What are you trying to say?" we asked him.

"Oh, I've been calculating," he replied. "Every year we have an import-export exhibition in the city of Guangzhou for which visitors come from all over the world and are entertained with some kind of a song and dance or opera or something like that. Well, I've been thinking that we've exhausted the repertoire of top-class operas, so now they will have to stage the play *On the Docks*, and that play can't be staged without me.[1] It's only about two weeks before they open, and so within a week I'm sure someone will come from Beijing, get me out of here, and take me to Guangzhou so we can get the show together."

We all felt slightly uneasy about such a person who obviously believed what he was saying, and days went by with no sign and no news of any *On the Docks* with him in it.

Finally he said, "Well, it will have to be tomorrow that they come—otherwise it will be too late." And the next day it was clear that he hadn't slept through the night, and he got himself all dressed up, but nobody came.

After that he fell into a deep depression. Nobody wanted to talk about it with him—we tried to distract him, but his attention wasn't there; it was obvious that he was still waiting for the last-minute summons, which never came. There was nothing he could do but make up some story about why he was passed over. It was really pitiable to see his illusions shattered. Similar things were happening all over the prison, in response to the fact that people were arrested and detained without any reasonable excuse.

As time went on, we discovered that this new prison had many advantages compared to Beijing. In Beijing we were under scrutiny all the time, whereas here nobody bothered. Who cared if we were studying or not? We just needed to have someone in the cell who could keep an eye on the sliding aperture on the door and warn everybody when the warden was approaching. Then each prisoner would take out his Little Red Book and start muttering, and later, whoever was keeping watch would say, "Alarm over," and we would all be at ease once again. It was like an air raid drill.

In terms of who would stand watch, we had a schedule all worked out, but nobody adhered to it strictly. Someone would just say, "It's your turn today," and that person would keep an eye out. The wardens couldn't care less anyway. As long as a drastic situation didn't arise—as long as no one killed anybody like the first night we arrived—there was no problem. Quite early on, I realized one has to find something to do to occupy one's time, rather than simply moping and staring into space, expecting to appear in *On the Docks*, because that's just not going to happen.

So I embarked on quite a few projects. The first of these was making some utensils, and the first utensil I made was a spoon.

At this point, the only possessions I had were Mao's Little Red Book, some toilet paper, soap, and underwear. My watch had been confiscated again a few days after we arrived. They say that watches are dangerous weapons—that for the prisoners to have watches and for them to be able to check the time leads to trouble. I suppose that is true, because in order to agree to hold an uprising at noon, prisoners need to be able to tell time.

To make the spoon, I had to first get the wood. There was a spade in the open-air bathroom, and I had my eye on its handle, which was quite long. I knew I could procure a piece of glass from the bathroom floor because there was no protection against the wind in there, so occasionally a strong gust would shatter a window and the broken pieces of glass would be left lying around.

Then I had to learn how to make use of that broken piece of glass. Using part of my clothing, I would hold the glass and try to break it—that way no glass was wasted and the edges would be sharp. I worked with it as one would a file. Whenever we were allowed to go to the bathroom, I surreptitiously went over to the spade handle and made the cut deeper and deeper and deeper. It took me two weeks to sever the whole wooden part of the handle, because these handles are made from very hard wood. The piece of wood was about seven inches long and I set to work carving it with my precious piece of glass. I ended up making a beautiful spoon, which I kept right up until I left the prison two years later. That spoon really came in handy for scooping things—it especially helped me eat the daily gruel, which was often all we were given. We were very hungry, and when gruel still remained in the bottom of the bowl at the end of a meal, scooping it up with my fingers was not totally satisfactory. That spoon became one of my most prized possessions. I was very sorry I couldn't bring it home with me, because it was a nice piece of workmanship.

The spoon, of course, whetted my appetite for embarking on other clandestine craft projects. I discovered that the special product for this area of Hengshui was writing brushes, the old-fashioned kind. By then we were more mixed up with the local prisoners, and I very politely asked them how I could make a writing brush. They said that I would need to have the proper hair first.

"Where can I get that?" I asked.

"You see that peasant wearing a blanket of fur as an overcoat?" one of them said, pointing to another prisoner. "That hair would be ideal. It's coarse—goat's hair, not sheep."

And that is where I got the hair for the writing brush. To hold it together, I started by making thread from old socks. Today's nylon strings are much better than what we used, which was cotton and broke easily. It was tough going, but I used those simple materials to make a writing brush.

Then the war scare came. China and Russia were in conflict on their border. So we were told to work and were given some fabric. We were instructed to dye the fabric black and then put it on the windows as curtains so that whenever there was an air raid alarm they could be closed and light would not show through. It was just like London during the Blitz in World War II.

While we were doing that, I tucked away quite a bit of the black powdered dye, which, when mixed with water, proved to be even better than the ink that was being sold outside the prison.

If somebody was ill in the cell they were usually given a bit of medicine in a tiny bottle, so I poured the ink I mixed into one of those little bottles. After a while, I had brush and ink and all I needed was paper—and in prison, you could always ask for paper because you were supposed to be writing down confessions of your crimes all the time. The hard-nibbed pens they provided for this task, however, were confiscated after a few hours, so in order to have something for my own use, I needed my brush.

We were given a newspaper every day in each little cell, and I started drawing portraits of Chairman Mao just like the ones in there. Of course, I didn't really want to draw pictures of Mao, because by that time I had lost all illusions about the Great Helmsman, and I even suspected that he wasn't quite right in his mind. But I needed some protection in case one of the guards caught me with my brush and ink.

One day, I was discovered by one of the other prisoners, a former rich peasant who had been arrested on the charge of fomenting class revenge after his son was accused of beating up a neighbor. When he saw what I was doing, I painted his portrait for him—and oh, how he prized it—he just loved it. He told me all his secrets after that. But he wasn't careful enough and the warden found the thing on him. He was literally in tears, kneeling on the ground, telling the warden, "I've never had even a picture taken of myself and this is the first time I've seen myself as a subject of a portrait. So, please give it back to me. There was no bad intention in this picture." Finally, because he was the designated prisoner who swept the courtyard and did the cleaning, the warden allowed him to keep that portrait I drew of him as a special measure of leniency.

Fortunately, I was not punished. The guards thought I had drawn it using the ink for writing my confessions. I had to have cover every step of the way—and that's why I subsequently turned to Mao, because then if I were ever caught, the guards couldn't pin anything on me. If they tried to, it might backfire on them, as if they were obstructing the study of Chairman Mao.

The small notebook covered in red cloth that I made in Jixian prison was my most impressive project. In it are three portraits I drew of Mao Zedong. One is a portrait of young Mao with a cap on—from a famous photograph taken by Edgar Snow at the end of the Long March, when Mao was perceptibly thinner than he ever was again. Another one of young Mao without his cap is from a meeting of the Politburo at the end of the Long March and was also taken by Edgar Snow. Snow seemed to own the only camera in those days. The portrait that comes first in my book, just after the title page, is the Great Helmsman's formal portrait.

The notebook is titled *The Poetry of Chairman Mao*. I'm surprised that after all these years the red ink of the title remains so red. I was afraid it might fade in color or become brown. Most of the writing is in black ink that I made from the curtain dye, but the title page is written in red ink. One day, I claimed that I cut myself and I was able to get iodine for my wound—actually, something even redder than iodine. And with that red liquid I inscribed "Beijing 1968, April" which is when I was arrested.

I was able to collect Mao's poems in prison because at the time the China Post Office issued a whole series of envelopes and stamps based on reprints of his calligraphy. Those were a real find for me, which prompted me to decide finally that Mao would be the subject of my work. The calligraphy I used in the notebook is an imitation of Mao's hand.

Some of the entries in the notebook include Mao's letter about his ideas on poetry that was reprinted in the newspaper. Some are copies of Mao's calligraphy. But most are his poetry.

My favorite was a love poem Mao wrote about his first wife, who was the daughter of a professor at Peking University.[2] The first line says, "I have lost my proud poplar tree"—meaning his first wife, whose family name was Yang, meaning poplar—"and you have lost your willow." Willow is the family name of one of Mao's former comrades, and he is writing this poem for the widow of Li Shuyi, who by this time must have been in her fifties. He goes on to say that the two trees have gained effervescence and go straight to heaven. Then he writes, "We ask Wu Gang"—he's supposed to be the man in the moon—"what do you have? And Wu Gang offers us the wine made from laurel blossoms." A laurel potion is a rather famous drink in China. The second verse of the poem says, "The lonely Chang E spreads her wide sleeves and dances for the loyal souls of her comrades. Suddenly news comes that in the world of men, the tiger has been conquered. Her tears flow like pouring rain." Chang E is the beauty who flew to the moon but was left to be lonely for the rest of her life. Here of course the metaphor is that Chiang Kai-shek has been defeated. So in the world of men, the tiger has been vanquished. The tears are tears of joy.

I think this is Mao in one of the rare moments when he suddenly and genuinely remembers his first love. His first wife was killed in Changsha, the capital of Hunan Province.[3] He wrote this about her, and for Li Shuyi, whose husband had also died. When Mao published his poetry and his calligraphy,

I'm afraid it was a losing battle for Chiang Kai-shek, who had nothing to publish.

I copied the poems by holding them to one side and imitating his writing. There are also printed sections that are in my own handwriting, not Mao's calligraphy. But everything in the book is directly from Mao's words.

I was sure to get into trouble if I kept drawing portraits of my fellow inmates; it was not what one would call straightforward political activity and so it was not permissible to indulge in such things. The safest thing was to link it with Mao. That way, even if I were discovered, people would hesitate before condemning me. By the time anyone saw the notebook, it was obvious that a lot of effort went into it. Both making it and designing the layout were painstaking processes. The other prisoners were full of admiration for it and very impressed.

The cover of the book was cardboard I made by wetting sheets of paper, laying them stacked on the bed, and sleeping on it with my body as the ironing instrument to press it flat. It took days for it to dry up. This process could not be hurried or wrinkles would appear. I got the red cloth for the cover from one of my friends in the same cell who happened to have this color on the underside of his blanket, and I persuaded him to share a small piece with me. I used some of our daily portion of gruel to glue the cloth to the makeshift cardboard.

I folded the pages so that in between the front and back of each page was a blank side, and a space where other paper could be tucked away and hidden. Sometimes they held my notes, but usually I stored those under my bedding. The characters my notes were written in were so tiny that few people would bother to read them anyway. The paper was very thin, almost transparent, with grids of blue squares intended for my confessions, whereas the paper for the notebook pages (and the paper I used to make the cardboard cover) was thicker plain white paper intended for our annual letters home.

There are several different kinds of notes, basically in two categories. One chiefly deals with methods of making food and other practical skills. I did not expect to be able to return to a civil life back in the city, so I would have to rely on myself for certain things I really liked—such as bread baked in the approved way of the French, or butter, cheese, and Chinese traditional tidbits of Beijing, which I couldn't imagine life without. Such tidbits were cheap to make and very tasty.

So, that was one kind of notes—foodstuffs, and so on. The second kind was my notes for my sessions at the pretrials. I didn't want to make a fool of myself by replying to something I had already been asked earlier with different answers on different occasions. So after each of these interrogation sessions, I would take notes to remember what I had said. I had to write them down in detail, including facts I thought I should remember in case I were asked again. For instance, the age of the playwright Cao Yu—I should have known that, but I didn't because I had never asked him how old he was. So I had to work it out from the beginning—calculating from when he finished his studies at Nankai Middle School and got into Qinghua University. It turned out that, much to my surprise, he wrote his first play, *Thunderstorm*, when he was only twenty-three years old. Of course, some of the interrogation notes were far more political and strewn with code names for Chinese and Soviet political figures. Those notes, if they had been discovered, could have gotten me into much more trouble than the food how-to's, which were themselves far more dangerous than you might imagine.

Comparing the two kinds of notes, however, I feel more nostalgic about the food, which was something quite essential for my future survival. One prisoner from a famous culinary shop taught me how to make *jiang* or soybean paste. The soybeans first had to be cleaned and washed thoroughly, then placed in a pot with enough hot water to immerse them all. After simmering for three hours, the beans would become a kind of a gruel. It was then taken out, dried, and placed on a stone mill to be ground into a paste. When accepting new apprentices, according to this older gentleman, "The big trick is to examine their hands. If someone has naturally moist hands, then get rid of him. He is certainly not suited for this kind of work. We want someone with totally dry hands so that his perspiration doesn't get into the beans."

The soybean expert was in prison for something in his history for which the authorities found it difficult to sentence him to any precise period of confinement. All the prisoners who remained in Jixian belonged to that category—the authorities didn't know what to do with these people, who were by definition—since they had been handed down from the former police—guilty of something. In his case, while he was out of a job, he had joined a warlord who collaborated with the Japanese. That way, he could have a decent uniform issued by the Japanese, receive a miserable monthly stipend—which was better than nothing—and could even send a few dollars back home.

Another interesting fellow I took notes from was a Catholic Trappist monk. A Trappist is not allowed to talk once he joins the order.

"Don't Trappists keep bees?" I inquired.

"I've been keeping bees all my life," he said.

So he started giving me instructions and I wrote them down word for word. He taught me about other things, too—how to make wine, how to make French cheese. He was good at all that Western stuff.

When I look at the notebook again after all these years, I think about how important and wonderful survival is. If I had to, I would do it again—copy down whatever is necessary to learn for my future survival. What I was trying to do in this project was quite simple: I thought I could carve out a little corner for myself and my family so that we could survive after prison.

It took me about a year to write the whole book. I never met anyone else either in prison or since my release who did this kind of thing. In order to pull it off, several conditions have to be met. First is the opportunity—if I had been kept in Beijing all those years, I wouldn't have been able to do it. Moving to Jixian gave me the chance. Second, I have always liked doodling and drawing pictures. If I didn't—if I couldn't draw—it also wouldn't have happened. And I was confident that one day I would be able to change my circumstances, to turn everything around. I can't say I was 100 percent sure that this could be done, but the hope was there—maybe just a lingering hope, but it was still something worth fighting for.

When I was leaving prison, I was afraid a search might be conducted and the book and all my notes from other prisoners would just be thrown into a furnace, but they were never discovered. Up until now, the only people I ever showed them to were my wife and son. Wu Shiliang was in tears as she looked at the keepsake, and young Ying Da thought it was great fun.

The important thing about Jixian is actually the amount of freedom we had—far more than Beijing.[4] For one thing, in Beijing they were not as understaffed as in Jixian. In Jixian, as far as I remember, there were only three persons looking after us: the head of the detention center, the jailer, and the woman who was supposed to be the doctor, although what she knew about medicine could be counted on the fingers of one hand. They all considered themselves lucky to be able to find a job like that. Since there were sixty of us, they couldn't keep an eye on us all the time. There were soldiers, of course, but they didn't interfere with matters of jurisdiction. All they did was patrol the prison, so they weren't in direct contact with prisoners.

Back in Beijing it had been different—the whole prison corridor was lousy with prison guards who would open the door and reprimand the prisoners if anything at all seemed out of the ordinary. If someone tried to sing or shout, make noise, or make a nuisance of himself (although, of course, this kind of thing almost never happened), the guards were there to scold us and suppress anything that might get out of hand.

I still remember the rules of behavior from the Beijing prison. They were all explained in four-character phrases such as "*bu yao bu xu*" (things not allowed): not allowed to "*zuo gu you pan*"—look to the left and right—or "*jiao tou jie er*"—whisper into each other's ears. So in theory we were just supposed to do nothing but study Mao's works from morning till night—basically, any time when we were not eating our corn bread. Of course, people still held interesting conversations, but in a subdued voice.

We were roused every day at six a.m. We weren't required to do any labor in the prison, because our cases were all pending. In theory, at any moment we still could be told, "Your case is clear now, go home." In theory, that is. It only ever happened to one prisoner, a student—because Mao suddenly felt a twinge of remorse, I suppose, for imprisoning so many students.

My wife, Wu Shiliang, was still being held in the same Beijing prison I had been in, but I didn't know that while we were both there. I didn't find out she was there until I had already been moved to Jixian. The building where my wife was incarcerated was all women; the conditions were cramped and damp, and it was very bad for her. Many of the women caught diseases. I'm sure the prison conditions had something to do with my wife's general state of health afterward, because dampness is very bad for a rheumatic heart. If she had gone to Jixian with me, perhaps she would have lived much longer than she did.

My wife shared a cell with the most prominent independent female capitalist on one side and on the other a pretty little girl who couldn't stand her mother-in-law and murdered her by pushing her into a well. It was a colorful cast of characters. In Jixian prison, there were only about ten or fifteen women and the rest were all men. Both the Beijing prison and Jixian prison stressed discipline and control. Thanks to the social system that had evolved in China by then, no one ever thought of trying to escape. Even if someone had opened all the gates, no one would have gone away. Where could they go? They would be spotted at once, because at that time everybody lived and worked within some sort of work unit organization and no one had any privacy.

The Jixian prison complex was originally a private home—it must have been the biggest house in all of Jixian, with quite a number of rooms, all of different sizes. Because of this, we were put in there in a rather haphazard fashion, unlike Beijing where everything was constructed to the specifications of a model prison. In Beijing, if there were eighteen prisoners in one cell, there were sure to be eighteen in all the others. But in Jixian it was a different story. The largest cell in Jixian could accommodate eight prisoners, and they had fun. We often heard laughter from the other end of the corridor after someone told a joke.

At Jixian, I was moved around at least ten times. I was there for two years altogether, about twice as long as I was at the prison in Beijing, which means I was moved to a different cell about every two or three months. Once I was placed in a cell with just one other prisoner, but not for very long. I think the poor guy was done away with, but I don't know for sure. He came from a doctor's family, and one day he heard an announcement on the radio—from the KMT station in Hong Kong—asking for volunteers. "All you have to do is write to us, tell us your name and how to correspond with you, and we'll take care of the rest," the announcement said. This young man was upset because his family of doctors was originally very respected, but by then they had been accused of being charlatans who were trying to cheat the people. So his parents were persecuted and the young man wrote a letter—according to the address given to him on the radio. And of course, he got in big trouble. The letter must have been intercepted, and they could trace him of course because he gave his address as instructed. He had been led around the whole neighborhood and "struggled against"—loaded onto a truck with other "baddies" and driven to a marketplace where people shouted slogans denouncing them.

The chief of the prison put me in that two-person cell with him, saying, "I am honoring you with a job. Watch over this young man so that he doesn't commit suicide."

I never found out what happened to that young man, but I am happy to say that nothing unpleasant occurred while I was sharing his cell. I tried my best to help him see the lighter side of things.

We prisoners received only sketchy details of what was happening outside, mostly from reading the *People's Daily*. But I could read between the lines much more than the other prisoners because I had been inside the Four Cleanups teams. I knew what had been happening before 1968, whereas most of the other prisoners had been there in their cells for quite a few years when I arrived. They couldn't imagine what this Cultural Revolution was really all about. So in order to pass the time, and at the request of my fellow prisoners, I told them about the movement's origin, how it proceeded, and what important things had happened up to the time I was arrested.

I became a leader not only because of my ability to explain political events, but also because of my ability to mobilize the prisoners. Only a few individuals who were theatre-goers knew my background or who I was. Most of the inmates were peasants and didn't even know what a modern play was, so I became very popular for another reason entirely. After we got to Jixian, I organized quite a few campaigns to steal carrots, potatoes, and—the one that made everybody especially happy—tobacco. I also explained how to light a cigarette without matches. Those things made me very popular indeed.[5]

Since rules were much more lax in Jixian than in Beijing, some things that could never happen in the previous prison could happen there. For instance, although prohibited from interacting, male prisoners and female prisoners shared a common courtyard. Two of the girls at Jixian—very young, very nice—had become friends of my wife at the prison in Beijing. They ate much less than the men, even though their ration was the same. So every few days they would wrap up a bun and some other nice food and put it on our windowsill with the instruction, "This is for Ruocheng."

I always shared these treats with fellow prisoners. One has to eat, but one also has to keep oneself busy, and one should not be selfish. That's how to win popularity and support.

Prison Projects and Pranks

Mobilizing prisoners to do things like steal carrots and potatoes is not simply a matter of popularity among peers. I had to establish myself with the authorities, too. Whenever the chief of the prison gathered us in the courtyard, he had a purpose, and usually it was because he needed skilled labor of some kind.

He would gather us and ask something like, "Now which of you is good at working with cement?"

And no matter what he sought, what demands he had, I always raised my hand up first. I did that because I knew that I would able to leave the cell and gain a little more freedom.

On this particular occasion he needed someone to work with cement, but didn't give any other details. I, of course, volunteered.

"Come to my office after this," he instructed.

And so everyone else was sent back to their cells and I was led to his office.

Once I entered, he said, "My superiors have decided we mustn't leave this place looking so desolate. We should have some sort of decoration in the front of this prison indicating that this is truly a school for remolding ideology. But we need something permanent. I've seen this in big cities—where the cement is made into huge Chinese characters, but in a way that the wall doesn't fall apart."

I nodded.

He continued, "What will you need to do it? Whatever you want, don't hesitate to say it."

And I said, "Well, of course, I need cement and I need quite a bit of salt." (Remember, they gave us very little salt in our food for fear we would get swollen feet, so salt was a valuable item.)

"Salt, and paint. Of course we need paint—we're going to paint it to make it look nice. And then we need putty."

He paid close attention as I listed the materials I would need.

"And I'll need fresh pig's blood."

"What for?" he asked.

"To stir in with the paint so that it sticks on the cement without peeling off," I said.

"Is that necessary?"

"Oh yes, it's a tradition," I replied. "That's the traditional way for professional painters."

Which was true, up to a point.

"And I'll need a little stove to heat it up a bit. Because when you mix the cement, the reason it cracks is because the weather's too cold. And so it's better to have some warm water to mix in with it." This was January or February 1970, and it was quite cold at the time.

"Sure, all this can be done easily," he said.

"Oh yes, another point," I added. "I need lots of bricks. The bricks must be rubbed together to make flakes, and we need the flakes to mix with the paint. The paint plus the pig's blood plus the brick dust will make it very sticky."

He asked me where he could buy brick flakes and I replied, "You can't buy them. But you have plenty of people here you can put to work, and it's not tiring work. It's easy enough that two girls can do it."

"All right," he said, jotting it down. "What else?"

I named my final request. "Paper, big pieces of paper, a pencil, a rubber eraser, and a ruler—in order to write out the characters first."

He complied with every request.

I must say it was very pleasant to have two women there. None of us had seen women for ages. The warden didn't like the idea of any male prisoners running around outside the cell blocks, and female prisoners were believed to be more docile. So, I knew if I emphasized that the brick-rubbing work was easy enough for girls to do, he would provide me with some female companions.

We started working. First I got the pencils and cut them in half. I sharpened both ends so that I had four points to a pencil, and I pocketed three of them. Pencils were very useful in prison. In comparison to all the trouble I had gone to making ink, this was so convenient.

The two girls who joined me couldn't help giggling, saying, "Is this true? That you really needed . . . ?"

And I said, "Of course it's true."

So they started rubbing the bricks together.

The fire was there to heat the little stove in which we boiled the water. So we were living like lords, actually having hot water.

And then the cement also came. And, finally, the pig's blood. That was difficult, because it had to be brought back from the butcher's after the morning slaughter.

The first time I said, "Sorry, this is not fresh enough. This blood has already congealed. I need real fresh blood." Actually I kept the blood, and ate it all up, together with the girls. We made a delicious soup of salt and pig's blood.

I learned the cement technique from one of the prisoners who was a professional mason, but who was so scared of officials that he wouldn't volunteer himself.

"You just tell me all the tricks," I said. And he did.

I was ordered to make enough space for eight characters. Someone who thought he was quite clever said, "Oh, it's ready made. Marshall Lin Biao's famous saying: '*tuanjie, jinzhang, yansu, huopo*'" (unity, intensity, earnestness, liveliness).

"Sure, sure, sure," I said, then went back and started drawing the characters.

This went on for about a week because I was trying to drag it out.

One day the chief came and said, "Are you ready?"

"Yes I am," I said. "But I have a little question—may I ask it?"

"Yeah, go ahead."

"Quoting Marshal Lin is all right," I continued. "And terms like *tuanjie, jinzhang, yansu* are all okay for prisoners—but the last two characters are *huopo*—lively. Is it suitable for prisoners to become *huopo*?" The implication was that prisoners could get agitated.

"Oh, I messed up," he said. "What would you suggest?"

I replied, "Well, it should be a slogan that we see in the papers all the time. Eight characters . . . let's see . . . how about *jiachang wuchan jieji zhuanzhi*—'devoted to the dictatorship of the proletariat'?"

He was really happy. "Good good good, let's switch to that!"

"That will take a bit more time though," I informed him.

"That's all right," he said.

So I kept the old paper for myself and asked for more paper. And then I started with the new slogan. The way to do it, as my mason friend told me, was to first make a framework of the entire wall, and then apply the cement, with the mixed cement on top—but flat, and pressed so that it sticks to the wall. On top of that I put my paper with the characters drawn on it. No glue was necessary because the cement was wet and the paper stuck to it. Then, I cut out the characters from this flat surface.

After this part of the process was done, I told the prison warden, "I'm sorry but we will have to wait a couple days for this to dry." And I enjoyed a couple more days until it was dry.

Then it came time for the poor man to run to the butcher's in the morning to get the fresher pig's blood. When he arrived, I poured the blood into the water, added salt, put it on top of the stove, and boiled it halfway. Then I painted the whole thing bright red—the color of revolution.

So that was that. And I even got a pat on the back. The two girls enjoyed it too, because it had been dreadfully boring sitting in their cells.

Not long after the cement project, we were again gathered in the courtyard and the head of the prison asked, "Who among you is good at making pickled green peppers? They are abundant now in this area. Our superiors want us to improve your diet. I know just eating those cornbread buns gets to be monotonous, so suppose we make some pickled peppers ourselves? I've got the vat. . . . "

And of course up went my hand again.

He was surprised. "You know that, too?"

"Yes I do," I replied.

"Where did you learn it?" he asked.

"One of my fellow prisoners was an apprentice in a famous pickled food factory," I said.

"Let's give it a try," he told me. "Now what do you need?"

And off I went again. "Green pepper, plenty of salt, bamboo chopsticks with pins or needles—four of them for each chopstick."

"Why do you need needles?" he inquired.

This was, of course, a very good question. I needed needles because needles are another thing valuable in the prison community. Everybody was in rags and we were only allowed to use a needle once every two weeks, which had to be returned immediately. Now I would be the man in there with needles!

"Why do you need needles?" he asked again.

"You see, the salt will stay outside the skin of the green pepper without getting inside it, and that's not tasty," I said. "So what you do is tie up four needles to one chopstick, and then each worker should be given one of these instruments to pierce through the peppers."

"Why four?"

"Well, that's what I was told, because if it's less than four you're wasting a lot of labor, but more than four is not necessary. So four is the right number."

"Okay," he relented.

So I was entrusted with the job. It certainly improved our diet. The pickled peppers came out very nice. I really did know a fellow prisoner from a pickle factory. While I was in prison, I was trying to squeeze all of my fellow prisoners dry about their special talents and knowledge.

The most sophisticated knowledge I gained came from an engineer from Hong Kong—it involved how to generate electricity from a local stream. The details included generating of the electricity, as well as storing it, and creating bathrooms, without the use of any modern equipment. I knew this might really come in handy later on.

The community of prisoners was large enough that I could find people with all sorts of secret traits, tricks, and talents they would hardly ever divulge to other people. When I saw someone who looked mysterious enough to have something up his sleeve, I would try to befriend him. And that is how I learned about all the different skills they had—skills that helped me volunteer for projects when the guards requested it, and skills that might help me get on my feet after prison one day.

I learned from one prisoner how to make soy paste and from another how to grow grapes. One really interesting lesson was on hatching eggs. This is what I recorded in my notes about that:

> When you have chicks, you don't need more than twenty eggs, just take twelve of them and with this trick you get out of this dozen eggs only one or two roosters, so you don't have to waste all that time and energy. There are three ways to recognize the sex of the chick. When the chick walks on the ground, the female chick will walk in a straight line whereas the male one will walk changing its direction from left to right and right to left [crooked]. The second method is to hold the chick with its two feet and if the head of the chick hangs down that means it is a female, and if the head of the chick goes in the contrary direction—that is, backwards and raising its head—then it is male.

The third method he mentioned is when the eggs begin to show cracks and the young chicks are trying to come out, those who come out first are probably female. I don't know where he got all this information. Even now, I am still mystified by how they make these gender distinctions among chicks.

Then there was a country doctor named Tian. When we were in prison, Tian was about the age I am now as I write this book—his early seventies. He was from a mountainous area north of Beijing, where they could produce gold from a tiny little mountain: they would blow up rocks from the mountain, and from pieces of the exploded rock, they'd start removing anything shiny with a pair of pincers. Gold doesn't get oxidized—well, not so easily anyway—so it is always recognizable in a piece of rock. Then these were collected together and put in a stream so that the gold would settle (because it's heavier than ordinary rock), and with that method finally they could get hold of some of the bits of gold. This was the first time I ever heard about this process.

In terms of medicine, this rural doctor instructed me about practices that were both legal and illegal. The legal part was how to make opium. It was legal where he lived, at least according to him. As a doctor, he couldn't do without opium—for coughing and asthma and things like that.

As he became friendly with me, one day he said, "I'll teach you how to make fake opium."

Of course, one was not supposed to do that—it was like making fake money. I remember he told me how to make it from some plants: how to put them in a pot, keep them heated until they become totally black and sticky, and how to make the fake trademarks on the bars of opium.

But at one point even he had to admit, "God knows what's happening nowadays outside—I've been in prison for the last five years. I don't know what the market is like—maybe it's not very safe to sell this, so be careful." The notes I took on making fake opium are very obscure because I thought it was too dangerous to write it down. I wrote in such a way that if someone else saw the notes, they would not know they are instructions for making fake opium.

I asked this doctor, just as I asked everybody, "Why were you arrested?"

He said, "You know, it was my own fault." And he proceeded to tell me about how, during the Four Cleanups when everyone was supposed to confess whatever wrong they had done in the past, he confessed that he was kidnapped by the Japanese during the war and had been forced to prescribe some medicines for a Japanese officer who was ill with malaria. After he confessed, he was told he could go home, but a few days later he was arrested again— for having collaborated with the Japanese by prescribing medicine.

Following those notes on making fake opium is a passage on how to induce an abortion. And then following that are details on how to castrate a rooster so that it puts on more weight—but that's pretty gruesome, so I won't go into it. At any rate, the abortion and rooster castration instructions came from a different doctor than the one who taught me how to manufacture opium. This other doctor was a surgeon and he was much younger than the traditional country doctor. People told me in whispers that he was arrested for real crimes—that he was practicing abortions on human beings, not chickens. Not only was he doing this without a license, but he had also caused some pretty serious medical accidents. He was from Miyun County in Hebei Province, an area north of Beijing.

A wonderful cook named Lin taught me how to bake crabs and shellfish. He was in his forties and lived near Peking University, where some foreign students had hired him as a cook. His Southeast Asian clients were impressed with his skills.

"Why do you stay here in this hole?" they asked him. "You could make a fortune in Thailand."

After being told this repeatedly, he finally made up his mind. He was also a tailor, so he took his sewing machine (which was one of those very old machines that turns by hand without a pedal), and went all the way to Ulan Bator in Mongolia, where he made quite a lot of money. But he was still thinking of Southeast Asia, so eventually he set off again, making the entire journey on foot to southwest China—and carrying the sewing machine with him, which must have weighed something, as well as fabric and pots and pans. He crossed the border somewhere in Yunnan and made a neat little pile of money in Thailand.

But he missed his wife and his children, so he came back—and waiting for him were the local police to arrest him. By the time we met in Jixian, he had been in prison for at least three years without being sentenced. It is very difficult to pass a sentence on someone who voluntarily returned, and whose only crime was sewing buttons and cooking food.

Lin was very good with his hands, so he was asked by some of the younger prisoners to make American-style dungarees. He cut up the material his "customers" provided and sewed it together with homemade needles. Now, to make a needle took at least two weekends. We had to get hold of some metal wire, the tougher the better. And then we rubbed the required length of wire against the cement portion of one of our beds until it became straight and shiny. If we were lucky, someone was wearing shackles in the cell, and we could persuade that guy to lend them as an anvil—the end of one needle had to be rubbed first and then struck with the shackle to knock it flat, and then sharpened again, knocked again and so on, until after quite a while, one end of the needle formed a flat shape. Preferably, the partially formed needle could be made red hot by rubbing it, and then dipped in cold water, so that it became harder and harder. While still relatively soft, the flatter end was knocked very lightly to make an indentation. With enough patience, sooner or later, this piece of flat needle would have one side of it protruding like a bud, and then it could be rubbed more on the cement—and, if one was lucky, with a few attempts a true hole would be formed. But even if one was unlucky, one could always do it over again, provided one had the time and the patience.

By this time, I had already won the trust of the prison authorities. In fact, at one point, I even gave the prison guards—especially the chief warden, a man named Xiao—regular classes on Marxism. Xiao didn't know what the party center wanted him to learn, so I helped him learn Marxism through the original texts written by Marx himself (of course already translated into

Chinese). We read Marx's writings about the civil war in France, and his collection of essays on the crisis in German ideology and things like that—of course, one couldn't expect someone in Jixian to know what all that was about. And I'm happy to say that Warden Xiao really made a name for himself.

By spring of 1971, I had managed to put myself in charge of prisoners' shopping. Unlike me, many of the prisoners arrived in prison with money on them. The prison authorities at the time had plenty of other faults, but corruption wasn't one of them, so each prisoner was given a little bank booklet on which was written how much money he had.

It was I who made a suggestion to the head of the prison one day, asking, "Why let them lie idle? We could do a little business. They all have money. Why not make a system where every month, they are given a couple of days and a list of things they could buy and then we'll handle the money."

"But this has never been done before," he said.

"So what?" I replied.

And he finally agreed. "It might be an idea."

Every month the prisoners were all given back their little bank accounts and they would fill out a form starting with, "I want to buy some . . . "

The first thing I bought for all the girls was a little mirror. Oh, they loved it. They hadn't looked at themselves for ages.

And then I told them something. "The mirrors aren't just for vanity's sake. This is a means of communication. Do any of you know Morse code?"

None of them did, so we had to teach them.

That way, when the sunlight was at the right angle, I could always flash it into the window of the girl who was talking to me and send messages. Rather convenient.

Eventually I had to start pulling a cart from the prison to the shopping center. A guard always came with me, but that was the most free I ever felt during those years of prison.

I myself rarely had any money to shop. Since I had been arrested unexpectedly, I had only twenty-seven cents in this whole wide world. We were allowed to contact relatives on rare occasions to request money, but I didn't want to involve my immediate family and risk endangering them. So-called letters home were censored and all one could write was, "I need a pillow" or "I need a new pair of shoes." We could write home only once or twice a year. Out of a sense of mischief, I suppose, I finally sent one of those letters to my elder brother, Ruocong, asking for ten yuan, a blanket, shoes, socks, and some history books. Up until then, my brother had no idea I was in prison. He hadn't heard from me in a long time, but he thought it only natural because during the Cultural Revolution people usually avoided corresponding with one another. He was shocked when he received my letter, and promptly sent me a very good woolen blanket, the ten yuan I had requested, and some books, which I never saw because they were confiscated.

I remember that blanket and how warm it kept me. Ten yuan was really something at the time, too. Things were truly cheap in China then: ten yuan could buy toothpaste, soap, and much more. But twenty-seven cents couldn't buy anything.

By the time my brother sent the blanket, I could more or less roam around the prison by myself, and I soon discovered where they kept the carrots and potatoes. At that moment, an idea was born, and that blanket played an important role.

Lin the cook assisted when I organized the great vegetable caper. It was truly a large-scale burglary. This was the spring of 1971, after all that practical or imagined learning from interviewing other prisoners had been recorded in my secret notebook.

"This has to be very efficient," I told my cellmates. "Someone has to be on the lookout for guards coming, and we must get enough warning so that we can run back to our cell."

The storeroom where they kept the carrots was actually just one door down, so the guards were asking for it. I instructed everyone to sew with the needles I had earned, using tough thread found in the cuff of nylon socks. Soon we had the blanket sewn up on three sides so that it became a huge bag.

The division of labor was painstakingly arranged. The younger, more agile members were to do the actual stealing, while an elderly man was keeping watch. This was crucial, because the soldier walked along the rooftop and there were windows that allowed him to peep in now and then. The old man we chose to keep watch had to calculate how long it took the soldier to make a full round and we had to be ready before he returned.

My plan was executed beautifully. Soon we had loads of carrots dragged back to our cell. Nobody could believe their eyes. I immediately recognized the need for discipline, because when eight people chew their raw carrots together, they make quite a racket. So we had to chew them in turns with the lookout man still at his post, and if he made a sign—even if someone had half a carrot in his mouth—we had to stop until the guard passed and then start chewing again.

We were only able to steal carrots once—they must have discovered something later on, because that room was kept locked from then on.

Man does not live by bread alone—he needs some entertainment. So I devised a number of games for us. I started teaching my cellmates how to play *weiqi*, a Chinese form of chess that the Japanese call *go*. The first thing we needed to make the chess set was a handkerchief, upon which we could draw the lines for the mini chessboard with my precious ink. And we had to make the chess pieces smaller than the regular size. For these, we started examining the soles of people's shoes. There were three kinds of soles in those days: the red, black, and white. We didn't need the red ones—we had our eyes on the black and the white. Sometimes it took a lot of persuasion to make someone donate his only pair of shoes. But we were very careful with them. We cut off pieces in a slice so that the owners could still wear them, though it felt a bit funny because the soles grew thin. Equal-sized circles were drawn and cut from those slices, all done with a piece of broken glass we found in the courtyard.

We had to make 180 white pieces and 180 black pieces that would fit onto the handkerchief. And with the slightest warning we had to be able to hide it all away. Handkerchiefs are easy to conceal in one's pocket. But the prison doors had peepholes, and sometimes the guards would peer in to see whether people were behaving. Once we were careless and the guard saw that we were playing some sort of a game, but he didn't know what it was. In order to enter the cell, he had to take the padlock off and pull the bolt, which made a lot of noise and took quite some time. So by the time he got in, not only had the little game disappeared, but we were all sitting in different positions. Oh, he was mad. And he picked on one of us, saying, "You come out."

This man was Zheng Zuocheng, a musician and composer who is still a very good friend of mine today.

So Zheng went out and the guard started interrogating him. "What were they playing? You were sitting in the middle. You should know."

Zheng shook his head.

People talk about torture and beatings in prison, but actually I hadn't seen it happen, at least not in that prison. It's very tiring to apply physical torture to a prisoner—one needs at least two assistants to help. But the guard devised a method of torture that forced Zheng to kneel in the courtyard on the ground, and this poor man had to kneel there for at least two hours. It wasn't very smooth ground—it was full of little sharp-edged pebbles. By the time he was allowed to come back, we could see the blood on his knees. This was an easy way for the prison guards to torture their prisoners without expending too much of their own energy.

People are funny. When I bumped into Zheng not long ago, I mentioned this incident and he looked quite blank.

"Really? Did that happen?" he asked. He had totally forgotten about it, or perhaps he had repressed the memory.

Of all the times I was moved around from cell to cell at Jixian, he was the only prisoner I was sad to leave. He is a wonderful man. I had always wanted to learn the intricacies of musicology and he was the one who initiated me, teaching me how to read music and the scales of "do-re-mi-fa-so-la-ti-do."

Zheng's wife was not arrested, and she was not yet married to him at the time of his arrest—they had just been introduced and had known each other for about a week. But she was there when Zheng was taken away. The last words he heard were her shouting, "I'll wait for you."

He had to stay in prison for eight years because his offense was looked upon as a serious crime—which it was. As a young man, he was trained as a dancer, and it was only later on that he started composing music. But in the summer when the dignitaries and other big shots were enjoying themselves at the seaside resort at Beidaihe, he was among the youngsters hired by Jiang Qing to dance with her at the parties she threw.

Well, when the Cultural Revolution started, several of them were joking about these experiences, and one of the people present reported them for making fun of Her Majesty. They were all arrested. I knew at least three of them personally, and they had to stay in prison right up until 1976, when Jiang Qing's case was fully investigated and she herself was sentenced.

When Zheng was released, who was there waiting to welcome him home but his girlfriend—now his wife. She actually did wait for all those years. So this world is full of tragedies, but some of them have happy endings.

"Spying" for Peng Zhen

After some time, I finally came to understand why I had been arrested and what all my interrogators were trying to find out. It became apparent that I wasn't arrested and imprisoned solely because of my foreign contacts—they were concentrating on my connection to someone else, an important person who was by then already designated as an enemy of the Great Helmsman.

In Russia, the ruling elite became so old that they had to replace their leadership after Stalin's death with a younger man, Khrushchev. This move in Russia ignited the seeds of ambition in the heart of a man in China named Peng Zhen. Peng attained the same position in China's Politburo that Khrushchev held in Russia's, becoming the party secretary of the capital, Beijing, just like Khrushchev was in Moscow.

As is the fashion with all Communists in the world, the Chinese Communists put a lot of value on the order of names. So whose name came first? In this case, of course, Mao. Who came second, third, fourth? I can rattle it off: "Mao, Liu, Zhou, Zhu, Chen, Lin, Deng"—Mao Zedong, Liu Shaoqi,

Zhou Enlai, Zhu De, Chen Yun, Lin Biao, and Deng Xiaoping. Those were the big seven. Now, Deng Xiaoping had a very peculiar position: he wasn't included in the group of six—Mao, Liu, Zhou, Zhu, Chen, and Lin—but he was general secretary, so his name came next. "Mao, Liu, Zhou, Zhu, Chen, Lin, Deng": anyone who knows anything about the politics of China knows that by heart. And Peng Zhen, the party secretary of Beijing, was known within the party as Peng Laoba: Peng Number Eight.

"Mao, Liu, Zhou, Zhu, Chen, Lin, Deng" . . . and Peng, number eight. The Eight Immortals of the Chinese Communist Party.[6]

Now, in 1965, Mao sensed the possibility that someone under him refused to obey his wishes, and when Yao Wenyuan published his essay attacking Peng Dehuai, Mao wrote a comment on the original article saying something to the effect that "Peng Dehuai is just a figure of speech used by some people to attack me. Hai Rui was dismissed by the emperor Jia Qing just as Peng Dehuai was dismissed by me. And now there are some people who wish to turn the tables, change the verdict."[7]

As evidence that Peng Zhen was one of those trying to turn the tables, Mao pointed out that Beijing's newspapers were the only ones that did not reprint Yao Wenyuan's article. Of course, Mao approved very much of Yao Wenyuan's article and wanted it circulated throughout the country.[8]

Meanwhile, at about the same time, Peng Zhen published an article of his own. Peng had just been appointed as *wenhua geming xiaozu zuzhang* (head of the Cultural Revolution Small Group) by the Central Committee. This group was established toward the end of 1965, before the Cultural Revolution actually started.

In his essay, Peng went out of his way to emphasize the importance of free discussions, saying that before the truth, everyone is equal (*"zhenli mianqian, renren pingdeng"*). This was his Declaration of Independence, so to speak, but it sounds more like something cooked up in the French Revolution.

Nobody really believed what Peng was saying. With Mao still in power, who would be such a fool? In more ways than one, Peng Zhen tried to emphasize his new idea of equality before the truth, but before the infamous May 16 Politburo meeting that launched the Cultural Revolution, Peng Zhen disappeared from public view.[9] Mao's message was obvious: everyone was free to say what they wanted to say, but only he himself could declare what was suitable for the party.

Other high-ranking cadres also vanished from the political scene around this time. They included Luo Ruiqing, who for years was the head of security in China; Lu Dingyi, who was the long-time head of propaganda; and Yang Shangkun. Along with Peng Zhen, they all disappeared.[10]

By that time I was already a notable actor in the Beijing People's Art Theatre. But my association with Peng had started much earlier, in 1952, just after I had joined the theatre. We were performing *Dragon Beard Ditch* (*Longxu gou*) and at twenty-one years old, I played an old man of seventy, which required considerable makeup. One night in the middle of our performance, I was approached in the makeup room by a man I had never seen before. He asked me to please wait after the show because someone wished to talk to me, saying he already had the authority of the theatre company's personnel department. So I finished my makeup and, after my scene, I waited backstage for the curtain call at the end. In the meantime, I checked in with the personnel director.

"Oh yes, yes, we heard about it," he said. "Go ahead with him."

He must have known who was sending for me, but he didn't tell me. In those days, although we were supposed to be the cadres of literature and art, we were actually under very strict control. When we had a play to rehearse, we rehearsed and performed, but otherwise we were sent out to promote various political movements and anticorruption campaigns. We much preferred being occupied doing plays.

That night, after the curtain call, this man was waiting to take me away from the theatre. I wasn't nervous, but I was curious.

"This must be a high-ranking cadre who wants to see me," I thought, guessing that it had something to do with my father being in Taiwan and my potential value to the United Front being attempted between the Nationalists and Communists.

The car took us to a *hutong* not far from the theatre, with a huge courtyard surrounded by many single-story dwellings. When we arrived, I was offered tea, and I still remember the taste of it because it was very fine green tea of a kind not usually found in shops or teahouses.

I was asked politely to wait in the room where I was served the tea. There was carpet on the floor, and a set of sofas and armchairs, and a little table with cigarettes on it. I was offered a cigarette, and I noticed that it was a very expensive brand, so I smoked one. Our play hadn't ended until after eleven o'clock, so by this time it was past midnight.

Then someone came in. I recognized the man's face and the way he walked, and suddenly I realized it was Peng Zhen himself, the highest authority in Beijing.

He was very affable. "Well," he said. "*Lao Ying*."

That form of address—"Old Ying"—is rather chummy.[11] After greeting me, he made small talk. It was still very fashionable in those days to get small talk going: how's the theatre, is the theatre you play at very far from here, are the tickets selling well?

Then he got to the real purpose of summoning me.

"We have seen the list you handed in about your foreign acquaintances and classmates," he began. "It could be very useful to the country, to the party, and to the army if we could enlist your help—especially now when Japan is beginning to have ambitions again."

I was overwhelmed by his proposal, and I responded, "But I'm a totally nonpolitical person. I don't see how I can be of any help."

"Oh yes, you can be," was his reply. "We don't want you to do anything mysterious. Just go on associating with these people, and whatever their reactions are—especially when it's about some big event—give us a nod so that we'll know and be prepared. We don't want to be taken by surprise." He continued in this vein, and talked quite a bit about Japan. "I've read your resume. Your father is someone we respect. He is a good scholar—a famous scholar—and was imprisoned by the Japanese for quite a few years." Nobody had ever acknowledged that to me before. The Nationalists never said it, even though it was them my father was supposedly working for both times the Japanese arrested him.

Still, I hesitated. "I may not be able to fulfill your wishes because my foreign acquaintances all know I've joined the new People's Art Theatre run by the Communist Party."

"Never mind," he said. "Don't be worried about that. We won't come after you to ask you for any details. Just give us some idea of what these people are thinking—that's enough."

I agreed, but of course not without reservations.

I was impressed by the respect Peng Zhen seemed to have for my father.

My father had only been in Taiwan for a few years. I thought I would see him again, but I wasn't altogether certain because the relationship between the two sides of the Taiwan straits were very strained at the time, with the Nationalists expecting the Communists to take over Taiwan as they had Hainan. My father had been able to send some money through businessmen based in Tianjin, so I held out hope of our family being reunited again.

I agreed to Peng Zhen's request. But actually they made very little use of my services. I suppose they didn't need me. Soon all means of communication were opened up—including newspapers and radio broadcasts—which offered more information than I could provide. They continued to call on me from time to time, though they didn't ask me to do anything out of the ordinary.

As long as Peng was still in power, they seemed to have use for me. Sometimes I wouldn't hear from them for two years. Peng himself appeared very few times. Most of the time it was Luo, the security man. They would call me first on the phone, and then send a car for me later. Usually, I was treated to a really good meal.

The topic of conversation would vary depending on the current situation. For instance, in 1959, when the mainland started bombarding Quemoy with what was exaggerated as ten thousand guns (*wanpao qihong jinmen*), I was asked to go to one of these obscure dinners, but that time there was no big shot around, just functionaries who asked me if I had heard anything. So I told them what I had heard, which was mighty little. As far as I can remember, the sensitive part was regarding whether or not the United States would interfere with us in Quemoy.[12] I hadn't heard much at the time. My conclusion was that I thought the word *brinkmanship* was important—that John Foster Dulles was playing this game to the hilt, meaning that he was not really serious about launching an attack on the mainland.

I learned this term *brinkmanship* because some people—just ordinary people—had approached me, saying, "I saw a term in the newspaper today: *bianyuan ganzheng bianyuan yishu.*"

"I've never heard of such a name," I said. "I'll look it up for you."

I went to the library and looked it up, and the term *bianyuan* turned out to be brinkmanship. It came up again when Dulles made a speech that was printed in the *Cankao xiaoxi* (*Reference News*) about *heping yanbian*—"peaceful evolution." I didn't know what that was either. This *heping yanbian* idea arose in 1964 or 1965, just before the Cultural Revolution began. It was in the papers, and this friend of mine in the theatre asked me what it meant. I looked it up and told him what Mr. Dulles was trying to say, which was that by peaceful means you can topple a government without war.

My English-language skills gave me access to foreign materials as well as foreign people. I was probably getting as much information from the newspapers as from foreigners I knew. Take the Great Leap Forward, for instance. I read in a British periodical, *The Economist*, an estimate of the number of people who had starved to death during the Great Leap, and my reaction at the time was, "This is pure slander! The Communists couldn't be that bad—they wouldn't have allowed so many people to starve to death." It was only many years later that I realized I was wrong.

The Economist estimated that millions of people had died, but the official number in China was zero! I didn't tell the authorities about all that starvation business because I didn't want to get in trouble. I knew from what had happened in the Anti-Rightist Movement that one could be sentenced to a prison term for fabricating news against the interests of the state, even if the news wasn't necessarily fabricated. (Later on, in fact, Peng Dehuai was labeled and demoted when he persisted in his estimate of the losses in the Great Leap Forward, in a long letter to Mao at Lushan.)[13]

I didn't consider it spying, but I also didn't want to lose the ability to put my hands on all sorts of foreign publications for my personal use. Over dinner, they would ask me if I had been talking to my foreign friends, and if I knew what people were thinking in the West, things like that. And I was hardly able to tell them anything. But they had to be content with that. In the course of about ten years of this, increasingly, I was left more or less alone, but my position gave me access to a wide range of English-language publications.[14]

It took me a while to figure out that the reason I had been arrested was because of my relationship to Peng Zhen. From the earliest interrogations after my arrest, the questions all seemed to center around what Peng had said to me. They mentioned him early on, and I was a fool not to realize that he was the reason for my arrest. I thought it was because of my associations with foreigners—the same reason Peng Zhen had approached me in the first place. Peng had already been denounced by then, but who would think that I was connected with him? We had no personal relationship and I simply was unable to figure it out.

When I was first arrested, I thought it was probably a misunderstanding or a mistake and assumed they would release me. But when they started asking me about Peng Zhen, and didn't release me even after I told them what I knew, I wondered if it was something else. I answered them as truthfully as I could when they asked me repeatedly what Peng had said to me. By this time I didn't have much affection for Peng either. I told them about the night I was taken to his office, about the dinners, and that I hadn't provided much information. But that didn't satisfy them.

Then I thought it was because Peng's last wishes were to let us write an original drama at the People's Art Theatre. I had been appointed as the main writer to create a play about the Number Two Woolen Textile Factory, where there was a case of corruption within the accountant's office involving mishandling of money. At first they seemed interested too. I told my interrogators how four of us had been summoned by the Municipal Party Committee to write this play, and how the theme of the play had been predetermined— and that, as far as I could see, Peng was ready to do something really big. The theme he gave us for the play was that the real problems of our society came from the old, corrupt ways, and not from the newly born rich people who are unscrupulous. Mao saw through this at once, because his entire premise was to prove that the country had gone to the dogs—that the people in responsible positions, beginning with Peng himself, were corrupt. And Peng was retorting by saying, "No, no, no, we are not the corrupt ones—the corrupt ones are the old generation of baddies." Peng ordered us to write this play before he wrote the essay about "everyone being equal in front of the truth."

The others who wrote the play with me are all very old now. I was the youngest. Zhang Tong is now in his eighties. Tong Chao was a famous actor at our theatre, but unfortunately he has now lost the power of speech due to a stroke. The three of us were considered to be gifted actors, and were also versed in dramaturgy. The fourth member of the writing team was the the-atre company's Communist Party secretary, Zhao Qiyang, who later died of cancer.

The play was called *The Struggle Has Not Ended* (*Douzheng meiyou jieshu*). We rehearsed all the way through dress rehearsal, but we never performed it publicly. By the time we were ready, it was already June, and people looked at each other at the dress rehearsal, nodded meaningfully, and said, "Maybe another day." It was after May 16, so judgment had already been passed on Peng Zhen by then—he had already been arrested—so we couldn't perform the play.

It took me a long time to finally understand that the cause of my impris-onment was not so much the forms I had filled out listing all the foreigners I had known when I joined the theatre, or the play *The Struggle Has Not Ended*, which I had been commissioned to write by Peng Zhen, but rather the fact that Peng himself was in deep trouble.

My Release from Prison

Some prisoners, after the long process of pretrials and eventually a more proper trial, were sentenced and departed, usually sent to labor camps. Life in the camps, difficult as it was, was much better than in prison. At least one could get decent food and openly smoke cigarettes in a labor camp. The re-sult was that prisoners were eager to be sentenced and would sometimes con-fess to their crimes and gladly accept the sentence. I never actually wished to go to a labor camp, so it never occurred to me to make something up or of-fer a false confession just to get out of prison. Many passed through the sys-tem this way while I was at Jixian. During my earlier year in the Beijing prison, nobody was ever sentenced or moved away, but of the sixty or so who were moved to Jixian with me, only about two thirds were still there when I left, and the others were sentenced to ten or fifteen years of hard labor in a camp.

I became a free man on June 21, 1971, which just happened to be my forty-second birthday. When I had been approached in my cell at Jixian several days before that, I had no idea I was being released. All I was told was, "Your accusers are now here, so get your things ready—they're taking you back to Beijing."

They had a jeep ready to take me. I was escorted by several men in uniform, who were very easygoing with me. When lunch time came, we arrived in a place called Pasen, in between Jixian and Beijing, where there was a huge marketplace with various food stalls.

The uniformed men turned to me and asked, "You got money?"

"No," I said.

"You got any food coupons?"

"No," I replied again.

So they gave me a half catty coupon, worth about one yuan. "Go find yourself some food and then come back to the street."

With that, they all went to enjoy themselves, and I was left alone in this strange marketplace, which gave me the first inkling that the end was in sight.

Food was already becoming scarce, but they did not hide the fact that they were buying goods on the way. They stopped the jeep where some peasants by the roadside were selling sesame oil, and with no coupon, each of them bought a huge jar of this oil. They didn't care. They weren't secretive about it. To me, that was another good sign.

But then I had a huge shock when we arrived in Beijing. I was thrown back into the original prison and held in the row of cells for individual prisoners—usually that's death row. This cell was much better equipped than the ones I had been in before. A wash basin was provided, and a piece of soap. There was even a toilet seat, and the walls were padded. When mealtime came, the food looked so rich (at least it looked that way to me at the time). It was a large bowl filled with meat—I hadn't seen so much meat for years.

After the meal, I was left alone, but I couldn't sleep. Was I going to be released or were they going to put a bullet in my head? Two days later (the day my wife was released from that same prison, though I didn't know at the time) I was interrogated by an army officer who had taken over the theatre company.[15]

All of his questions were about Lin Zhaohua, one of my younger colleagues at the theatre.[16] The army officer wanted to know what Lin had been doing during the beginning of the Cultural Revolution and who he had been associated with. The officials suspected that Lin had ties to the May 16 Group, which was supposedly a secret society within the Red Guards that had diabolical designs on the CCP and Mao himself. They thought Lin was involved because he was a leader among the younger men.

The army officer named several people and asked me if Lin had links to them. Throughout the interrogation, he kept up a very harsh front. I didn't tell him anything, and there was nothing to tell anyway. I always sympathized with Lin Zhaohua.

This questioning about Lin went on for three days. On the fourth day, it was not the PLA officer who came to my cell, but rather the man who was responsible for personnel administration of the theatre company.

He came alone, all smiles, and said, "You're going home."

My wife and I never found out whether we had been released because of lack of incriminating evidence or, as an insider later explained to us, because of a change in top CCP leadership.

On the way home, I discovered Beijing was in a terrible state. When we passed through Tiananmen Square and Dongdan, I noticed there were hardly any pedestrians and very few bicycles. The whole city seemed deserted.

"Where are all the people?" I asked the personnel administrator.

"Oh, they've all been sent to the countryside or cadre schools," he replied.

Students above the age of fifteen (including my daughter Ying Xiaole) had been sent to the countryside for reeducation by the poor and lower-middle-class peasants. I knew this had been going on, because it had started before I was imprisoned, but I didn't know the full extent of it. I was worried about my daughter and my son. Xiaole had been sent to Inner Mongolia. It was one of the most difficult areas, but she could earn some money and she felt she had a financial obligation toward her younger brother. When Wu Shiliang and I were arrested, Ying Da was only eight years old, and during our imprisonment he lived first with my brother and then with my mother. He turned into a wild kid in the streets, just like millions of other children left to their own devices at that time.[17]

While riding in the jeep through the streets of Beijing during the final minutes of my captivity, I was informed that my wife had been released four days prior and was waiting at home.

The moment I walked into the room and saw Wu Shiliang for the first time after three years, I was a little shocked. I hadn't expected her to have aged so much. Her hair had turned gray and her face had shrunken. I insisted that she go to the hospital and see a doctor, which she did the next day. The place they delivered me to was not far from where I used to live, but now we had only one tiny room. So I started building—first I built a collapsible bed that could go up against the wall for storage. That winter, I was given the job of managing the heat for the theatre company, so of course when I saw all that good wood, I brought back quite a bit as lumber to make furniture. I built a huge bookshelf. I also made a table where my friends could come and play bridge in that very limited space. Most of that furniture is gone now, but I still have the bookcase. Ying Da was home with us, but my daughter didn't return from Inner Mongolia until later. The two of us—my daughter and I—built an extra little room when she returned. There were bricks all over Beijing at that time, because the city was being dug up to build air raid shelters. The room Xiaole and I built together with those bricks is where we kept all our belongings, and the bedroom was reserved for playing bridge.

In 1976, when the huge Tangshan earthquake shook Beijing from a hundred kilometers away, our ramshackle house with its leaking roof collapsed and we had to move again.

As promised by the personnel man, I was given a stipend of one hundred yuan each month. I couldn't imagine how to spend it, when so recently I had had only twenty-seven cents to my name. I still remember my first meal with Wu Shiliang and Ying Da, which we decided would be a reunion celebration. I went out to shop for food, and at the grocer's I ran into two of my colleagues from the People's Art Theatre. They nearly fainted when they saw me, because they all thought I must be dead by now. I looked over all the goodies on the shelves and decided to buy a small bar of chocolate for my wife and son, which cost about twelve cents, and I also bought one ounce of liquor, which was seven cents. So altogether I spent less than twenty cents that day. I couldn't even finish the liquor—not having had a drink in so long, just half of it was enough to get me intoxicated.

Neither my wife nor I could sleep that night, and we stayed up talking till morning about our lives in prison and the people we knew there.[18] Ironically, even though there wasn't too much to tell to begin with, for years afterward we never tired of talking about it.

Aside from the brother I wrote to early on who sent me the blanket and ten yuan, I had no contact with my family while I was in prison. They did not know where I was or what had happened to me, nor did I know their circumstances or whereabouts. When I was finally released after three years, I reconnected with them.

"You're still alive," they each said, surprised.

And that was no joke—not at the time, anyway.

PART TWO

FAMILY HISTORY
AND EARLY EDUCATION

CHAPTER THREE

~

The Ying Legacy

Like Father, Like Son

Nearly thirty years before I was released from prison on my forty-second birthday in 1971, my own father had also turned forty-two in prison, at the hands of the Japanese. During my prison years, I felt a close connection to my father, even though I hadn't seen him or had any contact with him in the twenty years since he had been shuttled off to Taiwan—and despite the fact that his residing there was the cause of so much suffering for my family during those politically chaotic times.

My father was imprisoned by the Japanese on two separate occasions: the first time, he was arrested on December 30, 1941, and released in April 1942. This original capture was by collaborators, not the Japanese police. His second imprisonment was directly at the hands of the Japanese, and lasted much longer, from 1943 until the end of World War II in 1945. During the years spanning his two imprisonments, I made countless trips to the prison to bring him food and clothing, doing what little I could to help him survive.

My older brother Ruojing had died in the spring of 1941 at the age of fourteen, several months before my father's arrest. At age twelve, I became the eldest son living at home and thus was responsible for delivering food and clean clothes to my father and his cousin, who had also been arrested. I brought bundles for another relative, too—an uncle-in-law—and for someone else as well. To this day, I still don't know who the other person was, but I always carried four portions of food. I rode my bicycle all the way across the city of Beijing to the prison. This was a rather special group—they were all more or less well-known scholars—and my mother used whatever connections she had to get them preferential treatment while in prison. Through her efforts, their assigned chores were in the laundry facility, which meant they enjoyed access to some hot water and heating.

During all these journeys to deliver food and clothing for my father, I was only allowed to see him once, and that was near the end of his imprisonment. On this particular occasion, my mother accompanied me and took me inside. The reception area was at the end of a long dark corridor. Before my father emerged, we could hear his shackles and chains. He had lost a lot of weight. When we tried to comfort him, he deflected our efforts, saying, "No . . . this is to be expected." I think the visit lasted half an hour, if that. The prisoners were not allowed to use their own names, but each one was given a number. I will remember my father's number until I go to my grave—it was 770.

Aside from that one day when my mother was able to escort me inside to visit, I made the trip to the prison with my deliveries alone. Most of the other families who could afford it hired a rickshaw coolie to do this job. As the member of a privileged family who actually came in person, I was a rarity. The others were all very poor. There were always many families doing the same thing I was, waiting outside the prison for our turn to hand over what we had brought, so before long we got to know each other rather well. Thinking back on it now, it was a good opportunity for me to understand how the destitute in Beijing lived, and what they had to cope with from day to day. I can still see some of their faces, even though it was more than half a century ago.

Then the Japanese surrendered in 1945, and the city was just like it was in 2001 when Beijing won the bid for the 2008 Summer Olympic Games. It was like a big celebration, and everyone was smiling. Suddenly, all the goodies became available that we hadn't seen for years. One of the first things we did was buy a whole bag of fine white sugar. I still remember putting the bag on the living room table, and all my brothers, including the youngest, were staring at it because they had never seen anything like it—they thought it was snow.

My youngest sister, Ruoxian, was born in 1944, so she was still a baby at the time. She was not breast-fed as an infant because my mother was too old to produce any milk, so we fed her on soybean milk and she managed to survive on that, along with some boiled millet. But when the good days came back, all her elder brothers thought, "We must give that little girl some real milk." So we went out and bought some for her. She tried one mouthful and started vomiting. To this day, she still won't drink milk.

My father was released about two weeks before the Japanese surrender. He was warmly welcomed by the community when he came home. He flew to Chongqing, where the newspaper my grandfather had founded, the *Dagong-bao*, bent over backward reporting about him, and he became a great hero overnight.[1] When he returned to Beijing he was made the commissioner of the municipal education bureau by the KMT.

When my father talked about his imprisonment, it was always in a very humorous way.

One day he said to me, "See if you can solve this problem: how do you pull trousers on and off when you have shackles on your ankles with a chain in between?"

This really is quite a problem, of course.

I thought it over, and finally I came up with the right answer.

"In summer or in winter?" I asked him.

"Okay, you guessed it—summer," he replied.

Then I told him how to do it.

He smiled at me and said, "Exactly."

I'll bet by now you're wondering how it's done. Well, summer clothes are thin. Between the leg and the shackle, there is a small crevice that the material must be pushed through little by little until the whole trouser is on. Then the other pant leg is maneuvered the same way. It can't be done in winter because the pants are thick and padded. I knew the answer because I was the one who always brought my father his clothing, and one of the items was padded trousers that buttoned up from the outside for easy maneuvering.

Not long after my father's release from prison, I entered Qinghua University, and while I was living there, my father was flown off to Taiwan by the KMT. At that time, even many important officials could not escape, because the airfield had been surrounded by the PLA. The planes had to take off from the fields at Dongdan Park where the foreigners played polo. The city wall at Chongwenmen was still standing, making the runway quite short, so they had to use very small planes—and thus no luggage was permitted, only a tiny briefcase.[2]

We were never officially told that my father had been taken to Taiwan, but we knew. This was toward the end of 1948, and we believed that because the KMT and the CCP were negotiating, it would only be a couple of months before the family was reunited. But we never saw my father again.[3]

The KMT was concerned about these individual scholars whom they had "rescued" at the last minute. Most of these last-minute survivors did not really want to go. In fact, several managed to come back. But the KMT kept a very strict watch over those like my father who held important positions—he was appointed head of Western languages at Taiwan University.

The last time I saw my father was one morning when I happened to be home from university and we ate breakfast together. I was nineteen, an age when one tends to be haughty. He had received a letter from the underground CCP asking him to stay in Beijing. Many prominent people received such letters.

He showed me the letter, and I said brashly, "This is quite right," meaning that he should stay and cooperate with the Communists.

My father looked worried and said, "What about my religion?"

"No one would interfere with that," I said.

But I was mistaken on that count, or at least naive.

Nevertheless, I believe my father intended to stay. In fact, by the end of that conversation, he had promised me that he would. I don't think he thought in precise terms that he would leave the Nationalists and take up the Communist cause, but he probably felt that in the new society he would still be given a job as a teacher or a professor.

Some people believe it was my father's choice to flee to Taiwan, while others claim he was forced to go. I don't think either is completely accurate—but I know he never intended to be permanently separated from his family.[4]

Had my father stayed in Beijing, I think he would have been safe, because there were quite a number of people like him. But then again, later on they all got into trouble during the Cultural Revolution. Perhaps my father and I would eventually have met in prison.

I'll never forget December 30, 1941—the day my father was first arrested. I was twelve years old and home for the Christmas holiday from St. Louis Collège, a boarding school in Tianjin. We were all awakened early in the morning because the men who came to arrest my father entered our house by climbing over the wall. I was still in bed when they came. It was quite cold, and I remember the feeling of the heavy blanket on me.

My mother was a strong, level-headed woman. Right after my father was taken away, she told me, "I'm worried about one thing. There is a list with names of anti-Japanese resisters hidden in one of the books in your father's study. They haven't found it yet, and I know where it is."

In old Chinese books, the pages were folded with the ends absorbed in the binding, creating a gap between each facing page. The list was tucked in between two of the pages this way.

"You must get that list out of the book before it is found," my mother told me.

"Leave it to me, Mom," I said.

The entrance to my father's study had been sealed off by the men who arrested him, marked with characters indicating the year, month, and date when it was officially closed up. We weren't allowed to break the seal, and they might be back any minute.

The first challenge was to get past the sealed door. Using a little water, I wet the sealing paper to loosen it. After I'd done that—with my mother nearby the whole time, watching the courtyard—I managed to find the book, and sure enough the list was there. I took it out, brought it to my mother, and carefully pressed the piece of sealing paper back into place.[5]

The second time my father was arrested, I was back at boarding school, so I was not a witness to the whole incident. Several of our friends got into trouble as a result, because the Japanese left a group of special agents behind, actually living in our house, and if there was a visitor—any knock at the door—they would answer and promptly arrest whoever was there.

My wet nurse had been with us since I was a baby. All of the nurses for the other children had gone back to their homes in the countryside, but this one preferred to stay with our family. Every day the special agents accompanied her when she went to the market. Soon, of course, the whole street knew about this. All the shops were very quick in serving our needs, even though at that time some of the goods were already disappearing from the market.

On one of these routine outings to the market under surveillance, the nurse was as usual the last one to enter the house when they came back. As she was closing the door, she saw an old friend of our family obviously coming toward our home. So she said in a loud voice: "Who are you looking for? This is Ying's house, not Li's! You are mistaken." Realizing that something was wrong, the friend apologized and went away. He has always remembered her for saving his skin—if not his life.

The boarding school I was attending in Tianjin was run by French Catholic missionaries—I had been sent there by my father after having been expelled from previous middle schools in Beijing for my bold behavior. Coincidentally, when my father was twelve, he too had been shipped off to boarding school by his father—but he was sent much farther away, to Europe, and he would not return home until he was twenty. During those years he could not visit, because World War I was being waged in Europe and travel was very difficult. He couldn't even come back in 1918 when the war ended, because there was so much controversy about whether China should regain sovereignty over Shandong, which had been a German concession since before the war.

So my father had to stay in Europe longer than expected. He first lived in Belgium, then in France. When the war broke out, he went to Ireland and from there to London. In spite of the time he spent in England and the fact that he was an English professor, my father always maintained that his French was better than his English.

During his time in London, he was brilliant in his studies, attending the London School of Economics. My siblings and I were told since childhood how he excelled in his scholastic efforts, coming out number one in the British matriculation examinations. By the age of twenty, he was already well known among the overseas Chinese for being the son of the *Dagongbao* owner and editor, and also by virtue of his own efforts.

Finally in 1920, my father came home by sea. It took a hell of a long time to get to China from Europe on a boat. He was my grandfather's only child, and he came home on his father's orders for an arranged marriage. My grandparents prided themselves on being very modern, but at the time, arranged marriages were still the orthodox thing to do. And even though my father had lived in Europe and had met other women there, he came back to China and went through with it.

My grandfathers on both sides lived in Tianjin, and they were friends. When both their wives were pregnant, they said, "If one of us has a son, and the other has a daughter, let's get them married." And they stuck to it.

My maternal grandfather, Cai Rukai, was the founder of what is known today as Tianjin University, called Beiyang University in those days. Even though he had little education himself, he was appointed minister of education by Yuan Shikai right after the republic was declared. He had previously been governor of Shandong. My mother told me that my grandfather had many concubines, most of whom were high-class courtesans. So, after he died at the age of fifty-three, each of the concubines had to be given quite a bit of property. Every now and then I meet someone who claims to be my cousin. My grandfather had a number of sons, but only one child with his legitimate wife, and that was my mother, Cai Baozhen.[6]

My paternal grandfather, Ying Lianzhi, was a Catholic and a Manchu—so no concubines for him, though he was popular among the ladies just the same. He and his wife also had only one child, my father, Ying Qianli. He founded the *Dagongbao* soon after my father was born.[7] He would later help found Furen University in Beijing.[8]

Since one man was the editor of the only newspaper in Tianjin and the other was the president of the only university in Tianjin, it was a good match.

My father knew as a child that my mother had been chosen as his future wife. And my mother knew it too. My paternal grandfather was Catholic, so my mother was duly baptized, and sent to learn English at a school for girls run by nuns in Tianjin called St. Joseph's. That was part of her dowry, and my mother's wealthy family could afford it. Apparently my paternal grandfather didn't mind that his daughter-in-law would come from a family with concubines, in spite of his Catholic faith. It was just one of those facts of life.

Around the same time they married, my family founded a school for girls and my mother became the head of it. It was quite a responsibility for a nineteen-year-old, but one of the things that both my father and my grandfather insisted on was that women must have a vocation and must work. Their views were quite progressive for the times, even by Western standards.

The wedding was held in a Byzantine cathedral in Tianjin that was built at the beginning of the twentieth century. A huge temporary arch was built in front of the cathedral for the wedding, and everybody who was anybody came to the ceremony.

By the time my father returned from Europe to marry my mother, their fathers were barely on speaking terms, partly due to differing views on Yuan Shikai. Yuan hated my paternal grandfather because he was one of the reformers, and the hatred was mutual because Yuan had betrayed the cause of reform. He played some pretty dirty tricks during the transition from the empire to the republic, first making himself the prime minister and then usurping the highest position by pushing Sun Yat-sen aside and making himself the first president. Yuan tried many times to buy off my paternal grandfather by offering him money and position, but to no avail.

My two grandfathers were not getting along, but both sides adhered to the original agreement for the arranged marriage. It was too late to change it anyway—in addition to already being baptized and sent off to a missionary school to learn English, my mother had moved in and cared for my paternal grandfather after he had a stroke. One source of great pride for my grandfather was that, in spite of having suffered a stroke, he was still recognized as one of the outstanding calligraphers of the new century at the time.

When Furen University was established in 1925, my grandfather Ying Lianzhi was appointed president but was already quite ill. Even in his last days, he still showed his colors as a rebel by nature, naming as his successor the great scholar Chen Yuan—a Protestant being appointed as a leader of a Catholic university was unheard of in those days. Chen Yuan lived into his nineties; a book was published after his death including all his correspondence, and among them were letters he exchanged with my grandfather.

After my parents married, my father went back to England to finish his degree, and he stayed there for quite a few years. My oldest sister was born in the interim, and my father must have made a return trip back to China in 1924 to visit my mother because my brother came along in 1925. My father was away for the better part of the first six years of their marriage, leaving my mother to look after two children. She lived with my paternal grandfather until 1926, when he died and my father returned from Europe for good.

My father came back with a degree in economics, but he certainly wasn't interested in economics—he was interested in the romantic poets like Shelley, Keats, and Byron.

My mother once confided in me, saying, "Men are fickle." At the time she made the remark, Furen had just started a girls' college, and because they were my father's students, some of those girls visited us at home more often than necessary. My mother, of course, was her usual tolerant self, but said to me, "I know what they're after." It wasn't the sons of the household they wanted to meet, but their father, who was indeed very young for his position.

I don't know if my mother ever knew about an Irish woman my father had met long before he returned to China for their arranged marriage, but I found letters exchanged between them among my father's papers. The letters mention the war, so they must have been written before 1918. My father wrote of how he missed her, and asked her if she could come to London for such-and-such a holiday. Judging from the letters I saw, it seems she was in Ireland, so perhaps they met there, or perhaps they met in England. She was a student, probably a year or two younger than my father.

I don't remember her name, and I never mentioned it to anyone. As far as I know, I am the only one who knows about it. There was one letter in which she told him that she was willing to come back to China with him. I suppose if that had materialized, I wouldn't be here today.

From Warriors to Gentlemen

In his love for poetry and his popularity with women, my father seems to have taken after his father. There is a photograph of my paternal grandfather on which he wrote in eight-character phrases:

> You are tall enough to impress ladies.
> You are handsome enough to attract a female crowd.
> But it is only you yourself who knows how romantic thoughts torture you.

This inscription is a small glimpse into my grandfather's soul.

He was an extraordinary person in more ways than one. He came from a family of Manchu Bannermen, who all had military careers without being literate. Our clan most likely came to China in the seventeenth century with the first Manchu emperors. My grandfather was born in 1866 on the outskirts of Beijing, several miles north of the present-day Summer Palace in the vicinity of Heishan Hu. I have never been able to find the exact house where he was born, but I know that is where he grew up. Heishan Hu was where the Bannermen had their military training, so in his youth, my grandfather was trained in weight lifting, horse riding, wrestling, and bow and arrow, following in the footsteps of the skilled warriors in his family.

My grandfather's name as he was known to most people was Ying Lianzhi, but he was called Ying Hua before that. And actually the true form of his name was different, and its history is a long, long story because, as Manchus, our family didn't have a typical Chinese name. Ying Hua is a Han name, and not a common one at that. To begin with, the surname Ying, using the particular character our family uses, 英, is very rare. I have never come across anybody else with that surname.[9]

Our Manchu name, or the name of the clan, was Hesheli, sounding somewhat like Huxley. Of course, Hesheli is too long for a Chinese surname, which should be one character, or in some rare cases two, but never three. Originally, however, my grandfather was called Hesheli Yinghua. And then he changed his name later on after he joined the Reformists' school, at which point Ying Hua was his name and Lianzhi became his *zi*. The Chinese usually have two names. One is the official name, listed on all kinds of registers and documents. But the second name, or *zi*, is self-assigned and tries in just two characters (or sometimes only one character) to convey the essence of what one is really seeking in life. My grandfather's official name was Ying Hua (*hua* meaning flower or exuberance), and his chosen *zi*, Lianzhi, means "don't show off, try to hide it" (the word *lian* means to suppress—it is a polite way of being self-effacing and hiding one's emotions). One can tell that this name, Ying Lianzhi, was chosen when he matured because the custom is that when one makes a statement like that—"don't show off"—it conveys that one is not calling attention to oneself anymore like younger people do. He also chose for himself a *hao*, which is a kind of pen name.[10]

I have never traced my family back past my grandfather.[11] I know that my great-grandfather made a living by making a certain kind of coal briquette. There is a coal mine not very far from where our clan lived, which I believe is still functioning. There was always a lot of coal dust, so the Manchus in the borderlands took up this trade of mixing the coal dust with loess soil and making it into little balls that could be burned as fuel in the winter and all year round for cooking and hot water. Legend has it that my great-grandfather made a living by that, making him the lowest of the low in that society at the time, hardly any better than a rickshaw coolie. But he had five sons, and my grandfather, the second boy, was very much out of the ordinary. He wanted to learn how to read and write.

His family couldn't afford to buy paper, of course. There was a river just near where they lived, and a huge teahouse at the end of a bridge. As a boy, my grandfather would go to this teahouse to gather up the wrapping paper for tea that customers threw away. He gathered the pieces, took them home, and practiced calligraphy on them. And he made his own ink, too. Perhaps my resourcefulness in making my prison notebook came from him.

One day he met an old Taoist drinking tea at the teahouse, who asked him what he needed the paper for.

"To practice my calligraphy," he answered.

So the Taoist became interested and had a long talk with my grandfather, which finally ended up with the Taoist declaring, "I'll take you as my disciple. But now since you are my disciple, you have to leave your home."

In China this is called *chujia*. *Chujia* literally means to leave home, but colloquially it means to become a monk or a nun. And my grandfather seemed to like the idea, so the two of them set off from the teahouse and walked all the way to Beijing together. He didn't tell his parents—he just took off.

By the time they reached the southern part of the city, they hadn't had any food for quite a few hours, so the Taoist took him to a small noodle shop. There they met another man who was a professional teacher for impoverished Manchus. This man was quite lonely and since he was acquainted with the Taoist, he came over to talk to him.

"What are you doing here?" he asked.

The Taoist shamefacedly told him, "I just got a new disciple."

"What?" he exclaimed. "*You* having a disciple? What nonsense! Leave the child with me!"

So my grandfather had to leave the Taoist and go with the other man to become a kind of apprentice called a *shutu*, a boy who serves as an assistant to a teacher who specializes in going to people's families to tutor their children. Every morning my grandfather had to follow the teacher carrying heavy bundles of ink, stones, copper inkpads, paper, and books. He did this for several years.

He was so bright. Before the regular students of this teacher could learn their lessons, he knew them all by heart. And his calligraphy became quite impressive as well.

It so happened that there was an old, poor Manchu who still retained the title of *jiangjun*—general—but he didn't have a single soldier under him. He invited the teacher to his house to give lessons to his daughter because there were no schools for girls. One thing led to another, and my grandfather became more than a little friendly with this girl. He was in his teens by then and had been with the teacher for quite a while. The two of them—this boy and this girl—started secretly exchanging letters in the Chinese style of bound books. But then, unfortunately—or perhaps fortunately—it was discovered by the master of the house, who became very angry. He locked his daughter up and wanted to chase my grandfather away.

The teacher who had adopted my grandfather as his apprentice took the general aside and said, "You want my advice? Here it is. These days, we Manchus are not held in very high regard with the common people because we've been losing so many battles with foreign countries. What we need to restore the glory of the Qing is to be able to spot real talent. And let me assure you, you are lucky to have this boy as a paramour of your daughter. He is the most capable of all my students. At least think about it."

And by the next day, he must have thought about it because he sent a message to the teacher that amounted to, "All right, I agree."

So my grandfather and my grandmother were married. It must have been quite a daring thing to do in those days. This was in the latter half of the nineteenth century, a time that corresponded to the Victorian era in the West, when people were still very straitlaced about sexual relationships. In those days, marriages in China were arranged. It was only through the efforts of this teacher that my grandfather married the lady after his heart.

In so doing, he married into a royal clan. My grandmother's surname was Aixin Jueluo—the imperial family name—and her given name was Shuzhong.[12] On my grandmother's side, we are direct descendants of Qing dynasty Emperor Yongzheng, the third emperor who was the son of Emperor Kangxi. Her father, as I mentioned, was a general. My grandmother died in 1925 at the age of fifty, and it wasn't considered a premature thing—people had short life spans then. She had made, for a woman, the full round of her destiny: she had fallen in love in her teens and rebelled against the society of the time by marrying my grandfather, who at the time was nothing, an assistant to a teacher who himself wasn't rolling in riches. My grandfather hired this teacher as a journalist for the *Dagongbao* when he created the newspaper, so this old-fashioned teacher became among the first generation of reporters to write freely about what was happening in the news, and he even wrote editorials.

It was sometime after my grandfather's marriage that he became a Christian, converting to Catholicism. According to my father, my grandfather was listening to a priest in the streets haranguing the crowd with calls of, "Repent ye sinners, the Kingdom of God is near!" It was a foreigner doing this—he had a big beard and he was preaching in Chinese. The missionaries had very strict training in those days in order to be sent to China. They usually landed in Macao, went to school there to learn Chinese (either Mandarin or Cantonese), and worked very hard at it. And some of them found favor with the imperial family. Emperor Kangxi himself learned geometry and trigonometry, and even Latin, from some priests. Members of the imperial family all received proper Church burials after their deaths. Their tombs are still in Beijing, in the courtyard of the Beijing Communist Party School.

In any case, it was one of these missionaries that my grandfather heard preaching in the street that day, and he got interested. He began to study the doctrines of Catholicism and finally received baptism. As for my grandmother's faith, women didn't count in those days. She had to believe in whatever he believed in.[13]

Though my grandfather had wandered far from home as an apprentice to the tutor, he did eventually see his family again. After his conversion to Catholicism, he found a job, and made enough to feed himself and sometimes went home to visit. But he did not go back to the wilderness. He lived in the city proper, where he joined all kinds of social and political activities—the most important, of course, being the Reform movement, which won the support of the Emperor Guangxu.

My grandfather became very active politically. He joined some of the Reformist organizations, and he refused to sit for the imperial examinations, which used to be the only means in China for intellectuals to be promoted to officials. He condemned the system of demanding that all scholars write treatises strictly according to the eight-legged essay (baguwen) structure, saying, "This is a sure way to smother talent. People will just become machines writing according to a set formula."

The imperial exams were abolished in 1905. It was during Emperor Guangxu's Hundred Days of Reform in 1898 that many temples were turned into modern schools based on European models. Delegations were sent out to the West to observe how to put a constitutional monarchy into practice. But after one hundred days, Guangxu was betrayed in a coup and imprisoned on an island in today's Zhongnanhai, and six leaders of the Reform movement were beheaded. Those who could escape from Beijing did so. The famous Kang Youwei and Liang Qichao both set off—and so did my grandfather. He fled first to Hong Kong, and then from Hong Kong to Vietnam. My father was conceived and born during this period of flight from the mainland. From Vietnam, my grandfather came back to China, but hid himself in a corner of the empire in Yunnan before it was safe for him to migrate inland to Shanghai, then Tianjin, then eventually Beijing once it was safe.[14]

In 1902, the Empress Dowager returned to Beijing, and as a gesture of amnesty, she issued an edict that said something to the effect of, "Apart from two persons, everyone who joined the Reformists is hereby forgiven—you were just being foolish."[15] In that edict, my grandfather was referred to as simply Ying Hua without the Manchu clan name attached, because the authorities could not imagine that a Manchu would join in the movement against the Qing. They thought he was Han.

To my knowledge, this is the first time my grandfather's name comes up as Ying Hua, and of course his family all felt this was a very good opportunity to get rid of the Manchu shadow over their lives. So they all dropped the last name Hesheli, and adopted part of his first name as the family surname. Even his own father did this, and from then on, they were all called Ying.[16]

My grandfather and his friends, who were by then rather independent (because they did not support the Boxers in 1900), came back from Yunnan after the pardon in 1902. Some money had accumulated in the hands of this group of the new middle class in cities ranging from Shanghai to Guangdong and Yunnan, and they all felt their voices should be heard. The plan was to start a newspaper, modeled after those in the West. They wanted the newspaper to be in Beijing itself so that it could wield the greatest influence, but of course the Empress Dowager wouldn't hear of it, and finally they had to compromise by choosing the city of Tianjin. Tianjin was a good location for the newspaper because it had distinct areas that were concessions of foreign countries. The Dagongbao was set up in a building in the Japanese concession and was later moved to the French concession. It even had a French name: l'Impartial. It was the only newspaper of its kind north of the Yangtze River. My grandfather was the general manager and the first editor-in-chief, and he wrote one editorial every day. He was a hard-working man.

The newspaper itself was based in Tianjin, but the funding for it came from bankers and big traders in Shanghai. My father was raised as an only child in Tianjin. He told me that he was a very naughty boy, a holy terror in the courtyard of the Dagongbao in fact. In those days, people still lived in houses that had paper windowpanes, and just when they had finished decorating their windows with paper, my father would get a stick and tear up every pane. He was always getting into trouble for things like that.

In 1912, the family moved to Beijing, where my grandfather was entrusted with the area known as the Hunting Park at Fragrant Hills (Xiangshan). All these places around the capital—like Qinghua University or the present day Peking University—were originally imperial gardens, and Jingyi Garden was the Hunting Park.[17] Because my grandfather enjoyed considerable prestige as a new-styled scholar, he was entrusted with the whole area to create modern industry for the local destitute Manchus. That was a place where a lot of Manchus lived.

Thirty years ago, I visited the Hunting Park, and I met an old man and asked him if he remembered my grandfather. "Oh yes," he said, "we all remember him. He was the man who modernized the place." They were the first to have electricity in that entire region, including Beijing itself. Those must have been quite exciting times.

It was there that my grandfather founded Jingyi Girls Middle School (*Jingyi nuzhong*), of which my mother became president at nineteen. It was named after the Jingyi Imperial Garden—the same way Qinghua University is called Qinghua because it is the site of the former Qinghua Imperial Garden.

He also helped start an orphanage for the victims of a flood that had occurred a year earlier. The orphanage was called *Xiangshan ciyouyuan* (Fragrant Hills Philanthropic Kindergarten). Out of that orphanage came quite a number of future Communist leaders. These kids were orphans, so none of them had families and, as a result, a lot of them began to read radical books and progressive literature, and later became revolutionaries. I don't think my grandfather expected that—he must have been surprised to see such a thing result from his philanthropy.

My grandfather created a rather important institute called *Furen xueshe*—the Furen Learned Society.[18] It was established in 1913 in the Hunting Park of Fragrant Hills, and operated until 1918. Concentrating on the liberal arts, meaning classics—classical literature, classical history, and various other branches of classical studies—it became the basis for Furen University. All these institutions were created in one way or another out of my grandfather's religious beliefs, and Furen University itself was founded by decree of the Vatican.

The Furen Learned Society and subsequent university came about as the result of a violent quarrel between my grandfather and the French Catholic archbishop of Beijing, who thought the best way to propagate the faith was to become a respected member of the upper class and buy up land through both legal and illegal means. This was after the Boxer Rebellion and Europeans could dictate their own terms, so the Church in north China became one of the region's most powerful landlords. The more progressive citizens like my grandfather were against this establishment of a social system that positioned foreigners as powerful landlords who could then bribe Chinese peasants into becoming Christians. (The Chinese peasant, by the way, is a very cunning animal: he may pretend to go through all the rituals taught by the missionaries, but at home, he still offers paper money to the gods of money and war and so on.) This tension was at the root of a lot of trouble between China and the foreign powers of the time.

Together, my grandfather and his close friend Ma Xiangbo wrote a letter to Pope Pius X in 1912 about the state of affairs in China.[19] They felt that the teachings of people like the sixteenth-century Jesuit Matteo Ricci were being forsaken. Ricci had befriended the intellectuals and Qing court in China and introduced Western science and technology, and was fondly remembered all through the first half of the Manchu dynasty for his contributions. In place of his doctrines, my grandfather and Ma Xiangbo saw something very backward taking hold, symbolized by the perpetuation of the landlord system with foreigners buying up the land. They felt this was damaging to the spread of true Christianity, and they also saw that it was stirring up trouble.

The pope answered my grandfather's letter.[20] He was very supportive, and soon after the first Vatican-instituted Catholic university opened in Beijing and was officially named and registered. My grandfather was posthumously knighted by the Vatican for his contributions to the Church in China, becoming Sir Vincentius Ying. Many years later, my father was also knighted by the Vatican as Sir Ignatius Ying.[21] I'm afraid the line has broken now with me, so perhaps someone should remind Pope John Paul II that Sylvester Ying should be a "Sir," too![22]

In 1925, the pope entrusted the American Benedictines with the project of founding and administering a Catholic university in Beijing, and they eventually retained the title of Furen, appointing my grandfather as the university's first president. Furen still exists in Taiwan, where it was reestablished in 1960 by the Jesuits. When Furen was restored there, my father was already quite old, so they made him the vice president under Archbishop (later Cardinal) Yu Bin as president. Even now in Taiwan, the university memorial room features exhibits showing my grandfather, Ying Lianzhi, and his friend Ma Xiangbo, as well as my father, Ying Qianli. When I was there in a touring production with the Beijing People's Art Theatre in 1993, I was invited to give some lectures at the university, allowing me a brief moment to follow in their footsteps.

My grandfather and Ma Xiangbo were both obsessed with the idea of modernizing China according to the Western model—which, in their case, meant a constitutional monarchy like England. Ma was a Jesuit at one point, and was well versed in foreign languages, especially Latin. He is credited with the translation of various litanies and prayers. Ma was a full generation older than my grandfather, and one of the legends about him is his longevity—he was born in 1840, making him twenty-six years older than my grandfather, and he lived for exactly a century.[23] He died during the Japanese occupation, and was very patriotic and outspoken against Japanese aggression. Because Ma was such a political figure and wielded great influence over public opinion, even people like Mao Zedong and Zhou Enlai wrote memorial pieces in memory of him when he died. He was widely known at the time as the patriotic patriarch of China.[24]

Ma Xiangbo came from a highly educated and extremely wealthy family in Shanghai that owned the best land and buildings in Xujiahui (Xujia district), and Ma donated much of it to the Jesuit missions. The great Xujiahui cathedral built by the Jesuits stands on that land donated by Ma Xiangbo. I believe that my grandfather's adopting the Catholic faith had a lot to do with his friend Mr. Ma. Ma came to Beijing as an appointed official after passing the imperial examinations. He trained as a Jesuit, though he never actually became a priest—but he also never married or left the Church. He completed his studies and was a very pious person; on the other hand, it is well known that there was no lack of women who were fascinated by him and who fell for him—including a few in the Ying family.

I remember Ma Xiangbo as a very old man. The first time I met him he was already in his eighties. He had a white beard, and on that occasion he wrote a couplet for our family, as both a bestowal of good wishes and simultaneously an admonition to behave. He used classical Chinese to compose a couplet of four phrases, the first three of which I remember clearly: *yanzheng lishen* (严正立身), *kuanren jiewu* (宽人接物), *zhonghou chuanshi* (忠厚传世). Now, for the last four characters, I can still recall the meaning, but I can't remember the text. Altogether, the couplet said to be generous and uncompromising, and to carry on the family tradition to its logical end.

My grandfather built up the Ying clan from a group of illiterate soldiers to men worthy of carrying on the family tradition. The family migrated from Manchuria as part of the army at the beginning of the Qing dynasty— perhaps they were even among those who came in with the emperor to take over China. People often wonder how the Manchus could conquer a country the size of China. It sounds so ridiculous because, by all accounts, the Manchus numbered only about 280,000 foot soldiers. But the first three Manchu emperors were extremely capable rulers. The population—a barometer of prosperity for those times—increased to 300,000,000 by the end of the reign of Emperor Qianlong. People were well fed, and the country was united. The eventual corruption of the Manchus came much later with the Opium War.

From a litter of illiterate soldiers, my grandfather emerged as a man of letters who founded a university, a modern newspaper, a progressive school to educate girls, and God knows what else. Only recently, I discovered that he was even friends with Li Dazhao, one of the founders of the Chinese Communist Party. Li was chief librarian at the newly established Peking University when they met. My grandfather was also close friends with Yan Fu, the university's first president, a fellow reformer, and a celebrated scholar and translator.

My grandfather provided for the entire Ying family, giving each of his four brothers and his sister a piece of property and the means to make a decent living.

He was the Number Two Son, but he was promoted to the position of family patriarch through the murder of his elder brother. This great uncle was a true hooligan in the sense that he always got into fights. Because his wrestling skills were so good, nobody could beat him—but he was stabbed to death in a dark *hutong* one night by one of his adversaries. He wasn't important enough for the police to ever find his killer, though. Lately we've been trying to identify his descendants, and so far we've traced them to a very pretty and famous actress during the early days of the film industry in Shanghai who is supposed to have been his daughter. She kept her surname, Ying, and was known as Ying Yin. She committed suicide in 1938, at her prime, similar to Ruan Lingyu. Women had only just then been liberated, and practically overnight. So, the pressure—the social pressure and the pressure of public opinion—was quite fierce. And some of these young beauties like Ruan Lingyu and Ying Yin got into unfortunate marriages with bad men, and ended up taking their own lives as the only way out.[25]

Another of my great-uncles, Number Four, was named Ying Jie, and I remember him with quite a bit of fond nostalgia. He was not a rambunctious rogue like his late elder brother, but was actually a professional Manchurian wrestler who, as legend has it, won a decisive match against a famous wrestler when he was only fourteen years old.

Number Five, the youngest, was a skilled hunter, but he was also a good-for-nothing, a typical spoiled young man. He couldn't fight, not like Number Four. He just kept some dogs and falcons for his hunting outings. He loved to hunt, but he couldn't make a living that way. My grandfather saw that this brother was a good-for-nothing and wondered what he should do to help him. Eventually, he gave his brother fifty rickshaws so he could rent them out to the coolies in Beijing. And Number Five made quite a living that way, too. A coolie had to pay at least ten coppers per rickshaw for each daily rental, and that amounted to quite a sizeable sum in those days. My great uncle would collect the rental price from the coolies, and the coolies would keep the fares paid by their passengers—so you can see why the rickshaw coolies would try their best to wheedle out as much money as possible from their customers.

My grandfather shared what he owned with all his siblings. Nobody else had a cent to his name. He started the rickshaw business for Number Five, whose name was Ying Hao, and to great-uncle Number Three he gave the family businesses, including a grain route from Zhangjiakou to Beijing along with its corresponding grain shop in Beijing. He ran a pawn shop as well. Pawn shops were notorious for taking advantage of poor people, their only customers, who pawned rather than selling their possessions in hopes of retrieving them at a later date. Even though the prices were usually low, most of these people could never retrieve their belongings. Not surprisingly, these two businesses—the pawn shop and the grain shop—were among the first to be repressed by the new regime after 1949. Perhaps fortunately, Third Uncle died before he lost the two businesses—his adopted son had taken them over by then.

Great-uncle Number Three, Ying Shifu, had been introduced to society at large in Tianjin as my grandfather's brother. The legend goes that he was looking for a wife at the time, and many matchmakers were saying, "Well, if he's Mr. Ying's brother, then there can be nothing wrong with him." So the best families were trying to get their daughters married to him—and he ended up with a beauty, a very cultured lady from a prestigious family in Tianjin. But soon he was diagnosed with syphilis. Of course that was a taboo thing for a family like the Yings. The couple could not have children of their own, so they adopted a son, who appears to have also been a member of the Ying clan, a cousin of some sort.

In addition to setting up his brothers Number Three and Number Five, my grandfather also arranged a livelihood for Number Four beyond his professional wrestling career. Number Four served as the supervising operator of the printing press that my grandfather had purchased and brought from Europe to run the newspaper. When my grandfather left Tianjin for Beijing, Number Four was told to dismantle the huge, heavy machine and move the whole damn thing to Beijing—and he did, whereupon he became the owner of a factory with Beijing's first modern printing press of its kind for making high-class reproductions of calligraphy, paintings, and the like. So great-uncle Number Four became influential in his own way.

My grandfather had only one sister, Ying Di, who had caught smallpox when she was very young and was severely pockmarked as a result. Behind her back, malicious people would say she was so ugly that no one would marry her. And it was true—she wasn't very pretty, and she did not marry. She stayed single for her entire life. When I played the role of Pockmark Liu in *Teahouse*, quite a bit of my understanding of pockmarked people came from my great-aunt.[26] She was never without her huge, dark glasses. In fact, she stayed in her room most of the time wearing them. I think it was something psychological—I suppose the glasses gave her a false sense of security, as if no one could peep at her behind them.

But she was a brilliant woman, and she was fierce. She was headmistress of my first school, and she made it a rule to employ only unmarried women as teachers, who more or less all had somewhat warped characters. The school was founded by my grandfather and he immediately installed his sister as headmistress. My mother always claimed that this great-aunt of mine was illiterate, but I can hardly imagine an illiterate person being a successful school mistress. She used to make speeches every Monday morning to the entire school, sometimes for up to three hours. The school was called Peigen, sounding like "Bacon" for Francis Bacon, but it also has an appropriate meaning in Chinese—"to raise from the roots." Originally it was a school for girls from primary school up to the end of senior middle school (around age seventeen or eighteen). Several of these progressive schools for girls were founded by my family in different locations. The one in Inner Mongolia still exists today.

Of my grandfather's siblings, I was closest to great-uncle Number Four, the wrestling champion. He had an official name, but everyone knew him as simply Ying Siye, or Fourth Master Ying. He took his career as a wrestler very seriously, building up a reputation for himself in those circles. The professionals all admired his technique. They would gather together and all applaud at the end of a match when he threw the other man to the ground. I loved to go with him to Tianqiao, where all the popular entertainments took place. He would be greeted by the itinerant wrestlers there, which was great business in Beijing, and he'd be given the best seat, a special cup of fragrant tea, and snuff, which he loved. He took each of my two older brothers out to the matches a few times before he took me—but every time he did that, the next day my mother would complain to him, saying, "Where did you take him? The boy is sick, he ate too much." I, on the other hand, never complained. So, in the end, I won the honor and amusement of accompanying him to the matches, not my brothers. He even preferred to take me rather than his own sons.

I never saw my own grandfather alive, but all my elders claimed that as Fourth Master Ying grew older, the likeness between the two became more and more marked. When I played the role of a seventy-year-old man in the stage adaptation of Lao She's *Rickshaw Boy*, I made myself up to look just like my great-uncle, and my mother and all my relatives of that generation were tickled by the similarity—they could see from my makeup and from the way I played the role that I had him in mind as a sort of inner image.[27] His head was usually shaved, because he had all his hair cut off after the 1911 Revolution and remained bald ever since. He also had a kind of beard, though we Manchus could never grow full beards like Westerners.

Until his last days, Fourth Master Ying was tough. One of the things he loved to do when he came to our place was to show off the muscles on his legs. He'd say, "Come over and feel that." It was like a rock. That's part of the reason he was such a good wrestler. The Chinese traditional style of wrestling was a very popular form of sport in Beijing in those days. After the 1911 Revolution, the former professional wrestlers who had been paid by princes and the chief eunuchs from the city were all out of jobs. Many of them gathered to form clubs and entertain crowds who loved the sport. In addition to taking me to watch, Fourth Master also gave me lessons in wrestling.

Part of his training as a wrestler was in massage and the use of various drugs for healing injuries. I still remember once when I was eight years old, I jumped off the top of a high wall as the result of a bet with a friend. When I hit the ground something happened to the muscles in my leg. My mother was so worried that she took me to the Peking Union Medical College Hospital. It seemed to be very serious, a bad muscular sprain. When Fourth Master came to our house, my mother told him about it, and he said, "Let me take care of the boy." He made a mixture with alcohol as a base and some herbal medicine added to it, then rubbed my leg with the concoction and even lighted it with a match, which ignited the alcohol. It looked rather frightening. He prayed over my leg while it was on fire, and sure enough the next day I started walking freely—and in about three days the pain was gone and the injury was healed.

Fourth Master Ying was a very interesting and rather impulsive person, with a natural, independent character. When Japan invaded China for the first time near the Great Wall in today's Inner Mongolia, he was so furious that out of his own pocket he hired a crew of people to be stretcher bearers. He himself led them to the front to carry away the wounded, like a male Florence Nightingale. Because of his associations with the underworld, he had great admiration for a kind of people in old Peking at the time who were more or less carefree hooligans. These people formed gangs and collected protection money from shops, and they had their own moral code. He used to tell stories about them, mostly involving their ability to withstand pain. This was a great achievement, because physical torture was still regarded as the official way of defeating the unruly elements of society. Anyone involved in a criminal case or even a misdemeanor would be beaten upon arrival at court. These people prided themselves on their tolerance for pain. They'd never shout, never make a sound, but would silently endure all these punishments until the torturers had no choice but to admire their courage.

Fourth Master used to tell us horror stories about two factions of these people who were competing for a section of the city to extort money from the shops, each faction having its own sphere of influence. They arranged a bizarre duel in which iron pokers were placed in the stove until they were red hot, and then they took turns holding them with their bare hands. He said he could smell the flesh being barbecued alive. Sometimes they would pick up red-hot coal balls—the kind my great-grandfather made for a living—and place them on their laps with a pair of pincers. They did this to see who could stand the greater pain without begging for mercy. My great-uncle was in one of these gangs himself, and I imagine he must have been one of the winners in these grotesque competitions.

During the years when he took me with him to the matches, we had a routine. We'd go to Tianqiao in the afternoon, watch the wrestling, and then listen to some storytelling. After that, he would always take me to a favorite restaurant in the commercial downtown area. We'd usually have hot pot, individually cooking thinly sliced mutton over a steaming pot. He'd tell every waiter and passerby, "Look at my grandson—fourteen plates!" He was very proud of me. The empty plates were placed on the table for the final count of how much had been consumed in order to tally the bill, and according to him, I did once consume that many plates at one sitting.

Fourth Master Ying admired appetite and he admired strength. Even in his later years, he could still pull a bow and arrow. His bow was so tough that even two children together couldn't pry it open. He was brawny, but not very tall. Our clan had all intermarried in the past with Mongols, so characteristically they all had rather short necks and legs, but very tough upper body muscles. There used to be a photograph of my grandfather himself seated on a chair, on which (in one of his more playful moods) he inscribed the words, "When sitting down I'm taller than anybody but standing up I'm short. Perhaps that is the trait of a hero who loses his heart to a beauty."

My great-uncle Fourth Master Ying died in December 1948. I was already a student at Qinghua University when I attended his funeral.

Many years later, after I was released from prison in 1971, I was sent to a cadre school to grow rice for one year. There was an old man there who recognized my family name.

"May I ask a question?" he started.

"Please," I said.

"Ying—" he continued, "—this is a very rare name. Do you happen to be related to Fourth Master Ying?"

"Yes," I replied, "he was my great-uncle."

"He was my teacher!" the old man informed me with delight, explaining that he had been my great-uncle's apprentice at the printing press.

In the early years of the Republic, new-style model schools were set up, giving quite a number of children from big cities like Beijing and Shanghai the chance to learn reading and writing. At that time, it was difficult to find apprentices who were literate. To work with a printing press, one must be able to read.

This man at the cadre school told me his life story. After apprenticing with Fourth Master Ying, he eventually became the foreman of the press, and then was promoted even further. By the time of the Cultural Revolution, he was considered a member of the ruling class, so he was sent to the cadre school for reeducation. If he had never met my great-uncle, he would never have ended up in the labor camp where I met him.

Fourth Master Ying had a son, Ying Xiliang, who while still in his teens had an illicit affair with a maidservant in his family. When I say maidservant, I don't mean someone you hired, I mean someone you bought. The elders of the Ying clan felt that this behavior was too shameful, so they kicked him out—he was more or less excommunicated from the family. He did all sorts of things to make a living, including, finally, becoming a professional trader who roamed in the streets preying on families who were trying to sell the little bit that remained of their belongings. There were lots of families like that in Beijing at the time. Beijing used to be the capital for the Ming and Qing dynasties, so there were quite a number of officials who lived in Beijing, and Manchu Bannermen as well, who by then had all lost their incomes and had started selling off their possessions. Some of these things were quite valuable objets d'art, bronze pieces, and the like. So Ying Xiliang became one of those who went around in the *hutong* plying a trade that was not entirely legal. For instance, he never paid taxes for his income. But I must say that I owe him quite a bit for his influence on my acting. When I acted in *Teahouse*, he was my chief model for the pimp Pockmark Liu. In fact, he once took me with him to a teahouse while I was preparing for the role. All the tradesmen had their particular teahouses—one for masons, another one for carpenters—and this one happened to be for pimps.

The atmosphere at this teahouse was very interesting. When they got together, these traders would all boast about their acumen: one would say he spotted a treasure that all the others had missed, and then he would brag about the pile of money he made. Of course most of it was not true, but I was utterly impressed with their quick changes of mood and expression, especially when they were bargaining with a would-be seller. They would treat the man who was trying to sell something through their brokerage with full sympathy and pity, but then become disgusted if he got too stubborn and claimed to have a treasure when it was really something worthless. And they could really bully people.

This was the trade my great-uncle's good-for-nothing son got himself involved in. And his wife busied herself with bearing him child after child after child—at least a dozen—so many that they couldn't come up with new names for them anymore.

We had a cemetery handed down from a fourth-generation ancestor, where my grandfather's parents were buried. The land was collectively owned, because it was supposed to be a family plot. Then after 1949, the government published notices in the newspapers that went something like this:

> The areas mentioned below can be purchased by the State because the State needs the land to construct new buildings. Each family will be compensated with the price of the land.

The notice was followed by a list of land area properties. None of us paid any attention to this advertising offer, of course. But Ying Xiliang, without telling anybody—and after he had already been kicked out of the Ying clan—went to the government and showed his ID, saying, "I am a representative of the Ying family and we support the government's directive. How much are you gonna give?" He took away a few thousand dollars—at that time land was cheap. We didn't find out about what he had done until ten years later, but by that time it was too late. The government sent surveyors to the property and started building modern buildings, and all the remains in the family tombs, including the coffins—even if they were rotten—were moved to a new site north of Beijing that was given to us as compensation.

Summers at Warm Springs

The Summer Palace at the northwest corner of Beijing was the private retreat of the Empress Dowager Cixi. Ten miles north of the Summer Palace is a place called Wenquan (Warm Springs), which was our family's summer retreat, and I still own our land there. On a huge piece of rock, in characters over six feet tall, the phrase "*Shuiliu yunzai*" is carved in my grandfather's calligraphy. The phrase means "The water flows by, but the cloudy mist remains."[28] The rock is on a very prominent hilltop and is a tourist attraction nowadays. Several years ago, I spent a good deal of money to restore it, as a tribute to this extraordinary man. And then I spent even more building a new residence on this land, where I hope to live in my old age.[29]

My family's original residence there was lovely. We were quite wealthy, and there were three or four other families like ours who built summer homes in Warm Springs—but our houses were quite some distance apart. The other residents of the area were all local villagers.

Sometimes the few well-to-do families vacationing there would pay courtesy visits to one another. What I remember most vividly is that when the other families came, the men were usually dressed in full formal silk gowns, and the first thing the host would say was "Aiya, kuanyi, kuanyi," a very polite way of saying, "Take off your coat." Beijing can be really hot in the summer, and there was no air conditioning in those days. So each guest would be handed a fan, and special semitransparent Chinese jackets were worn by the gentlemen.

We children thought this phrase kuanyi was part of the grown-ups' own funny language, and it always made us laugh. Children, you know, are really sensitive to these things. We actually used to make collections of all the quaint sayings uttered by these self-styled gentlefolk who envisioned themselves as separate from the poor people surrounding them because they could afford to have a summer house there. And then later, behind their backs, we would imitate them.

Another phrase we children thought was awfully funny was the typical greeting, "Today I brought my unworthy relative to pay you his respects." We hardly ever heard phrases like this in the city. Back in the city, we were surrounded by the new liberals who were trying very hard to behave like civilized people by imitating foreigners or novels they were reading in translation. These neighbors in the countryside, however—the rich ones who owned summer homes there—were trying hard to seem sophisticated without knowing how to appear as civilized as the urban residents. So their attempted niceties were more old-fashioned, even feudal. Some of them were wealthier than my parents, but money alone cannot afford one a cultural education, so in terms of social status, my family was highly regarded.

Usually, just the adults would drop in for a visit, but sometimes they brought their children. My parents were very progressive and welcomed the poorer local families into their home as well. So when I went out and played with the children, it was more or less a mixture of rich children and poor children. We weren't divided by class out in Warm Springs to the degree that we were in the city proper, and situations arose that were hard to come by in the city. For instance, during the summer we had the freedom to catch grasshoppers alongside our little neighbors who were socially quite far behind us.

But the wealthier families sought us out—especially because of my brother, Ruoqin. He was four years older than I was, and we teased him quite a bit because he was the obvious desired match for all the girls out in Warm Springs. People there thought of him as a Prince Charming, and it was up to all the mothers to entice him, so he would sometimes go with the grown-ups to the other families' homes at their special invitation. Of course, we children thought that was very funny, because none of us ever dreamed that we would take a wife from this place. It might have been less obvious in Warm Springs, but class was still very important in China at that time.

Our summer house was rather high up on the side of a hill, and there was a local family that lived in a house below ours with a little girl about my age. She was a lively girl and we children liked to play with her. One day when we were seven years old, she simply disappeared. We went to her home to try to find her.

We could hear her mother's voice scolding her through the paper windows: "Don't make so much noise! Every girl goes through this!"

We expected her to appear the next day and play games with us as usual, but she did not—and it took her about a month to reappear. We looked for her, we asked for her, but we heard nothing.

"She's busy," the grown-ups told us, as though that explained anything at all. She was only seven years old—how busy could she be?

Several weeks later, she emerged from her home and wobbled along the mountainous area. We all stared at her feet, which seemed to be the cause of her trouble.

We surrounded her and asked her, "What happened to you?"

"My mom forced me to have my feet bound," she replied.

We were all so curious. "Can we have a look?"

"No," she said. "No one is supposed to look at them."

The binding of feet was still going on in the countryside at that time, even though it had already been banned. I only vaguely understood what it was. All of the elderly women in that village had bound feet, of course, and I knew that these women had the procedure done when they were very young.

We children continued asking this little girl about why her mother had done this to her. She answered bashfully, "My mom says no one will marry me if I don't have my feet bound."

Just then, her mother appeared and shooed us away, shouting her own answer to our question: "It's quite true. Who'd marry a girl with huge feet? Dajiaopian! Big Flat Foot! Who'd marry a girl with feet like that?"

We children scurried in all directions.

"And you're not allowed to play with her anymore!" her mother called out after us.

I never did get to play with her again. Her mother treated me a bit more carefully than the other boys, however. They were just local neighbors, whereas in her mind, I was a possible future suitor for her daughter's hand.

That poor girl did have a pretty little face.

It was a long journey from Beijing to Warm Springs back then, and moving the family out there every summer was quite an undertaking. Sometimes, if my father could manage it, he would borrow a friend's car, and later on we bought one ourselves. Cars were rare in those days. Most people rode on donkeys for transportation, which were quite safe, but extremely slow. I remember making the trip by donkey when I was very young. And I remember one particular incident while traveling by donkey—about the same year that that little girl got her feet bound—that became one of my many small crimes as a child.

I was a cheeky boy, and I always wanted my donkey to be faster than my elder brother's, which of course was a little too ambitious of me. One day we were all going out to a missionary church in the Western Hills from Warm Springs—a journey of about five miles—and I chose a lively braying donkey. I loved to hear that donkey bray. And while we were waiting at the foot of the hill, my aunt, Ying Ruiliang (my father's cousin), was seated on another donkey just in front of me. I didn't have the patience to wait for my brothers to catch up, so I started to beat the donkey with the handle of a whip, and the donkey was not very pleased about it. This donkey became so angry that it bit my aunt's leg. She howled with pain and tumbled to the ground. The entire trip to the missionary church was abandoned, and I was in a lot of trouble. It was a rather frightening experience.

My aunt was carried up the hill, and doctors were summoned. She had to be sewn up right away. I still remember that donkey: he was black and fierce. And he just continued on his way after biting my aunt—nonchalant, as if it was just part of a day's work. I tried to stop him, but by the time I succeeded, I was a hundred meters away.

The grown-ups pulled me off the donkey and said, "Do you know what happened? What did you do to that donkey?"

And of course I answered, "I didn't do anything. I just wanted to go faster."

My parents were the modern type, especially my father, having been educated in London. So when we children were disciplined, he always behaved like a gentleman. He never beat us children. None of us were ever touched— except once, when my eldest brother, Ruoqin, was impolite to our mother. He was about ten years old, so I was six or seven. My father turned it into a real ceremony: he made Ruoqin bend down over a table, and he spanked him with a cane. It was purely a British tradition. We all had to watch and learn that we should never use coarse language around our mother, because my father would not tolerate it.

Ying Ruiliang, my aunt who was bitten by the donkey, lived into her nineties in Kunming, so apparently the donkey incident did not do too much damage after all. She was the daughter of my grandfather's good-for-nothing youngest brother, Number Five, who managed the rickshaw business. He had only one son, Ying Zhuliang, and he had intended to drown his two elder daughters, Ying Ruiliang and Ying Duanliang. This was a sort of whispered rumor in the Ying clan—and when my grandfather heard about it, he became so angry that he went over and bawled out his brother and took the two babies away. So these two girls grew up in my father's household. He was an only child, but they became like sisters to him, and later like aunts to us children.

I suppose the Ying clan made a habit of taking in pairs of orphans—my mother adopted two young women from the orphanage she ran in Fragrant Hills, and even though they were not blood relatives, they lived with us like sisters—we children called them Ruiqing Jie (Elder Sister Ruiqing) and Ping Jie (Elder Sister Ping) or just Jiejie (Elder Sister) for short. The two sisters were just permanent fixtures in our household, and I remember being surprised when they left to get married.

Ping Jie and Ruiqing Jie were in their teens when they arrived in our home and my parents managed to find husbands for them. They also had the responsibility of marrying off my two aunties, Ruiliang and Duanliang—the two that my grandfather saved from drowning. My father was trying to find husbands for them, but the only bachelors my father knew were teachers at the university. They weren't very brilliant girls, so what professor would look twice at them? It was through a lot of perseverance that we managed to marry them off.

I remember one summer day, we were having dinner under the big tree in our courtyard and the adults were discussing my aunties, and one of them said in reference to the elder of the two spinsters, "Did you notice? She's beginning to like spicy food." Another grown-up, probably my mother, replied, "Yes, it's time she got married. It's a sure sign." You see, when a girl suddenly loves spicy food, it means she is sex-hungry. That comment stands out in my mind because soon after that, I noticed my father bringing young, wise lecturers and professors to our home to meet the family. Quite a few of them fell in love with my oldest sister, Ruoya, instead of my two aunties, which created quite an embarrassing situation.[30] Ruoya was in her prime at eighteen—beautiful and intelligent, with lots of young men trying to win her hand—while my two aunties were well over twenty and not as attractive or intelligent as she. One of them was twenty-seven, which was quite old to still be an unmarried woman in those days.

Eventually Ruiliang and Duanliang did successfully marry, and they had Catholic weddings at Beitang (Northern Cathedral). I remember serving at one of the ceremonies with my little cousin as ring bearer and flower girl. My mother labored over our Singer sewing machine to make new clothes for the two of us for the special occasion—she wanted the little boy and girl to match at the wedding ceremony. Both outfits were made of light blue brocade, and I was very proud of my little costume.

Ruiqing Jie and Ping Jie were, comparatively speaking, easier to marry off, because they were both younger than my aunties. And Ping Jie was quite pleasant to look at. She married a neighbor of my maternal grandmother who lived in the southwestern corner of Beijing. We lent her out to that family for a period to help them with something they needed—a wedding or housework or something of that nature—and one of the young men in that household fell in love with her and married her. I can't remember who Ruiqing Jie married.

These two adopted sisters lived in our home for several years and really did feel like members of the family. And they came with us every summer to Warm Springs. My mother was a very fair-minded woman. I remember that when she would buy impressive clothes for my oldest sister—such as a newly fashioned fur coat—she would buy three of them, and give the other two to Ping Jie and Ruiqing Jie.

I was never well acquainted with their husbands, unfortunately. I believe Ruiqing Jie moved to inland China during the war and died in a bombing, but I continued to hear from Ping Jie up until the late 1970s. They never adopted our surname, Ying, but I never knew what their actual names were, because I only called them Sister Ruiqing and Sister Ping.

"Mr. Wang"

There was a rather manly woman who became a very close friend of our family, mostly because she chose to attach herself to us in various ways. She was quite a bit older than my father, but younger than my grandfather's generation. We children knew her by the name Mr. Wang (Wang Xiansheng) because that was what she preferred to be called. She was a rather unique individual: a devout Catholic, a progressive activist in Feng Yuxiang's Christian army, and a lesbian. She was one of the most interesting people I have ever known.

I was never able to understand how she reconciled her sexuality with her faith, but Mr. Wang was utterly devoted to the mission life, particularly in its goal at the time of establishing liberation and social position for women. And she was very successful in her work. Before I understood her true nature in terms of her sexuality, I only knew that she had lots of lady friends. We were used to having her around as children, and it became a ritual for her to take us with our family to buy nice fruits to eat. She would always make sure the fruit was of the highest quality before we tasted it. She must have been helping to feed the poor as well, because I remember that on days when we had had a feast the night before, she would come with little canteens to carry away the food that was left over. Most of my memories of Mr. Wang are from the late 1930s when I was approaching adolescence, but she continued to frequent our house when I was in my teens and living away at boarding school.

Due in part to her interesting hairstyle, Mr. Wang looked very masculine. Her forehead was shaved so that the hairline started very high, in the Manchu style of the queue. Manchu men were cutting off their queues by then, so such a hairstyle was very unusual, and it made Mr. Wang look just like a man if viewed from the front. It was clear that she had formerly worn the male Manchu pigtail and had cut it off near the nape of her neck. In its place, the hair atop her head was pushed back to that spot and held in place with a brooch.

Mr. Wang served as a low-ranking officer in Feng Yuxiang's army. Feng Yuxiang was the powerful warlord of the northwest. After converting to Christianity himself, he baptized his soldiers using a huge water hose, proclaiming, "I baptize thee in the name of the Father, Son, and Holy Ghost" as he sprayed them all with water.[31] The various responsibilities that Mr. Wang assumed in Feng Yuxiang's corps are difficult to translate into modern terms. One of her titles was head of the office of inoculations, and she had all the soldiers vaccinated to combat major diseases like smallpox, cholera, and typhoid.

After the Japanese came in 1937, she led a platoon of women who specialized in searching female civilians at railway stations; by then it was the new collaborationist regime that employed her, not Feng Yuxiang. The Japanese were very nervous about cholera. She and her platoon of girls were given the job of issuing injection certificates to people at large throughout Beijing. So everyone on the street had to carry, among other papers, their inoculation certificates.

This was also one of her favorite topics when she came to our home—she would go on and on about her certificates. She would come to our place every spring, and earnestly hand my mother a bulging envelope filled with certificates for all sorts of diseases, so that we could never be stopped in the street without possessing proof of a particular inoculation. Every year, she gave us enough for the entire family. We did not actually have these shots, of course, so we were quite privileged. The needles used for the shots were so dirty that it was more dangerous to have an inoculation than to go without—the Japanese, in their paranoia about disease, apparently never figured that out. Or if they did, they didn't give a damn about infecting the local Chinese, so long as the local Chinese were not spreading contagious diseases.

Most of the time as she went about her duties, and when she visited our home, Mr. Wang wore some kind of army uniform on her petite frame, at first in gray or blue and much later, against her wishes, in army green. It was strange in those days to see someone dressed that way, and to my young eyes she looked very funny. She was the only person I had ever seen wearing such outlandish costumes, and she was the only military woman with a substantial leadership role at that time—or at least the only one my family knew of.

Mr. Wang was also the only Chinese open-and-out lesbian I have ever met, even to this day. She lived with her companion, Ms. Fan, whom she pampered. Ms. Fan was a teacher at the Peigen School, where I had attended primary school, and at times Mr. Wang worked there as a teacher, too. I don't think I realized as a child that she was gay; only later did I and my brothers start to understand that there were people who not only tolerated but actually enjoyed homosexuality. As boys, we were kept away from such ideas.

I think my realization that Mr. Wang and Ms. Fan were lesbians came later, when a propaganda campaign against homosexuality was mounted during the spring of 1949. It was actually a rather weak campaign as political campaigns go. But homosexuals were targeted again at times such as the Anti-Rightist Movement of 1957 and the Cultural Revolution of 1966–1976. Whenever there was any kind of political campaign afoot, it seemed she had to pay for her choice of lifestyle by enduring public humiliation. She was quite an old woman by the time of the Cultural Revolution, but during the Anti-Rightist Movement she was stripped of her dignity and forced to make shameful confessions.[32] Mr. Wang had many influential friends, and none of them, including Feng Yuxiang, would come out and accuse her of anything. But when those being struggled against were brought out for public display, she would be positioned against the gate post so that she was easily visible to everyone around. In response to the interrogations she received, she would simply say, "I can't help it." She apparently did not consider herself a freak or feel that she was a corrupting influence among the younger generation. At times when she was cornered, she actually defended herself and what she believed in, even when her accusers credited her lifestyle to mental illness. And even as she endured this kind of humiliation, she remained devoted to her mission of earning a position for women in society and continued her work with great determination. She was truly a very courageous person.

Along with her supervision of inoculation papers, she also organized efforts to enforce the abolishment of foot binding for women, which had been declared in 1902 with only partial success. The height of all of her activities was during the period of resistance to Japan after 1937. Ironically, by the time the social upheavals of the Cultural Revolution began, I think Mr. Wang had won new dignity for herself. Her attitude by then seemed to be, "I couldn't care less. Call me what you will."

She still kept up her rounds to families of her own choice, or people whom she felt should be protected and respected. Our family was one of those, of course. Those who knew her like we did avoided the subject of her sexuality, saying, "I don't want to interfere in her private affairs. She has a right to do as she pleases."

Mr. Wang and Ms. Fan stayed together into their old age. We had been told since childhood to respect this couple. We even heard stories about how Mr. Wang had sold her family heirlooms for a few miserable yuan to buy fruit for the needy. And although there were Red Guards during the Cultural Revolution who tried to use radical discrimination against her, they never got very far. Also, because she had organized so many social campaigns to help China and women, she must have had some strong *guanxi* (connections) with important people, which likely provided protection during those chaotic years.

Feng Yuxiang was one of her faithful supporters, and he was always very highly respected. He died in 1948, so he was long gone before the Anti-Rightist Movement and the Cultural Revolution. When Feng went to the United States on a friendship mission to sell his cause in the West, Mr. Wang was one of those people he talked about as a model citizen and kind soul who should be admired and protected. On one of his travels, he died when his personal boat, which was being tugged by a large American ship, caught fire on the ocean. People had actually begun to sympathize with Feng Yuxiang, regarding him as a possible alternative to the dictatorship of Chiang Kai-shek, and there were elaborate commemorations of him when news of the tragedy reached China. Mr. Wang, of course, was devastated, but she continued her travels both within China and abroad to further the causes Feng had inspired.

Recently, I visited a hillside in Warm Springs, and on one of the hilltops, there was an edifice in memory of Feng Yuxiang.

A Risky Exit

The official start of the Anti-Japanese War was the Marco Polo Bridge Incident on July 7, 1937.[33] At the time, I had just turned eight, and because it was the summer holidays, the family was in Warm Springs—but my father was in the city that day, so we were all stranded out in the country. There were no adequate roads back then—especially in the summer, when there was a lot of rain, and the muddy paths became treacherous. At first no one knew exactly what was going to happen. Would this be a major war, or just a skirmish emanating from the troubled China-Japan relationship?

When the Marco Polo Bridge Incident occurred, everyone was talking about it. People came to our summer house every day bringing us news of what was happening here and there, saying all sorts of weird things, such as, "The Japanese are so well-equipped—they have a cannon that can hit a cow across the mountains!" Most people were convinced that the Japanese meant business this time, and that they were using their concession in Tianjin as one of their bases to start an attack on north China. By that time, the Japanese had already taken Manchuria.

People often warned one another not to provoke the Japanese, saying things like, "They might do anything—they eat babies." Everyone was very nervous, and no one dared venture out from his own home unless it was absolutely necessary to buy a box of matches, a pound of salt, or some sugar.

After the Marco Polo Bridge Incident, all-out war with Japan began, and my father came to fetch us and return us to our home in Beijing. He finally borrowed a car from one of the embassies, though I don't know which one. It might have been from the Italians, but I don't recall precisely—I just remember it was a Ford and had the equivalent of a diplomatic license plate. My father had many foreign friends, and I think he was a member of the International Club at the time. Cars were extremely rare in those days. The whole family had to be crowded into that tiny car. Piling in, we children had no idea what was really happening, and we thought this was great fun. Children are always excited about changing the plan or breaking a routine.

When we arrived at Xizhimen (West Gate), we were all aghast at the huge crowd there trying to get into the city. The Japanese soldiers were already posted on the garrison, and they were not allowing anybody to enter. Back then, the city of Beijing had immense walls that were very effective when the city gates were closed. Nowadays, one might visit some big cities in the world as an honored guest and be presented with the keys to the city, as a purely symbolic gesture. But it was literally true in those days: to open the West

Gate, you really had to use a mammoth key. And the wall surrounding the gate was a double wall, so it was impossible to penetrate.

The West Gate was composed of two huge gates. The lower part was made of iron and the upper part was made of wood. They looked like giant double doors, and on the gates were large knobs. There is a famous Beijing snack named after those knobs—a pastry made of flour with a meat filling. It is bigger than my hand and formed in the shape of that original doorknob, called *mending roubing* or "doorknob meat pie." *Mending roubing* are still being sold in Beijing but very few people know that the origin of the name is the great city wall, because the city wall itself has disappeared.

As we approached the West Gate, the crowd was frightening, and we were nervous. The city gates had already been closed to anyone from the outside. Our car was stopped, and we had to wait at the edge of the moat where the canal was. My father had managed to secure a special pass from some kind of foreign friend, and when the garrison saw the pass and the diplomatic license plate, we were reluctantly waved through. By that time, the car itself was extremely crowded because everyone had piled in, wanting to get into the city.

Two university coeds who had been stranded just outside the city wall had come running up to the car when they recognized my father. "Professor," they pleaded, "please take us with you into the city so that we can return to our families."

And of course my father agreed.

"Okay, we'll try our best," he said. And the two girls somehow or another squeezed themselves into the already packed car, sitting on other people's laps.

There were seven children in the car, and my father, my mother, my two aunties, and the adopted orphans. That was a dozen people already. I suppose when you are desperate, you can do anything. My father was worried that the tires might burst before we entered the city, so he hired some people at the West Gate to help him push the car through. Finally we made it. Just inside the city gate on the right was a Catholic church, and acolytes and parishioners came out to help us. Fortunately our home was not too far from the city gate. So it was a happy ending for everybody.

Ying clan on Ying Di's birthday at Peigen School, 1937. Ying Ruocheng is in the front row, second from right. *Front row, left to right* [children]: Ying Ruozhi, Ying Ruoshi, Ying Shuren, Ying Jialiang, Ying Mulan, Ying Qiliang, Ying Ruocai, Ying Ruocong, Ying Ruocheng, Xiaolin. *Second row, left to right* [one young girl standing, seven elders seated]: Ying Zhongyu, "Fifth Great Uncle's Wife," "Fourth Great Uncle's Wife," "Third Great Uncle's Wife," Ying Di, Ying Shifu ("Third Great Uncle"), Ying Jie ("Fourth Great Uncle"), Ying Hao ("Fifth Great Uncle"). *Third row, left to right* [ten women, three young boys]: "Ninth Aunt," "Eighth Aunt," Li Jing'an, Ying Yuliang, De Yuzhen, Ying Mengzhao (Ruoya), Cai Baozhen, Ying Duanliang, Che Chengxuan, Ying Mengwan; Ying Ruoqin, Ying Ruojing, Ying Zhuliang. *Fourth row, left to right* [five men standing]: Ying Chunliang, Ying Qianli (Ying Jiliang), Ying Qiliang, "Shubo gege," Ying Jialiang. *Note.* Ying Ruoxian was not born yet and Ying Ruiliang was not present. Courtesy Ying Ruoshi

Aixin Jueluo Shuzhong and Ying Lianzhi, 1900. Courtesy Ying Ruoshi

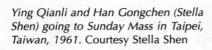

Ying Qianli and Han Gongchen (Stella Shen) going to Sunday Mass in Taipei, Taiwan, 1961. Courtesy Stella Shen

Ying Ruocheng in his first professional stage role as Old Liu in Dragon Beard Ditch, *produced in 1951 and 1953.* Courtesy Beijing People's Art Theatre

Ying Ruocheng (second from left) as Liu Mazi Jr. in Act III of Teahouse *(original production 1958, revival 1979). Yu Shizhi is on far right.* Courtesy Beijing People's Art Theatre

Portrait of young Mao Zedong drawn by Ying Ruocheng in his prison notebook, 1968–1971.

Mao's 1936 poem "Snow," copied by Ying Ruocheng (imitating Mao's calligraphy) into his prison notebook beside Mao's portrait.

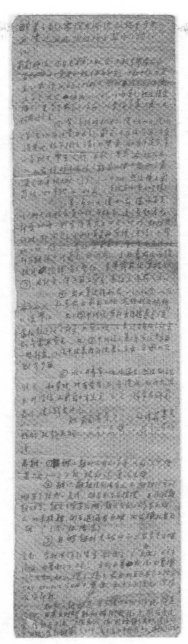

A strip of paper with notes written by Ying Ruocheng that was originally folded and hidden between the pages of his prison notebook, 1968–1971. Notes include excerpt translated into English on page 43 of chapter 2.

Ying Ruocheng (front, center) with coworkers at the Foreign Languages Press circa 1975–1978. Courtesy Ying Da

Wu Shiliang and Ying Ruocheng circa 1982. Courtesy Ying Da

Ying Ruocheng as Willy Loman (with Biff and Happy) in Death of a Salesman, *directed by Arthur Miller in Beijing, 1983.* Courtesy Beijing People's Art Theatre

Arthur Miller, Cao Yu, Wu Shiliang, Ying Ruocheng, and Inge Morath celebrating after opening night of Death of a Salesman, *1983.* Courtesy Beijing People's Art Theatre

Princess Diana, Lu Yan, and Peter O'Toole with Ying Ruocheng at the premiere of the film The Last Emperor *in London, 1987.* Courtesy Ying Ruocheng

Ying Ruocheng (kneeling, on right) as Lama Norbu in the film Little Buddha, *1993.* Courtesy Ying Da

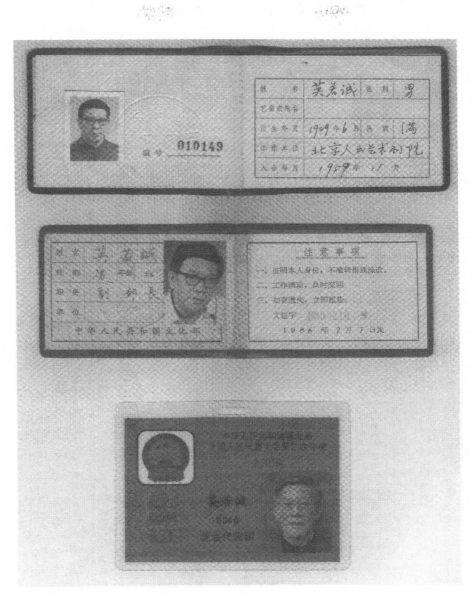

Ying Ruocheng's identification cards for the Beijing People's Art Theatre (1959), Ministry of Culture (1986), and National People's Congress (1999). Courtesy Ying Da

Ying Ruocheng holding his grandson Xingxing (Jin Xinghan, son of Ying Xiaole) in 1985 at their home in Qianchang hutong. Courtesy Ying Da

Ying Ruocheng at his father Ying Qianli's gravesite in Taiwan, 1993. Courtesy Ying Da

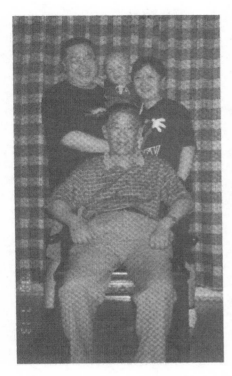

Ying Ruocheng with Ying Da, Ying Rudi (Bayan), and Liang Huan, 2000. Courtesy Ying Da

Final photograph taken of Ying Ruocheng (with his grandson Ying Rudi) at Peking Union Medical College Hospital, December 2003. Courtesy Ying Da

Pu Cunxin and Ma Xin with Ying Ruocheng's son, Ying Da, and daughter, Ying Xiaole, at the posthumous memorial held in January 2004 at Beijing People's Art Theatre. Courtesy Beijing People's Art Theatre

Portrait of Ying Ruocheng with his grandfather Ying Lianzhi's calligraphy, taken by AFP photographer John Giannini in the mid-1980s. Courtesty of Getty Images/ Ying Da

CHAPTER FOUR

~

A Princely Childhood

Home Sweet Home

It is highly unusual for a commoner to be brought up in a prince's palace, but I was. And it was the palace of the notorious Prince Qing at that, who was quite corrupt and probably the richest of all the local princes.[1] Before him, the palace belonged to He Shen, who was by far the greatest villain in the entire Manchu dynasty. It was not until He Shen was finally arrested and his property officially inventoried that the emperor realized there was someone in the empire even wealthier than himself.[2]

All major cities in the old days used to have a drum tower and a bell tower. The bell tower was used to declare the time every day: at noon sharp a gun was fired on top of the tower, making a hell of a big boom, and people who had watches would set them to twelve o'clock. Near the bell tower and the drum tower in old Peking was Coal Hill, a man-made mountain that had accumulated throughout the ages from trash and other materials from the Forbidden City. Prince Qing's palace was in this area near Coal Hill, surrounded by several small lakes, which were favorite spots for the idle rich during the Manchu dynasty of the Qing (1644–1911). In the summertime, temporary sheds were erected along the lakes for circuses, operas, and other popular entertainments.

In his epic novel *Hongloumeng* (*The Dream of the Red Chamber*), the author, Cao Xueqin, describes a very interesting street near the northern lakes in Beijing, on which there are no businesses, but only three princes' palaces.

95

It is on this very street that I was raised—and some say that it is Prince Qing's palace in particular that appears in Cao's masterpiece.[3] During our seven years in the palace, my siblings and I frolicked among priceless antiques and treasures. It was in this setting that we prayed for our brother and sister as they succumbed to tuberculosis. And it was there that we created and performed little plays for the entertainment of our parents' neighbors and friends—my very first acting roles.

Prince Qing's palace happened to be located just beside Furen University, the university my grandfather had helped to create, where my father was a professor. By the mid-1920s, the imperial household had dissolved, and the princes began to sell off their personal properties. The compound that is now the Peking Union Medical College Hospital belonged to one of them, and the one that now holds the British embassy belonged to another.[4] Furen University purchased a compound adjacent to Prince Qing's palace for its campus. At that time, the prince would not sell his private palace because he was still dreaming of making a comeback. In order to be safe, he relocated to Tianjin for the shelter of its foreign concessions, and he asked the Furen priests to send some reliable professors to occupy his furnished mansion. About ten families moved into the huge palace compound, and the prince did not charge them any rent. His preference was for a few foreigners to be among the professors in residence so that a flag could be hoisted, preferably the American stars and stripes, protecting the site from invasion by the Japanese. Several years later, the prince sold his house to the Japanese and moved permanently into their concession in Tianjin, for which he was derided.[5] After the occupation began in 1937, it took some time for the Japanese to establish their control over Beijing, so it was 1940 before they confiscated the palace and made it the headquarters of the military police in the city.[6]

My father was an obvious choice for one of the palace's occupants, because he spoke English and he was more or less in charge of the fledgling university next door. In 1932, when I was less than three years old, the whole family moved into part of the compound, and we lived there until I was eleven. It was a paradise for children. My siblings and I enjoyed free run of the place—and in the process, we absorbed quite a bit of history and culture. The furniture was huge and of the finest workmanship. Before the emperor had abdicated, the prince was in charge of foreign affairs and had amassed a fortune out of his position.

Our section of the palace included five rooms facing south, and we occupied another courtyard attached to it with rooms to the east and west. We had plenty of space. There were residences on every side of the courtyard, which was recessed so that if you went to a room, you had to walk up about one story on stone steps, just like in the Forbidden City. I remember being with my older sister and our neighbor (the daughter of another professor) when they would play tennis in that huge courtyard. The center room of the five big rooms—more like a reception hall—was large enough for us to stage plays. It had a hard rosewood couch twice the length of a typical modern sofa, where the prince received his underlings at the height of his glory. We children used it as our stage, and there was enough space in front of it for the audience to sit on chairs we placed there. There was also a spacious garden where the prince used to keep his sedan chairs, and it had a stage for performances like the ones in the Summer Palace.

Prince Qing must have left in a hurry, because none of the furniture had been moved, and there were gigantic cupboards with drawers inside half-filled with cash (the old coppers with square holes in their centers). The main room where we held our theatre entertainments had an enormous chandelier. I remember we devised all sorts of tricks to reach it because it was decorated with tiny crystal multicolored ornaments and we wanted to play with them. We would carry ladders inside the room and climb up, keeping the little glass gems to offer as presents to our friends.

The experience of living in the palace left such a deep impression on me that I twice managed to sneak into the compound years later to have a look. The first time was soon after Mao's death, when I organized an outing with all my younger siblings and gate-crashed the place.[7] It had become a kind of hodgepodge residential area of the Beijing army. I remembered as a kid turning to the left upon entering the main gate before coming to the second gate, which led to our living quarters, so that is how I proceeded out of habit. I was quite moved to once again stand in the place where I had been raised from my infancy up until my early adolescence, and many old memories were renewed in vivid detail. A decade later, I went back again with my brother from Shanghai and some of my other siblings—we had all gathered in Beijing for my mother's birthday shortly before she died. At this family gathering, we all got nostalgic about the palace, so we just decided to go over there and have a look. When we arrived, there was a guard at the gate telling us it was closed to the public, but we talked our way into the place. I was prepared to find everything much smaller than it had all been in my imagination, because I was just a little kid back then. But even today, when the whole compound is falling to pieces, I look at that place and can't help being impressed by the grandeur of the ruling classes in those days.[8]

Performance and Prayer in the Prince's Palace

My father loved classical Chinese drama—he took us to the theatre every Sunday. On coming back, we children tried to imitate what we had seen, holding our own performances of *jingju* (classical Beijing opera) and sometimes vaudeville. We usually chose the military operas, because we couldn't stand the parts with singing. *Monkey King* was a favorite, and also *Wusong Killing the Tiger*. We five brothers devised our own costumes and makeup, and sometimes my two sisters would join in on special occasions, but Ruoya only watched. She was about sixteen, and the other children were all between the ages of twelve and two (this was before Ying Ruoxian was born). I was seven or eight when we started holding these performances.

We invited our neighbors to come and charged them one copper. Some of them were erudite professors who were quite cultured. At Chinese New Year, our cousins from other branches of the Ying family would come. In a sense, even though I was often in the show, my siblings were performing for me as well because I served as a kind of manager or producer, organizing the performances and paying the actors. It is customary to give each child some money in a red envelope at Chinese New Year, so each of us was given his share. After I paid my siblings for the productions, I was the poorest of the children, but I knew I could get the money back by sulking in front of my mother.

"Why are you sad?" she would look down at me and ask. "It's the New Year—everyone should be happy. What's wrong with you?"

"Nothing, nothing, please don't ask me," I would mutter.

"Come on, tell me the truth," she'd say.

And I would reply, "Well, my money has been given to big brother and second big brother . . . and I don't have any left."

"What?" she would ask in disbelief.

"They said they needed the money for the performance," I explained.

And my mother would fly into a rage and ask them all to come to her.

"You took his money?" she demanded.

And all they could say was, "Yeah, but we worked for it."

"What nonsense!" she retorted. "Pay him back!"

So, all the money was returned to my little hands.

My brothers and sisters would be very mad at me, of course. They wanted to murder me. But I was just getting back at them. They didn't really need any money for the performances—there was nothing to buy—they were just trying to fleece me. I was too smart for them. In the end, whether they took the money from me or whether I gave it up voluntarily and then recovered it was a rather ambiguous matter.

Usually this situation arose when I bribed them, saying, "If you play the pig and I play the monkey, I'll give you money . . . " I always wanted to play the Monkey King.

I suppose I was directing even back then, and already securing the plum roles for myself, too. My brothers gave me a nickname—Xiao Cao (Little Cao)—after General Cao Cao of the Three Kingdoms period, who was the most cunning of all the generals and eventually defeated the two other kingdoms.

It was my father who introduced me not only to Chinese classical opera but also to Western theatre and forms of stylized athletic movement like boxing. He had a friend who was a professional exercise coach, whom we called Su Laoshi or Teacher Su. My father had great interest in Western boxing and hired Su to teach at Furen Middle School where he was head-master. Su devised a system called Technique of the Twenty-four Positions, which utilized twenty-four body positions as the basis of any exercise. I was about three years old when my father first brought this man to our home in the prince's palace to teach them to me. We practiced these exercises for about five years, until the Japanese nearby became curious and started drawing pictures of us, which made my father nervous. These body exercises by Su Laoshi were my earliest introduction to any kind of theatrical training.

My father started writing plays—mime scenarios, really—to utilize the training. I remember some of them being quite funny, based on Charlie Chaplin and the like, and I loved performing them for him.

My earliest performances, however, were in the Catholic church as an altar boy. It was our parish priest who first employed me to sing solos for different Masses. As an altar boy, I knew the Latin litany by heart, and countless hymns as well. The best singers were always teenage boys, before their voices deepened. Oddly, with so many brothers in our family, I was the only one who sang at Mass. The reason was very simple—money. When the parish priest would spot me, he would break into a huge smile and rub his hands together. Then he'd take me to a corner and hand me ten cents to sing a funeral Mass or a wedding. My talent came pretty cheap.

I remember at first I felt a little embarrassed taking money from the priest, but he was very businesslike about it, saying, "This is what you earned by singing. You have a good voice." So I took the money, and sometimes I brought friends along to try their luck, too.

Ten cents in those days was real money—ten cents was twenty-three big coins, and it meant I could enjoy my favorite Beijing snacks after Mass. When the emperor abdicated in 1912, the original imperial kitchens were disbanded and their cooks, some of them with very special skills, were set loose. They established businesses in Beijing, and when I was around ten years old and doing most of my paid singing, my favorite treat was a pastry made from a kind of bean, with honey inside—it was formed into various shapes so you could play with it, and also finally eat it. They are long gone now, and what we have in their place are Western cakes with a lot of cream. Though they are not easy to come by anymore, a shop called Fang Shan (meaning Imitation Imperial Kitchen) still offers some of those old-style snacks—it was one of the establishments started by groups of cooks who were disbanded after the abdication, and they were very particular about what kinds of raw materials they used. Fang Shan's main branch is in the Beihai area by the lake, but there are outlets throughout Beijing.

Even before I was hired by the priest to sing at Masses at the age of ten, I was hired to simply walk down the aisle at Western-style Catholic weddings when I was about six years old. Apparently, I was an extraordinarily beautiful boy—though no one would believe that now—and I had a female cousin half a year older than I who was extremely pretty. She had naturally curly hair, which is rather rare for a Chinese girl. The two of us were always invited by people to appear at their wedding ceremonies because such a pair—a tiny angelic boy and a girl—looked so heavenly. My mother never let us appear on these occasions without new clothes. One time I took the book *Little Lord Fauntleroy* to the seamstress and told her my mother wanted her to make clothes for me just like that. My cousin and I actually received some publicity—which probably had something to do with my father being a man of rank and my late grandfather having been knighted by the pope. People in the parish community looked up to my family, so it was an honor to have me and my cousin appear at their weddings. All we had to do was look cute. We were not the ring bearer or flower girl—we were just told where to walk up the aisle, and that was it. It was bloody cheating actually, because we got paid and provided no service at all. But, technically, this was the first professional acting work of my life.

I started making quite a bit of money singing solos at Mass after I was eleven years old. Sometimes I would sing *Ave Maria*, and on one occasion I remember a special number called *La Donne Mobile*.[9] The most memorable performance I gave was when I was chosen from among the singers in a Christmas play to do a solo. There were two thousand people in the audience at this particular Christmas concert, and at the last minute, nobody wanted to sing, so I was asked to volunteer by the president of Furen University. For this particular occasion, I sang:

Nobody knows the troubles I've seen,
Nobody knows but Jesus . . .
Sometimes I'm up,
Sometimes I'm down,
Oh, yes, Lord . . .

Prayers and hymns were part of my life at home too. My siblings and I grew up saying the rosary together. My father would gather us in the parlor and conduct prayer services. During some periods, we would do this quite often, depending on our circumstances. My brother Ruojing and my sister Ruoya both died of tuberculosis during the Japanese occupation of Beijing, and my father was arrested and imprisoned during that time, so gathering in family prayer was quite a normal occurrence in those days. My father always led the rosary, except when he was in prison, when a priest came to lead it instead.

When my father conducted, sometimes we would sing and sometimes we would pray. He would beckon the children to come over to him, and then he would count the number of children and the number of stands on which we could place the sheet music. The whole business of singing with my father conducting was more sacred than mundane, because of its intent: if we sang well, maybe next week big sister would be home, and maybe my brother would be able to play soccer again. When my brother's illness was at its worst, we gathered every evening to pray for him.

Ruojing was only fourteen when he contracted tuberculosis. We had already moved out of the prince's palace to a different residence in Beijing, and the weather was getting warm after the passing of winter. Like everyone else, he started to change into lighter clothes for the season, and people started noticing that he was too thin.

One day, some students from the university came to my mother, saying, "We showered with your son yesterday after the game, and we saw that he has lost so much weight!"

So my mother took him to the American hospital—Peking Union Medical College—which was still functioning because this was just before Pearl Harbor was attacked. At the hospital, they diagnosed him with tuberculosis. After that, we prayed for him every day, but his death came quickly. He was not allowed to come into other rooms in our living quarters, but he was allowed to come into the courtyard to get some sunshine. One day we were all outside, and Ruojing was trying to put on his jacket, but he could not button it up.

"Ah, he's put on some weight!" we declared.

But that was not true—the weight he had seemed to gain was the advanced tuberculosis that had gone to his tummy and distended it. The disease was discovered in his body too late—and everything moved so fast from there. It was less than half a year between his diagnosis and his death.

Ruojing was sent away to a half-hospital, half-sanatorium—a Catholic one with lots of foreign nurses. I believe they were the Little Sisters of Mary—the nuns wore big white hats that Beijingers always jokingly referred to as *huntun punr* because they resembled giant wonton.

My sister died a year after my brother, at the age of twenty-one, when she was at the top of her class at the university. With her intelligence and culture, she had been a very attractive catch pursued by several young men. In those days, it was rare for a girl to even attend university, let alone be such a brilliant star. My mother would say years later that she felt sorry for Ruojing and carried tremendous guilt for not discovering his condition until it was too late, whereas regarding Ruoya, she would say, "I did whatever I should have or could have done for your sister."

Ruoya was eight years older than I, and we had a special relationship. When I was still very young, she would chat with me in English, and when she was in college, she would talk to me about her classes—especially the romantic poets like Wordsworth, Coleridge, Byron, Shelley, and Keats. She was also a great theatre fan, and taught me Chinese opera pieces, many of which became the performances my brothers and I staged in our home.

During my brother's illness, I had to leave Beijing to attend boarding school in Tianjin, and it was there that I received news of his death and promptly returned for his funeral. But when my sister died, I remained at school in Tianjin because my mother knew how dear she had been to me and feared it would be too painful. My father had not yet been released from prison. Both my brother and sister had Catholic funerals, with priests sprinkling holy water, and prayers recited and requiems sung, and they were buried in our ancestral cemetery.[10] When my mother died in 1989, we went through the same rituals again in the Northern Cathedral. My mother's funeral was well attended, because she was acquainted with much of the Catholic community there. People offered prayers, and some of my father's college students—who were all of quite an advanced age by then—even contributed to paying for the ceremonies.[11]

Ruoya had a promising future ahead of her when she died, whereas my brother Ruojing would have had a real problem if he had lived. At a tender age, he was befriending the priests at the new university next door. He would get up very early every morning while the rest of us were still snoring away, and quietly put on his black robe and go to Mass. His ambition was to become a priest—even an archbishop. What would I and my siblings have done later on if we had had a brother who was a priest? Surely, we all would have suffered politically for his choice. Even back then, we thought it was rather odd—what boy at that age entertains the ambition of becoming a clergyman?

My brother's devout faith must have been influenced by my mother. Even though she converted to Catholicism to marry my father, she was far more sincere in her faith than he. There was a time when she would go to daily Mass, which meant she would get up before six o'clock in the mornings—and on those days we usually had a very poor breakfast.

We used to fast on Fridays during Lent, and on Wednesdays too—not just Ash Wednesday, but every Wednesday. Everyone in the house pulled long faces because of the fasting, and no one would mention food. We had other regulations during Lent, too, like keeping up the "great cleanliness" (zhishou dazhai)—that meant, among other things, no meat at all, just vegetarian food. And then there were various "little cleanlinesses"—shouzhai, which is a Buddhist term after all, not Catholic. In addition to Masses, for instance, we had extra ceremonies—Benedictions—in the afternoons in our home. In any case, it was generally a miserable time.

Unfortunately, we didn't follow the Russian Orthodox tradition, like some of my classmates at school. They always celebrated the end of Lent in a gluttonous manner, with a huge meal featuring a suckling pig with an apple in its mouth. In my house, all we got were very uninteresting red eggs on Easter Sunday. And we went to church together, of course.

The Ying clan—not just our family, but the whole clan—all considered themselves pillars of the Chinese Catholic church. Several of them were more devout than we were. They would add all kinds of rules to their lives during these important holy days, so I always avoided them at those times, because I knew it was going to be unbearable.

The daughter of my father's cousin (from Number Five Uncle) became a Catholic nun. She was born about three years after I was, right when the Japanese were starting to invade China—and her father was a rather patriotic person who wanted his daughter to grow up and fight the Japanese, I suppose, so he named her after the female warrior Mulan. He was a university professor—only an intellectual would dare to name his child after a heroine like that.

But Ying Mulan lived up to her name. During the 1950s, she was imprisoned for religious reasons—she had belonged to an organization at her medical college called the Holy Virgin's Fighters (Shenmujun)—and that organization was treated pretty much the way the Falun Gong is handled these days. The girls involved were arrested because it was an illegitimate religious organization, and a very interesting thing happened in prison. A huge chimney, about forty meters in height, had just been built and somehow got clogged with soot. So one day all of the prisoners were gathered and the guard said, "This is an opportunity to redeem yourselves. Who will be the first to dare to climb the chimney?" None of the men wanted to risk their lives, so my cousin volunteered. She climbed to the very top and cleaned the chimney with some kind of instrument they handed her, and it worked. One of her fellow prisoners later became a novelist and in one of the novels about their time in prison, a chapter is devoted to my brave cousin Mulan.

A Fluent Truant

Mulan and I were both adventurous prisoners. My own experience with pranks and pushing my luck with authority commenced long before I was jailed during the Cultural Revolution—it began when I was in primary school. I am ashamed to admit that I was expelled from not only one school, but three. Doubtless, these experiences enriched my education immensely and will serve as a source of great amusement to you, my reader—but they did not amuse my father. He was the secretary general of Furen University and head of the Foreign Languages Department, as well as headmaster of the attached Furen Middle School. My education began with kindergarten at Peigen, where, as with all my schooling, I started early and was younger than my classmates. Then, from about age six to age nine, I attended Furen, and then another Catholic school, Sacred Heart, for about two years. Finally I was shipped off to St. Louis Collège, an international Catholic boarding school in Tianjin with a British curriculum run by the French Marist brothers. It was quite an embarrassment being kicked out of three schools when I came from such a distinguished scholastic family.

It all started with a rather dramatic mishap with a slingshot. There was a teacher at Furen who was in charge of discipline, and we hated him. The Japanese were occupying Beijing, and this teacher was always declaring that the Chinese and Japanese should be friends, saying things like, "We must learn from the Japanese," so the students all despised him. The campus had started expanding, which meant there was a worksite with hundreds of bricks, and we boys thought it would be great fun to gather the bricks together and build a fortress. So we did—we built an impressive structure—and then we divided ourselves into two factions, one trying to seize the fortress, and the other trying to defend it. I brought in my new toy, a fine slingshot given to me by a grown-up friend of the family. My slingshot was strong—it used a rubber band made from bicycle tires, and it could actually kill birds.

One day we were playing around at our fortress, and along came the horrible teacher, shouting from the other end of the lane, "Now all of you get down from there!"

So naturally I took a shot at him.

And purely by fluke—because I wasn't that good a sharpshooter—the pellet I released struck his head and blood came trickling down. This caused quite a scandal, of course, and the school sent a small delegation to our home to report my unruly behavior.

My eldest brother went to eavesdrop by the guest parlor and came back, saying, "You better run away. All the faculty are here accusing you of hitting that teacher."

I tried to act as though I didn't care. I went out on my bicycle to visit a friend, and we decided not to waste our time waiting around to see what would happen, but to go see an American movie instead.

The film was *Angels with Dirty Faces*, starring James Cagney, about a gangster who has great influence in his neighborhood and is finally caught and condemned to the electric chair—a rather horrible story, considering my circumstances. The main character's childhood friend, who by then has become a priest, advises him at his last confession, "You still can do some good for the young. You can pretend that you're scared as hell because of the electric chair." So I decided to go back to my house and pretend I was scared as hell.

As headmaster of Furen Middle School as well as a professor at the affiliated university, my father couldn't very well allow me to continue as a student there when I had assaulted the teacher in charge of discipline. But Chen Yuan, president of the university and a colleague of both my grandfather and my father, looked upon the situation differently. The middle school was technically under his jurisdiction, so it bothered him when I was expelled because he didn't agree with the decision at all. My father, like all the Chinese intellectuals in cases like this, showed his impartiality by dismissing his own son, whereas Chen didn't have any such reservations.

He told everybody, "This is a big mistake, to have this boy kicked out. Just you wait—one day he'll surprise you people."

I remember Chen Yuan with great fondness. He was a very kindly old man, and very prominent in society. He was included on the list of people to leave on that last plane my father boarded in 1948, but refused to go. The new government appointed him president again when Furen and Beijing Normal University were amalgamated. After the age of seventy, he joined the Chinese Communist Party, and he lived into his nineties, dying during the Cultural Revolution. A Protestant approved by the Vatican as president of a Catholic university, who joined the CCP in his old age—he really was quite a legend.

After my shameful departure from Furen, I arrived at Sacred Heart Middle School (*Shengxin zhongxue*) when I was about ten years old, but my stay there was even shorter—less than two years.

Before I began my studies at Sacred Heart, Chen Yuan invited me to his home and sat down with me, encouraging me to make a new start.

"Now is the time when you can show them all what you're made of," he said.

So when I finished the first two semesters with top honors, my mother insisted that I go visit Chen and proclaim the good news that I had lived up to his expectations. My success was short-lived, however.

Although I did not learn English until my next school, I managed to enlarge my Chinese vocabulary to an unbelievable extent during my short time at Sacred Heart. I picked up a new hobby there—learning all imaginable swear words, especially sexual terms. Boys of my age were supposedly not even allowed to know that such words existed, but I learned them easily from fellow students.

This came to my father's attention in a rather unusual way—when there was a contest that year with all the primary school students, and I was chosen by Sacred Heart to give a speech.

"This kid's all right," the school officials thought. "He has a glib tongue, so he'll have no problem with words."

But after my presentation, the reviews came back from the judges saying, "Master Ying has proved himself very courageous. We would only add one little wish, which is that he should pay more attention to the clarity and cleanliness of his language."

Imagine how proud my father was to hear that!

Ironically, the assigned theme for the speech contest was what should constitute good behavior for a model student. My speech might have been a little original, but that doesn't mean I wasn't sincere. My father's disappointment was just as sincere.

That evening before I arrived home from school, he told my siblings, "Third Son has been up to his tricks again, so I'm going to have a talk with him tonight. I hope he knows how serious this is."

When I got home, my father immediately sent me off to bed, even though it was too early for sleeping and none of my siblings had gone to their beds yet. I lay there awake for what seemed like hours, terrified. This time I wasn't able to escape to the movies. But my father apparently forgot all about his decision—until one of my brothers gladly reminded him and he became furious all over again.

He struck the table with his hand, hollering loud enough for me to hear, "I'm going to teach you a lesson once and for all! I'm going to send you away from Beijing—away from all these bad friends who teach you nothing but curses!"

It was only then that I realized that what got me in trouble was the swear words. I had sensed I was in the doghouse again, but I didn't know precisely why.

The next day I discovered my father's plans for me.

He said calmly, "The only way to get this child under control is to send him to one of those French missionary schools where he is watched over by his elders twenty-four hours a day." My father knew they were very strict there because he himself had attended a European school like that during his youth.

That is how the news was broken to me. My father simply said, "Because you've done this and that, we're going to send you to a terrible place—a missionary school. And you better behave. All the other boys there are foreigners. If you're not careful, you'll get a beating—not from me, but from your fellow students." So I was sent to St. Louis. The French think very highly of their Louises.

Two days after delivering this news to me, my father took me on a train. It was the first time I had ever boarded a train, and I enjoyed it. I didn't care about the distance at all. I was even looking forward to boarding school, thinking I might enjoy that, too.

In order to save his dignity, my father had to teach me some proper phrases in English before we arrived. One of the instructions I still remember him giving me was, "If people ask you if you speak English, you should answer, 'Only a few words.'" Once he taught me that in English, I spent the whole trip chirping, "Only a few words. Only a few words."

I truly only knew a few words when I arrived at St. Louis at age twelve. I picked up virtually all my English there. As my father had described, it was an all-male boarding school run by missionaries, and almost all of the other students were foreigners who didn't speak any Chinese. There weren't any rules against Chinese students enrolling per se—it's just that most could never afford it. It was a very expensive school. All of the instruction was in English—math, science, history, everything.

They were very strict at St. Louis. During the week we were not allowed to leave the school premises. On Sundays in the afternoon, we were allowed to go out and do some shopping or see a film, but we had to be back before curfew.

The teachers disciplined students by beating them. If they committed some misdemeanor in class, they would be publicly humiliated—told to bend over and then whipped with a cane. That was supposed to frighten me, but it didn't.

In a short time I could speak English. I could even quarrel in English with the Western boys. We had to practice memorization every day without exception, and with no leniency. For example, we would be forced to memorize one modern literature poem and recite it perfectly three hours later. Most of the time when children are asked to learn something like that by heart, they don't even know what they are saying. But I still am a firm believer in the art of memorization and recitation. A lot of people with advanced ideas about language learning object to this, or think it is silly, but it did work for me, so I believe in it.

We also had to recite scripture at St. Louis—one passage of the gospel every day. By the time I left St. Louis, I had memorized the gospels chapter and verse. The passage that stands out especially is the episode of the Sermon on the Mount, where Christ fed something like fifty thousand people with two loaves of bread and five fish.[12] They could have used him during the Great Leap Forward. I must say, the gospels are well-written pieces of literature, in terms of structure and language, and the surprises. . . . I still feel that if you want to learn a language, to build a solid foundation, it is best to recite great works of literature.

The teachers at St. Louis were specially invited from abroad, so the tuition was very expensive. People who could afford to send their children there were very chic. One of my few Chinese classmates, who became a good friend, came from a family that owned the biggest winery in Shandong. Another went by the English name Bobby. His father, Wang Shijing, was head of the entire banking system in north China, so they were fabulously rich. Wang was shot by the Nationalists even though he tried to buy his life with two trainloads of gold and silver. His son Bobby ran off to the United States—he had attended the Peking American School before St. Louis, so he was pretty thoroughly Americanized already.

The students at St. Louis were very nice. When I first arrived, there still were quite a few boys who came from foreign English-speaking families, but half a year later, Pearl Harbor happened, and they were sent with their families to Shandong, where the Japanese had established internment camps for overseas English, American, Canadian, and Dutch citizens. I remember the day of Pearl Harbor very clearly. It was December 8, the feast of the Immaculate Conception—a Sunday morning, and we were lined up as usual to go to Mass in town.[13] On the way, we knew something was wrong, because usually there were no Japanese soldiers visible in the Tianjin concessions, but that day the streets were lousy with them. They were rather sorry to look at, and their uniforms never seemed to fit, in contrast to the American or German soldiers. Their helmets in particular were quite ugly.

I remember that my father used to read a news sheet from Reuters first thing every morning, and he would tell us over breakfast what was happening in the world. That is how he found out Prince Qing had decided to sell his residence to the Japanese. From there began another four years of hardship, beginning with our family being forced to leave the prince's palace. I was away at school when the actual move happened. My family relocated to Zhenrujing, a home near Beitang (the Northern Cathedral) that my grandfather had bought for his mother, who had lived there for many years, but had died by then.[14] It was a typical old Peking *siheyuan* (courtyard surrounded on four sides by single-story dwellings), much smaller than the prince's quarters. We occupied the whole thing, because by that time (since moving into the prince's palace in 1932), my younger sister Ruocai had been born, as well as the twins (Ruoshi and Ruozhi)—and my youngest sister Ruoxian came along a few years after the move to Zhenrujing. So there had been four additions to our family, and even though we filled a whole *siheyuan*, it felt cramped compared to the spacious compound we had become accustomed to over the past decade.

Even after the native English speakers left St. Louis to stay in the internment camps after Pearl Harbor, English was still the only language permitted in the school. I realized from about that time that I really had to make an effort from then on, if only because I was Chinese and there were only four of us Chinese boys in the school, ironically cast as "foreigners." So I applied myself diligently to my studies. Of course, at first I was placed in the lowest grade because I couldn't speak English, but soon they couldn't keep me there. I had already studied all the other subjects in Chinese and knew them well. They kept a record of past grades they had given out, and I quickly broke their record. Out of 1,200 possible points, I think I scored more than 1,150 points when my classes were tallied together. So they couldn't hold me in the lowest grade anymore, and they told my family that I should jump ahead. If I had stayed in the Chinese middle school, I would have finished my studies in five years, and in the end, because I skipped some grades in Tianjin and because the semester schedule was changed twice because of the war, I finished in the same amount of time—five years—before moving on to university at age sixteen. The completion of my studies at St. Louis and my entry into Qinghua

University in Beijing in 1946 followed on the heels of the surrender of Japan and the end of World War II, by which time our family was enjoying a short spell of prosperity in the wake of my father's second release from prison.

I did eventually graduate from St. Louis and move on to university, but not before getting kicked out of school yet again. Luckily, my dismissal was smoothed over and they took me back. This was because around the time I got in trouble, the school officials had realized that China was probably going to win the war against Japan and the French Vichy government. My father was still in prison at the time, but it was clear to the powers that be that when he was released, he would likely hold a post in some official branch of the government and education. Thus, they thought it better not to induce scandal by broadcasting everything I did. Also, we Yings had some influence with the Catholic church, and one of my relatives in particular intervened on my behalf to have me reinstated at St. Louis. In the end, I lasted longer at that school—about four years—than any other I had previously attended.

By now you are probably wondering what horrible thing I could have done to warrant being expelled. It was a silly incident, and it all happened because of another boy whose father was a manufacturer of hygienic soap that was very popular in China. I was about fifteen, and I remember the American students had just come back to the campus. The Marine Corps had landed in Tianjin, and that prompted a number of affluent families to send their sons to our school. Most of these boys were not boarders, of course, but rather day students, and thus they ate their lunches at school and their dinners at home. I was captain of one of the dining tables that term, which meant I was responsible for dividing up the food for each boy onto his plate before we began to eat. We used knife and fork at boarding school and ate our food off of our own individual plates, which was different than the Chinese way of using chopsticks to take food from communal dishes placed in the center of the table. During lunch one day, this boy complained that I had shortchanged him by giving him too little food. God knows he was fat enough already. But, because the boy's father was rich and a donor to the school, the teacher on duty came over and reprimanded me.

Of course, I wasn't about to take that lying down.

"What he says is not true," I said. "You can ask everybody else at the table."

At that, the other boys spoke up and supported me. But the teacher, who was a Marist brother, ordered me to stand in the corner.

Defiantly, I declared, "I will finish my lunch."

"You dare talk back?" he retorted.

"Of course," I said. "My family paid for this meal. Why should I be deprived of it?"

I don't think anyone at the school had ever seen a teacher quarreling with a student before. I was at my boldest at that age, and the teacher was a weakling. In fact, he used to make a point of telling us that he was born during the Weimar Republic days and thus since childhood had been badly fed and suffered from malnutrition.

I didn't give in. I sat down and went on eating my lunch. This made the monk extremely angry, of course. You could see the anger steaming out of his ears as he stormed out of the dining room.

The next day I was told by the school, "You are dismissed." So I had to go home, all the way from Tianjin to Beijing.

When I got home, my mother wept.

"How could you do that?" she asked. "You are already costing more than all the other children for your education and you're not making the best of it."

I suddenly remembered how a year earlier I had received an award for my studies and the whole family had been so pleased—and now because of my bad behavior, I had incurred the wrath of this teacher and was being expelled.

Fortunately we had considerable influence in the church—in fact, within the Marist organization itself. After being dismissed from St. Louis, I was actually getting ready to enroll in a Chinese-language missionary school, but the headmaster of that school—also a Marist brother—wouldn't agree.

"I'll fight this out," he said.

By that time China had changed from prewar days. The Vatican had decided that a relative by marriage in our family would be the next brother provençal—in charge of the whole province. This would-be provençal was the nephew of a woman from Tianjin who married my Number Three greatuncle, and his word meant something. The Marist brothers at St. Louis had to listen since he was going to be their next boss. So I was allowed back.

What I benefited from the most at St. Louis was learning English. Also being around foreigners for the first time—but of course, that caused me a good deal of trouble later on.

I was at St. Louis during the Japanese occupation, and I still remember how they took over the entire British concession and several other concessions in Tianjin. The Japanese were very efficient and well-organized. They assumed control of all the big foreign industries, American and British, and left only the French concession intact, because the French concession was still in the hands of the Vichy. My father sent me to St. Louis in the French concession precisely because it was safe from the Japanese.

For Christmas holidays and summer vacations, I left Tianjin and came home to Beijing. I was never totally innocent from "extracurricular activities" and always preferred the company of girls to boys. When I was about fifteen, we had a summer with a lot of thunderstorms, and there happened to be a young girl living in our house. She was a college student helping my father edit some kind of text, so she must have been quite a bit older than I was. Her family lived in Tianjin, and she didn't like living in the half-empty dormitories during winter or summer holidays, so my father generously allowed her to stay with us. That summer, whenever there was a thunderstorm, she would act like a frightened little girl who needed a man there to protect her. And boys of that age are very susceptible to things like that. We got to know each other quite well because of those thunderstorms.

Her family was one of the richest families in Tianjin. The large number of concubines her father kept was enough proof of that. She never said so outright, but I think she was the offspring of a concubine, and not of the legitimate wife. We kept in touch for a little while and she came to visit me sometimes at my boarding school when she was in Tianjin.

My Own Gang of Four

I kept in touch with one of my St. Louis classmates for a very long time, and together with two other comrades, we met in rather clandestine circumstances during the Cultural Revolution, referring to ourselves (only in private, of course) as the Gang of Four. This Gang of Four included myself and three others: a priest, a diplomat, and a helicopter manufacturer (my classmate). I need to exercise some discretion in talking about them, because they were quite a diverse bunch, and even today they remain rather prominent in China and Chinese politics (as do I).[15]

One is an Anglican priest and is a personal friend of the Archbishop of Canterbury. He is Chinese and even a Communist. Another member of the group has been Chinese ambassador to quite a few important countries such as Great Britain and the United States—today he works in the Hong Kong government. The third one lives in Texas and went into business manufacturing helicopters, and the bulk of his products are sent back to China. He has the necessary *guanxi* (connections), so he knows whom to approach on both sides. He moved to the United States after June Fourth, but he had been there before, and he speaks English like an American. The four of us kept in touch right up until 1989 and occasionally we are still in contact. We don't call or write, but we see each other in person on occasion.

We called ourselves the Gang of Four because of the way we exchanged information during that time. Take the diplomat, for instance. I was called on the telephone at six o'clock in the morning one day—I never get up at that ungodly hour—and suddenly found someone knocking rather urgently at the door of my apartment.

I turned to my wife and groaned, "Who the hell can this be? It's only six o'clock."

This was 1976, just after Mao Zedong died. As I opened the gate, there he was, this diplomat, breathing heavily because he had to run up all those stairs.

"Is something wrong with your family?" I asked.

"No, no, no, no," he said, barely able to speak because of his excitement.

Then he blurted out, "Finally, they're arrested, they're arrested!" He was referring to the Gang of Four—Jiang Qing and her cohorts.

This man worked high up in the foreign office, where he supervised an information center. Even if nobody else knew about something, he knew the moment it happened. So as a result, I became one of the first to know, too. It was like getting the news about the Japanese decision to surrender in 1945.

But for nearly a week after the whole thing happened, there was no sign posted about it in the streets, and nobody else knew. The Chinese are pretty good at keeping secrets. Finally a week later it went public, and our Gang of Four bought drinks and celebrated the demise of our namesake.

Our little group usually met at my home to have our private discussions. The helicopter man and I had gone to boarding school together, as I mentioned. He was a year younger than I was. As boys we faced a lot of fistfights side by side, chiefly against the "White Russians"—those who didn't have a passport and were not Soviet citizens: the Soviet government would not recognize them, and they would not recognize the Soviet government. They all claimed to be descendants of the aristocracy. They didn't have passports, but China was pretty easy to get into in those days. One of the games these boys enjoyed most was insulting the Chinese and calling us names.

The diplomat was a friend I met through my wife. She had been borrowed by the Ministry of Foreign Affairs to take care of a foreign visitor who was from the family that owns the *New York Times*. They were extremely short-handed because most of the English-speaking people had been sent to the countryside to cadre schools, so they didn't have interpreters or guides to accompany important visitors. It was in 1975 and Zhou Enlai was still around.

This visitor was the most important journalist from the *New York Times*, and his family happened to own the paper. The diplomat was obviously a well-informed person and was on rather close terms with Mao's interpreter, Nancy Tang, and Mao's cousin, who were both serving as translators along with my wife. Nancy Tang had a built-in loudspeaker system—without making the slightest effort, she could make everybody hear. She first made her name with Richard Nixon's visit to China in 1972.

The priest was introduced to me in 1972 or 1973 by the helicopter man.[16] Very few people in China after 1949 associated with those who were not from their own work unit or profession. So in order to talk about these political matters privately in a mixed group like ours, we had to be very careful because other people might see us together and wonder, "How the hell did they come to know each other?" You see, the four of us were not connected professionally or otherwise in any way.

Every couple of weeks, someone usually proposed getting together, and my wife loved cooking (and was a very good cook, too), so we would all have a nice meal, and of course exchange the latest news. It sounds very normal nowadays, but in those days it was not. If we were discovered—the four of us having a good time and talking about certain things we should not talk about—just the exchange of information itself could have been considered a crime in those days.

We would discuss the hottest news, to begin with—usually with some inside information one of us had heard. For instance, the helicopter man would say that he saw Mr. So-and-So the other day, who seemed very unhappy.

If anything was worth noticing, one of us would sit up and say, "Really? Now what could it be?" and it could go on for hours, with no conclusions reached.

These speculations happen even today. Right now, people are wondering about Ding Guangen, the chief of the Ministry of Propaganda, a very sensitive position. I would like to know what Mr. Ding did last night, because he failed to appear on an occasion he ordinarily wouldn't miss—Jiang Zemin making an important speech on National Youth Day. His absence registered somewhere in my head as I watched the television and read the newspapers today.[17]

This same kind of thing—that someone should have been somewhere, but wasn't—often came up in conversations among our little Gang of Four. We'd hear about the person in a week or two—and usually what we heard was not happy news for the poor fellow—though sometimes it was bloody good news for us.

I had a few close friends who were the usual sources of certain information I gathered. Why I went to all that trouble at such risk is something for a trained analyst to figure out, but we needed to protect ourselves. After so many years of political confusion and wasting our time with endless campaigns, we were conditioned to think things would have the worst possible outcome. Above all, experiences like the Anti-Rightist Movement and the Cultural Revolution made us realize the importance of keeping our mouths shut.

PART THREE

PROFESSIONAL LIFE
IN ARTS AND POLITICS

~

CHAPTER FIVE

My Stage Career

Center Stage at Qinghua University

My first stage role was at St. Louis in a play organized by one of the monks. Titled *The Cellar Door* and based on the social background of the Austrian Empire, the play was a melodrama in which naughty monks made surreptitious visits to the cellar in order to satisfy their lust for drink. My fellow students played the naughty monks who went to drink in the cellar, and I shot them to death. My character was a monk, too, so apparently monks were not supposed to drink, but it was fine for them to murder their fellow monks.

Though I was punishing others for drinking, I would be doing the same thing myself a short while later. At St. Louis, they had insisted that all the boys play soccer during recess between classes. I didn't particularly like the sport, but I was pretty good at it. When I moved on to Qinghua University, I saw that the other students were real novices and I didn't want to play soccer with them—so I took up drinking instead.

One of my neighbors in the dormitory at Qinghua was at least ten years older than I, and he loved to drink. He was a former KMT soldier who had been stationed in Xi'an before the civil war. Because of his proficiency in mathematics, he was appointed as an engineer in the army. After Japan surrendered and the war ended, he got fed up—he had been in the army for eight years and had had enough. So he got hold of his brother's diploma and sat for the entrance exams to Qinghua, posing as his brother. He was accepted, and he found that nobody cared whether he had a real diploma or a fake one. He had a little money, too, so he would buy 250 grams—small bottles of hard liquor—and invite me over in the evening to share them with him. I considered myself a grown-up at seventeen and fully capable of consuming hard liquor, and thus my drinking began.

I didn't yet know in high school that I wanted to become an actor, but I became engrossed in drama as a university student. One of the professors at Qinghua produced a full production of Shakespeare's *The Merchant of Venice*, in which I was cast partly because of my fluency in English. In the play, Isabella must choose between three suitors who must choose between three different caskets—one of gold, one of silver, and one of lead. This sticks in my memory vividly as a high moment of my adolescence because the woman playing Isabella was an amazing expatriate teacher and I still daydream about her today. She was only a few years older than me, and after my graduation, she went back to her native country (Turkey, I believe) to marry a teacher there. Theatre comes naturally to young people who have a romantic side in their mental and spiritual makeup, and I certainly did.

Another foreign drama teacher at Qinghua, Mr. Ronnie Parker, was sent by the British Council and had full training from RADA (the Royal Academy of Dramatic Arts). He never really had a chance at a professional career in the theatre because when he graduated from RADA, World War II started, and he was sent by the British army to very odd places like Afghanistan, India, and Iran. By the time he arrived at Qinghua, this heavyset man was in his thirties. The acting classes he taught were the first formal instruction in acting technique I ever received.

I entered Qinghua University in 1946 and graduated in 1950, which made me literally one of the first bunch of university students to graduate after Liberation.[1] I learned many things at Qinghua, but I didn't actually study very much. Those weren't days for studying—they were days for student movements and civil war.[2] That is not to say that the instruction at Qinghua was anything less than excellent—Qinghua was a top university and was *the* place for academic theater, especially because the Foreign Languages and Literatures Department (in which I was enrolled) was so strong. The classes I took in theatre were more academic than practical, but we did have a very active student theater group, and some of us became professionals in the theatre after we graduated.

We performed quite a number of propaganda plays as part of the student movements, writing such pieces collectively ourselves and calling them "living newspaper plays" (*huobaoju*). "Living newspaper" is actually a term borrowed from the United States, from the workers' movements of the 1930s during the Great Depression. We were inspired by Agitprop theatre and plays like Clifford Odets's *Waiting for Lefty*.

I was involved in other creative endeavors besides theatre as well. During my freshman year, I teamed up with a fellow student, Wang Zuoliang, who would later become the head of the Foreign Languages Institute in Beijing, to make study guides for the freshman English curriculum. We condensed answers to test questions from a huge textbook of essays into small pamphlets to make it easier for students to prepare for the test. We published them in the school newspaper, and the first year we did this, the exam results of the students were shockingly good.

Tiring of that after a while, Wang and I founded a literary magazine called *The Qinghua Tyro* and published a few issues. Tyro is a British word that means "beginner's notes"—very appropriate for a new venture like ours. By the end of my freshman year, Wang encouraged me to be more discriminating, so I started a magazine of modern Chinese poetry in English called, quite simply, *Poetry as Compiled by Ying Ruocheng*. I translated every single poem myself, typed each one on carbon paper, and duplicated about fifty copies. The journal became very popular.

It was during my third year at Qinghua that my father went off to Taiwan. My mother told me I would either have to drop out of college or find a way to work my own way through. I didn't want to leave Qinghua, so I found odd jobs and created some business opportunities for myself—long before China had anything resembling a market economy.

The Qinghua student body hailed from all over the country, with international students as well. Once enrolled, the first thing students wanted to do was send letters home to their friends and relatives. So I designed Christmas cards with designs in both English and Chinese. We had no printing facilities, so I used photographs, going around the campus with a camera and taking pictures of the more impressive buildings like the library, auditorium, gymnasium, and so on. Students were lining up to buy them. I became quite famous among the students for my stage acting and for selling these photo cards, and I also tutored students who wanted to improve their English. Qinghua was very strict about English proficiency. With the extra money, I was able to pay for school and graduate with my class.

My brother Ruocong transferred to Qinghua during my senior year. He had been studying literature at Furen University, but I convinced him that Qinghua was a much better place for him. He had a natural talent for drawing and he was a quiet boy—very different from me. He became a successful architect after college, but he suffered greatly several years later, being capped a Rightist during the Anti-Rightist Movement.[3]

At the moment I graduated from Qinghua in 1950, everything was coming into being, including the new government itself and various propaganda groups the Communists brought in. A vast number of actors and artists were holding "Congress of This" and "Congress of That," and that is when the Beijing People's Art Theatre was founded. I went to the theatre immediately upon graduation, so in that sense I am one of its founding members.[4]

Qinghua gave me a wonderful foundation for my career in the professional theatre. In our courses we read the foreign classics, including Greek tragedies and early British drama ranging from *Gammer Gurton's Needle* to Shakespeare. Instruction for many of the classes was in English and taught by foreigners, while others were taught in Chinese by local professors. Chinese and foreign students were mixed in classes, but not in the dormitories. As a rule, the foreigners were separated, especially the Americans. For a period after the war, it was mainly American students who came to Qinghua, and they were so wealthy. The American dollar was something that everybody was after, so they lived like lords even on very low budgets.

Qinghua was a special case, because the university was still being supported by the remains of the Boxer Rebellion indemnities. The Peking Union Medical College hospital was also being supported this way. The Boxers mainly were active in Hebei and Shandong—areas that we now loosely call north China. And China was paying out a huge amount of money in those days. I think it was the Germans who made the proposal, saying the crime of the Boxers was a national crime: China was estimated to have 450 million people at the time, so the idea was for each citizen to be charged one silver dollar, but that seemingly small tax adds up to quite a bit of money. It was President Teddy Roosevelt who was the first to propose that we shouldn't bleed China dry, but that it is much more in the interest of the West if this fund could be used directly for philanthropic and educational purposes. Qinghua University resulted from that, so the library never lacked foreign publications, including the things I loved to read in those days like *Theatre Monthly* magazine and new books published in the United States. Qinghua is where I first read Arthur Miller's play *Death of a Salesman*.

During my senior year, the librarian pulled me aside. She knew I was very keen on having a first look at the new books.

"There's a new play," she told me. "I don't know whether or not it's interesting."

I saw that the playwright had a name I didn't recognize—Arthur Miller— and that the play was one I had never heard of—*Death of a Salesman*. So I took it away, and started reading. I finished it that same night.

I was so drawn to the play, but immediately thought it would be impossible to produce at that moment in China. It was only a couple of months after the inauguration of the People's Republic, and it certainly wasn't—or didn't seem to me at the time—an appropriate time to introduce something like that. But it left a very deep impression on me.

Another book that fascinated me was called *Stanislavsky Produces Othello*—a Russian text that had been translated by a British scholar named Helen Nowak.[5] Another was Eisenstein's *Film Sense*.[6] These three—Miller, Stanislavsky, and Eisenstein—attracted me most during that period. But I remember my second reaction to all three books was misgiving, in the sense that I saw clearly it was not the right time to render these books into Chinese.

Of the three, I must say I liked Eisenstein best. He was such an erudite man. His analysis of Leonardo da Vinci's plans for the projected picture called *The Deluge* was so forceful, and his analysis of the modern Stanislavsky method of acting was very penetrating. He was definitely against the idea of all these ritualistic styles of acting. He depicted two scenes of a man in despair who has been caught in a case of corruption, detailing what went on in his mind. This is something I remember even today—how he described the man's mental process leading to his suicide. I was still using that bit of text many years later when I went to the United States to teach the art of acting, and I can't think of a better example of highlighting various images. Eisenstein made a sharp distinction between what he called a representation and an image. A representation is simply something like a picture, something that one encounters in daily life—but an image is something that is formed after the accumulation of a number of representations, which drives the actor to the inescapable conclusion of an idea. So it's no longer just one—or a few—representations, but it becomes a desire or a mood, much more than what the representation usually depicts.

Once I started working on Eisenstein's book, it became an obsession: How does one translate what one wishes to achieve as the end result of all the images that arise in one's mind? What can one create through the juxtaposition of representations? Each representation may only be a simple picture, but combined together they become a force independent of their sum, and then the image comes alive. That's how I approached my roles in Lao She's *Teahouse* and Arthur Miller's *Death of a Salesman*.

While I was still a student at Qinghua, I imagined what it would be like if only we could stage Miller's play. I remember toying with the idea, saying to my classmates, "But anybody can understand the plight of this Willy Loman. The circumstances may be a little different, but what he faces is the same all the world over. As a father, he is willing to give up his life for his children. This is something any Chinese would understand."

I was already quite prominent in the student theatre clubs by my senior year, and I had my mind set on three plays. One was *Death of a Salesman*.

Another was George Bernard Shaw's *Major Barbara*, mainly because I felt instinctively that what China needed was a few more Undershafts.[7] The third play, *The Corn Is Green*, was rather tame, and thus easier to get approved by the new authorities. It didn't have the potential of the other two plays to change the world, but it changed my world just the same—because my classmate Wu Shiliang was cast to play Miss Moffat opposite me as the young miner Morgan Evans.[8]

We produced the play in English with a cast that combined students from five different universities. The audience was mostly students, and the majority of them understood English well—there were also foreigners who came to see the play, because everybody was trying to feel the pulse of the new regime. Some low-ranking officials came, one of whom was instrumental in giving us permission to do the play. Wang Songsheng was an underground Communist during the civil war who was very friendly with our theatre group at Qinghua, and even directed some plays with us.

Another influential Mr. Wang was Wang Wenxian, one of our professors at Qinghua. He was from the United States, but was ethnically Chinese, and his great ambition in life was to become the George Pierce Baker of China.[9] Wang was a Harvard man himself and started a playwriting workshop based on Baker's model. Most of our playwriting work, however, was done in collectives because that was the fashion for propaganda plays of those times, and the pieces we created were highly political. We also produced Lillian Hellman's *Watch on the Rhine*, and everyone knew that the fascists Hellman was writing against in her play were, in our case, the KMT.

The Corn Is Green was an innocent choice in comparison—there's nothing very political in it beyond the popular theme at that time in China of the oppression of the poor in a class-divided society. So even though it was not espousing the ideas of the new regime as obviously as *Watch on the Rhine* or our collectively created propaganda plays, it also wasn't anything that could possibly raise concerns, like *Major Barbara* or *Death of a Salesman*. It was a safe choice.

Meeting My Match

The Corn Is Green was the first play I performed in English with Wu Shiliang, but we had worked together in the student drama group before, when we produced a series of four foreign one-act plays in Chinese, including the Soviet play *The 41st* about a White army officer who is captured by a Red army girl on an island. *The 41st* was the first play we performed in together, but *The Corn Is Green* is much more memorable because we played the leading roles and performed the play in English, and by that time, I was in love with her and she with me.

The first time I saw my future wife was at a gathering of the third-year students at the beginning of the 1948 fall semester to welcome *xin tongxue* (new classmates). She caught my eye, much to my surprise. I had never thought much of the girls in my class. To begin with, none of them had this girl's looks, and, even more important, they didn't have her learning and her aptitude for study. She had attended three universities in Shanghai before coming to Qinghua, so she was very well prepared. No other student—male or female—possessed the kind of knowledge with which Wu Shiliang arrived on our campus. Obviously, she made quite an impression on me.

In terms of what kind of impression I made on her, I think what struck her was my sense of humor. Of course, later on when I found that out, I told her, "I'll make you laugh for the rest of your life." And I did.

We didn't actually speak at the new student gathering that day. My first real interaction with Wu Shiliang happened afterward, in a cabbage patch of all places.

In those days, the boundary between boys and girls was still pretty strictly observed—this was only the 1940s after all—and at Qinghua, the ratio of male to female students was heavily weighted toward the former. As manager of the boys' dining hall, I oversaw about two thousand students, while when Wu Shiliang was elected manager of the girls' mess hall, there were only about a hundred female diners.

By September 1948, Chiang Kai-shek had driven the economy to ruin and inflation was at its worst, the real rock bottom. There were price tags, but no goods—you couldn't buy anything except toilet paper. Even rice was scarce. I was the experienced mess hall manager, so I went around to my old connections—the rice merchants, the oil people, and so on—to see what they could do for us. They said they could not sell to us at the price I offered, so I proposed a business deal with them.

"If you promise to sell your food only to us, I'll give you a higher price," I said, "and I'll protect you from pressure by local customers by posting a placard on your door that says QINGHUA UNIVERSITY—NOT FOR PUBLIC SALE."

I devised a plan to sign contracts with the merchants for meat and with the peasants for cabbages, and I agreed to pay the peasants in advance. They didn't have to supply any cabbages when they took the money, but they had to guarantee to supply them two months later when the crop came in. They liked this method because they got the money up front, and we were assured a fresh cabbage supply at a secure price. Apparently, no one had ever used this system before. And it worked—we always got our cabbages.

When the girls heard the news, they said, "We should do the same thing. Otherwise how will we survive the winter?"

So one day, I was out examining cabbages, and I saw this girl coming toward me. I had seen her before, of course, but only from a distance. She was very fashionable for those days, because she had come from Shanghai. She was dressed in a *qipao* (a traditional, tight-fitting dress with side slits), a style she insisted on wearing right up until we graduated, even though almost everyone else was in a uniform referred to as the Lenin suit. She just thought the Lenin suit was too ugly. It looked like a Western-style jacket, but with no filling or lining, just a single layer of cloth, and it was worn with pants. The school didn't care whether people wore this uniform or not—it just happened to be the fashion during those revolutionary days. Wu Shiliang was among a handful of girls at the university who preferred to wear a dress.

The day she walked toward me in the cabbage field was quite warm. Her *qipao* had a small flowered pattern with short sleeves and a long slit—only Shanghai girls had slits like that—and high heels. Her face was tastefully made up and she had a permed hairdo that was very fashionable. She looked one hundred percent like a Shanghai girl. Compared to her, all the other girls at Qinghua looked very clumsy.

She couldn't help laughing when she saw me standing in the cabbage patch sampling the crop. The field was on the edge of campus and I had come to taste the raw cabbage I had purchased to see if the farmers were making good use of their fertilizer.

"What are you laughing at?" I asked.

"Sorry," she replied. "I've never seen anyone eating raw cabbage before. You look like a rabbit."

So I offered her a bite. "It's quite tasty," I said. "Try some."

"Oh no, I couldn't," she answered, still laughing.

Even though she had lived in places like Yunnan, Nanjing, Chongqing, and Shanghai, Wu Shiliang spoke perfect standard *Putonghua* (Mandarin Chinese). She didn't have a trace of an accent, and that was part of the reason why we took her into our drama group.[10]

The following semester, in February 1949, we students were organized into two performing groups to herald the entrance of the PLA into Beijing. We were provided with a place to stay near one of the middle schools, near today's Chongwenmen. It was a nice enough middle school, and quite famous, started by American missionaries back in the prewar days.

We were sent out into the streets to perform a propaganda play we had collectively written for the occasion called *Kaishi Daji* (*Opening the Market with Great Fortune*). They gave us a huge room with a wooden floor to sleep on, and we all slept in the same room.

Early in the morning one of the boys came over and said, "See what I've found—a silver dollar."

I examined the coin with him and some of the other boys. It featured Sun Yat-sen's head, or what we used to call *xiaotou* (little head), whereas the Yuan Shikai coin was known as *datou* (big head). We boys held a hasty conference about the discovery, and I volunteered some information.

"I know that Comrade Wu's parents left her with some silver dollars," I said, "because they were ready to leave Beijing to go back to the south. This must be hers."

Since boys will be boys, we decided to spend the coin on some good chow. In those days one silver dollar was worth a lot. We rounded up our group—which totaled about thirty students—and we all went out together to a little restaurant. There were only three girls in the group, and Wu Shiliang was one of them, but she had no idea it was her silver dollar that was buying everyone dinner.

On the way back from the excursion, we boys started discussing things.

"We better tell her before she finds out herself—that would be bad," someone said.

So we started talking to her, going around and around what we really wanted to ask.

"Have you lost anything?" one of us inquired.

"No," she replied.

"You sure?"

"Oh, let me see then. . . . " She started looking through her purse. "No, it's all there."

And she was honest enough to tell everybody how her parents left her with the silver dollars.

Then we said to ourselves, "My God, whose was it then?" And suddenly one of the boys had a hunch. "Let's hope it didn't belong to the most miserly person in the group," he groaned.

One student actor was famous for his penny-pinching ways. Of course, it turned out it had belonged to him, exactly the person we were most nervous about. We were going to have to tell him.

"What do we do now?" one of the boys asked.

"Well," I said, "the only thing we can do is pay him back."

"But who has the money?" another boy wondered.

I knew I had no choice but to volunteer.

"When my father left, he gave me some silver dollars," I offered.

This was a lie. What he had actually given me was a gold watch. I still remember the brand—it was an Elgin. I went to a watch shop with one of the boys and asked the proprietor how much he would pay me for it. The man couldn't have been less interested, because the times were still uncertain. The PLA had just gotten into the city, and the ceremonies in Tiananmen Square to mark the official founding of the People's Republic had not yet taken place—that would not happen until October. The storekeeper offered a ridiculously low price, something like twelve silver dollars. The other boy told me not to sell it for so little, but I felt I had no choice.

So I sold my father's watch. I had to, you see, because I didn't want to leave a bad impression on someone I was intent on marrying later on.

Wu Shiliang never knew about the whole incident with the silver dollar until just before we were married. She thought I was foolish for selling the only possession my father had given me when he left for Taiwan. Of course, I had no idea then that I would never see him again.

In March, after about a month of touring our play at universities around Beijing, we were told that everybody could go home. The Political Consultative Conference was in session drafting a new constitution, after which the founding of a new republic would be announced.

Wu Shiliang and I had become more than a little friendly during these weeks of unsupervised time with the other students, and at this point we were about to be separated so that she could travel to Tianjin, where her parents were. They had hoped to relocate down south after she enrolled at Qinghua—they owned houses in or near Hangzhou, Suzhou, and Kunshan—but they couldn't go back to Shanghai because it was too risky for them politically. They were stuck in Tianjin as exiles of a sort, and to them it felt like they were in a foreign country.

I took Wu Shiliang to the railway station, and I bought a platform ticket to see her off on the platform. We stood there beside the train, and at the last minute, just as she was about to board the train, I told her, "I'm coming with you."

"What? What?" she said. She was shocked and happy at the same time. "But you don't have a ticket."

"I can buy a ticket on the train," I assured her.

So I accompanied her onto the train. I had nothing with me, but I didn't need anything. It was quite uncomfortable and extremely crowded. In those days, people were rushing around, not quite sure which direction they were going. All sorts of rumors were flying about—some people were saying the PLA was coming to liberate us from this direction and some were saying from that direction. Tianjin had already been liberated, but things were especially tense because they had had a real fight there, unlike in Beijing where there had been no real war and both sides had just signed papers.

When Wu Shiliang and I arrived in Tianjin and stepped off the train at the railway station, there were quite a number of rickshaws vying for our business. The two drivers we hired tried to cheat us on the price halfway through the journey, but I reported them to the police. Eventually, we arrived at the racecourse where the Kailuan Mining Association was located. Wu Shiliang's father had been appointed advisor to the association, which was originally owned by the British but was now back in the hands of the Chinese. He was there waiting for us, and that was the first time I met him. I liked the old man very much, but I had trouble understanding his accent.

I stayed with Wu Shiliang's family for only two nights, and then I went to visit a friend. Shiliang and I had not talked about getting married yet in so many words, but on that trip to Tianjin I think it was understood that that was our intention. I never actually asked her to marry me—it was just something that both sides took for granted.

We still had to finish another year of university, but I was intent on getting married as soon as we graduated. You may wonder why I was in such a hurry. Well, those were times when quite a number of former students and semi-intellectuals joined the revolution and went to places like Yan'an. And of course, if they could help it, they did not want to marry the local peasant girls, so many of them remained single. By the time they could see the light of day again, the whole country was liberated and they suddenly found themselves in very enviable leadership positions. There were plenty of these newly fortunate bachelors looking around for attractive, intelligent girls, and naturally, I was afraid these men would go after Wu Shiliang—I was not only afraid, I knew it was happening. University students were rare, especially in the arts. And girls with a university degree were even rarer. I don't blame those men, of course—after all, they gave up the best years of their lives for a cause.

Wu Shiliang was an exceptionally good catch, and she was an extraordinary woman. Everyone who knew her—including her university classmates at that time—admired her intelligence, and she was always first in her class. But she was never one to flaunt her knowledge or prestige—in that sense she was very Chinese. She had started learning foreign languages back when the Japanese first occupied Beijing. At that point, the entire central government moved inland to Chongqing, and she went with it, because her father was appointed president of Jiaotong University. Both our families were closely linked with the academic world—so I suppose my joining the entertainment business was really in some ways a step down.

Wu Shiliang spent a few years of her childhood in the town of Kunming in Yunnan. Her father, Wu Baofeng, was one of the first returned students from America who witnessed experimentation with radio. In the mid-1930s, he started the first genuine radio station in China—originally in Nanjing (when Nanjing was still the capital of the republic) and later in Yunnan. At that time, radio was young even in the United States, and Wu is recognized by those in the Chinese radio world as the man who started it all. Later on, when the war situation settled down, the wartime capital moved to Chongqing, so that is where Wu Shiliang spent the greater part of her youth—she was only in Kunming for a short while.

When his daughter enrolled at Qinghua University for her junior year, Wu Baofeng, president of Jiaotong University, was very sympathetic to the students. They were holding some kind of political movement at the time—against the Americans of all people—because the Texaco oil company had been responsible for the death of a Chinese student in a traffic accident. The municipality of Shanghai was on the side of the Americans, and students wouldn't take this sitting down—they protested, and the movement started to grow and acquire political significance. The whole country, beginning with universities like Beida (Peking University), Yanjing, and Qinghua, had already started protesting because of the Pierson case (the rape of a Chinese girl by an American soldier).[11]

Chiang Kai-shek was not happy about the situation, and he ordered Wu Baofeng to come to Nanjing because he wanted to talk to him. Jiaotong University specializes in engineering—so of course the students knew all about railways, and they began dismantling the Shanghai-Nanjing railway as a gesture of protest.[12] This line was the most vital link between the biggest city, Shanghai, and the political capital at the time, Nanjing. As an indication that they would not tolerate being bullied, the students were taking the railway apart, and Chiang Kai-shek got very angry.

"What do you have to say for yourself?" he asked Wu Baofeng.

Wu bravely replied, "I have some words of advice, Generalissimo. I think we ought to reexamine our position. I remember the way things were in 1927 when we started the Northern Expedition." (Wu was an old Chiang loyalist.) "In those days," he continued, "the students and the common people were all for us, but now they're against us—we really should reexamine our position."

Chiang responded by banging on the table and declaring, "I warn you, you're losing your sense of judgment. I want you out of Shanghai. You have too much influence in Shanghai as the president of Jiaotong University. If I see you around Shanghai ten days from now, I won't guarantee your safety."

So Wu Baofeng went home, immediately assembled the whole family, and made preparations to flee to Tianjin. He and his wife had five children, and he had given each of them a name representing the five Confucian virtues: *wen, liang, gong, jian,* and *rang.*[13] My future wife was the second child, so she was Wu Shiliang. The reason they chose Tianjin was because one of Wu Baofeng's former classmates from the United States had become the director of the Kailuan coal mines there. This old friend gave him the position as advisor for the company—basically doing nothing but reading newspapers and drinking tea.[14]

When Chiang Kai-shek ordered Wu Baofeng out of Shanghai and Wu moved the family to Tianjin, Wu Shiliang stayed behind alone to continue her studies. She was enrolled at Shanghai University at the time, which was her third university in as many years. During her high school days, she had been full of patriotic fervor and wanted to go to Jiaotong University when she graduated. Her own father, the university president, was against it, saying it was no place for a girl—but the more he said that, the more determined she became. She got very high marks on the entrance exams, and sure enough, she enrolled at Jiaotong. But she found taking nothing but engineering courses uninteresting—Wu Shiliang loved poetry and theater. So she transferred to St. John's, an American university that was known for its business school and humanities. (In fact, the Chinese Communists educated their most important diplomats there.) But she tired of that university, too—she didn't like it—so she joined another university called Hujiang or Shanghai University, which was a world-class university recognized by the authorities in the United States. But after a year she got fed up again.[15]

Finally, in the fall of 1948, she ended up at Qinghua, and finally she stayed put. She met me, I suppose, and thought, "The long march has ended."[16]

Her grandmother had always advised her, "You must find your young man while you are at the university. Once you graduate, it will be too late—you will meet only riff-raff." So, by the time she got to Qinghua for her junior year, Wu Shiliang was running out of time.

A New Theatre Company in New China

I married Wu Shiliang on July 17, 1950, between the time we graduated from Qinghua University and reported for work at the Beijing People's Art Theatre. I was originally hired by the Central Academy of Drama (*Zhongyang xiju xueyuan*) as a member of its spoken drama troupe (*huaju tuan*). The academy was the first spoken drama training institute in the People's Republic, created in 1949 by Cao Yu and Ouyang Yuqian.[17] At the last minute, they couldn't take me because a new directive stipulated that that year's college graduates must not be absorbed into a central government unit, and the academy had to obey these distribution requirements. As a result, a very young group of us was assigned to the newly established Beijing People's Art Theatre, with several of us right out of college.[18]

Wu Shiliang and I were hired to be in the resident acting troupe, but during our careers at the theatre we would both hold other posts as well. Not long after her arrival, Wu Shiliang became the personal assistant to playwright Cao Yu, who was also the head of the theatre. Cao Yu once remarked, "Wu Shiliang's classical education is much better than mine," indicating it was one of the reasons he chose her to be his creative secretary (*chuangzuo mishu*). I would later be hired to supervise the archives, and would also be appointed head of the creative office (*chuangzuoshi zhuren*), where I basically oversaw the efforts of the resident playwrights.

When I joined the theatre at age twenty-one, I was one of a handful of university activists who had taken part in the student movement during the last days of the KMT. We were a progressive, bright, young generation. Mao's policy at the time was that we should take over whatever the KMT had left in terms of the government machine, including the propaganda machine. We actually had among our ranks quite a number of people who used to belong to KMT anti-Communist propaganda groups. So then came one campaign after another, all aimed at weeding out the undesirable elements—and there were plenty of them. The new regime had to build a new China out of the rubble and the KMT and CCP had often used similar tactics against each other. Naturally, we young recent college graduates were the few people with clean pasts.

There were countless campaigns against corruption, with countless officials singled out. It was happening all over China—because every damned official was corrupt. But then Mao reiterated that we should keep these people within our ranks, so we had to form a kind of lifestyle where one associated with rather influential people in the former KMT, such as higher or lower ranking military officers. After a few years of these political movements, everybody knew who the targets were, and they were faced with the possibility of being singled out to be struggled against.

One of my first roles when I came to the theatre was in Lao She's *Dragon Beard Ditch* (*Longxu gou*).[19] I always cherished that particular production because it was handled by a great director, Jiao Juyin. Dragon Beard Ditch was the name of a neighborhood in the Tianqiao district of Beijing. According to Jiao's concept, the audience was supposed to hear Peking in its natural sound and habitat of those days. As part of our preparation for our roles under Jiao's direction, all of the actors visited the neighborhood and interacted with its residents, and Jiao required us to keep diaries with notes, using a Stanislavsky approach to creating our characters.

I played the role of Old Liu, a teahouse owner. I was a very young man in his early twenties playing a very old man in his early seventies. I had all my hair shaved off—my head was a shiny ball—and I had a white beard glued to my chin. I was a perfect replica of the typical elderly man of old Peking. Men like that wandered the streets selling big pots of tea for years. And for the price of two cents—quite a bit of money in those days in such a poor area—customers could also buy snacks like celery or seeds. What distinguished this old man Liu was how good-natured he was—he loved the neighborhood children and would sometimes give them a piece of candy or a handful of peanuts. The real-life model for my character was my Number Four great-uncle, the professional wrestler.

During our production of *Dragon Beard Ditch*, Jiao Juyin pulled me aside to have a talk with me. "I'm going to install you as the head of the archives for our theatre," he said.

I was a young man and not ready to be trapped behind a desk.

"Come on," I replied. But then, capitulating, I added, "Please don't deprive me of acting while doing this."

He laughed and said, "I won't do that—that would hurt the theatre."

So, since then, I had this double role. Jiao was very convincing when he told me, "This is a very important part of serious theatre—gathering all the archival material and producing a first-rate copy of each play after it has been seen by the public." With a strange light in his eyes, he added that he expected to see publishers only too glad to have a chance to publish such texts—which partly came true. We did publish a manuscript that I put together called *A Director's Plan to Produce "Dragon Beard Ditch,"* and Jiao was rather proud of it.

A combination of factors determined my becoming the archivist at the theatre. Some felt it was because I wasn't really cut out for acting.[20] But really it had more to do with Cao Yu and Jiao Juyin protecting me. As a Manchu, a Catholic, an intellectual, and an artist, with a father in Taiwan and associations with so many foreigners, I was a likely target in the various political campaigns that were brewing in the early 1950s. By putting me in an administrative position, I was better protected—it's much easier to get rid of an actor in the theatre than an archivist. Above all, of course, I was the best person for the job, and as archivist, I started collections on all the important members of our theatre company while they were still living—including Cao Yu, Lao She, and Jiao Juyin. People love to see themselves recorded and to be able to point to their accomplishments.

For two years, I was taken off the stage while serving as the theatre archivist, but later I returned to acting. At the time I was assigned to the archives, I had been cast as an industrialist in a play written by Lao She in 1952 called *A Family of Delegates* (*Yijia daibiao*).[21] In fact, I was cast in four plays written by Lao She or adapted from his novels during my first decade at the Beijing People's Art Theatre: *Dragon Beard Ditch*, *A Family of Delegates*, *Camel Xiangzi* (also called *Rickshaw Boy*), and *Teahouse*.

I was never officially removed from the archives—I suppose I am still on the staff there—but once the Russian experts arrived, I spent very little time there and I returned to the stage full-time.[22] The first Soviet expert to arrive at our theatre in 1953—Boris Kulinev—was a truly great actor, and he was the head of an acting school in Moscow.[23] At that time, all the actors were eager to know more about Stanislavsky's method as it was used in the USSR. Kulinev had an entire acting system based on Stanislavsky that took about six months to learn. He stayed at our theatre for three or four years, during which time he led many workshops for us and for the Central Academy of Drama. Those were the honeymoon years between the USSR and China. And I would have to say that most of our best senior actors from the Beijing People's Art Theatre went through Kulinev's training.

Kulinev directed us in Gorky's *Yegor Bulichov and the Others* (*Yege'er Buleiqiaofu he qita de renmen*) in 1956. The first scene he tried out with us, in order to take the pulse of the actors, was Act I, scene 1, with Bulichov, his mistress, and his business vendors, managers, and so on. I played a priest. Bulichov was a brilliant man, full of verve, who knew how to deal with things. The play begins when Bulichov and I both come in from outside—it is Russian winter, very cold. As an actor, I was at a loss about what I should do in this situation. I tried to remember—after all, I knew many Orthodox Russian priests during my lifetime. There was a huge fireplace on the set, as a rich man like Bulichov would have. Kulinev told us to begin the scene, and so we came in from this bitter cold, and what I did next I did instinctively—I stood with my backside toward the fireplace. All the other actors present burst out laughing. The Russian teacher, who had laughed himself, said to the whole class, "Now that physical action was not in Gorky's book, but it was a very good stroke and is representative of Stanislavsky's system." Kulinev wasn't one hundred percent pure Stanislavsky—he placed much more emphasis on physical action and on building characters, not just everything happening inside the actor.

The production was successful in spite of the scandal that China's foremost theatre in collaboration with a Russian counterpart would present a story about a Communist who became a capitalist. Kulinev realized the play was politically sensitive, but he was very proud of his choice. And this was the first time a Russian director had ever directed a play in China.[24]

Other Soviet experts came to Beijing too. There were additional acting teachers at the Central Academy of Drama who led workshops both there and at our theatre, and there was a lighting expert and a sound effects expert who worked with our designers. We were deluged with gifts from the Moscow Art Theatre. For instance, there was a huge roller that gave off the sound of autumn leaves falling and created a breeze. During these years, anyone entering the theatre company building could see a dozen or so Russians walking around, as well as a handful of interpreters from the Chinese-Soviet Friendship Association milling about translating for them.

We grew to be quite friendly with the Russians. Sometimes we would have picnics together, and they would bring us over to the compound where they were housed—the neighborhood near Peking Union Medical College. I had a Russian carpet in my home at the theatre—Moscow didn't make these carpets; they were from Siberia. The Russians had special travel permits, and would buy the carpets in Siberia as they passed through on their way to China. I remember washing our carpets together with the Soviet experts. We would beat them with a stick, then rinse them with water until they looked clean enough—but by the time they dried the next day, you could still see the dirt.

The senior-ranked experts brought their families over—and they had a hell of a good time. Some Chinese began calling them Russian carpetbaggers because they carried off all the goods they purchased in China with their Siberian carpets when they went away. I believe this expression was borrowed from *Gone with the Wind*, though given a slightly different meaning.

We could feel it coming when the tide changed and it was time for the Soviets to go. They started buying certain antiques—old vases, old pieces of furniture—and people were running around whispering about it. The Chinese were never very happy about national products being taken out of the country.

"The Russians must be leaving," someone would say.

"How do you know?" another would ask.

"I heard expert so-and-so discuss the future of his carpet. . . . "

Things were rather bitter when the Soviets left Beijing. The Chinese were making merchandise much finer than the Russian bears would ever dream of, and would point this out whenever the Soviet experts bought anything ancient or antique because they were proud of their handiwork. This understandably annoyed the Russians, who also had to sign papers agreeing to payment and taxation for whatever they bought in China.

The withdrawal of the Russian advisers in the arts and technology was all handled through very high-level diplomacy. We at the theatre did not understand exactly what was happening, but we could feel the tension behind it. A few of us did speak up and tell our own comrades that the Russians left behind a lot of good influence: Russian acting in particular had always been excellent and had a lasting impact on our theatre that is still felt today. And I liked Kulinev personally. He even sent me a Christmas card from the USSR.

Full House for *Teahouse*

Of all the productions I participated in as an actor, the most significant was *Teahouse*. It debuted in 1958, and the people of Beijing had never seen anything like it. At that time, a typical play might run for a week, and that was considered lucky, but *Teahouse* ran for over a hundred performances.[25] Beijingers continued attending plays after *Teahouse* opened in 1958, but by the early 1960s, it became very difficult to draw audiences to the theatre. Following the failure of the Great Leap Forward, the economy was very bad—a period we referred to by the euphemism "the difficult years."

After the early, heady days of the new republic, China's intellectuals embarked on a terrifying roller-coaster ride. Our leaders initially exhorted us to speak our minds during the 1957 Hundred Flowers Movement, but then, almost overnight, the leadership counterattacked, and those who had made the most scathing comments were singled out and labeled Rightists. During the nationwide movement, at least 300,000 people suffered this disgrace— my brother Ying Ruocong was one of them. Scientists, technicians, teachers, artists, and others who were targeted were demoted in rank, forbidden to practice their professions, and sent to the countryside to do manual labor. Many of them, like my brother, were rehabilitated only after two decades or more.

The whole affair shocked China's intellectuals and muzzled most of the malcontents. It also created the necessary political atmosphere for the next big movement—the Great Leap Forward. In 1958 peasants were told to double or triple their production quotas, with the theory that once certain ideological barriers could be breached, the working masses were capable of achieving miracles. The leaders realized the quotas were excessive, but it was an article of faith that the masses should never be doubted or discouraged. Soon the media caught up with this strategy, and in due course there were endless reports of miraculous harvests. Factories in the cities picked up on the fever and steel production quotas were doubled. The entire countryside was collectivized, with production teams upgraded to brigades and brigades transformed into people's communes, in which the collectives shared the work and its spoils. Family kitchens were abolished and everyone ate in communal canteens free of charge. It seemed that, overnight, China's problems were going to be solved.

Amid these glowing reports about the success of the Great Leap Forward, we in the theatre company were totally unaware of what was truly happening in the countryside. We went on blithely performing every evening and rehearsing new plays during the day. Then suddenly we noticed a surge of peasants on the streets of Beijing, some of them begging for food door-to-door. At first we thought this was due to natural disasters in isolated areas. But as the days went by, the number of what the newspapers called vagrants showed no sign of abating. We knew something must have gone wrong. Edible goods began to disappear from grocery store shelves, and the rules for buying grain products with ration coupons were strictly enforced.

It was now up to the state propaganda machine to explain away the food shortage, and each explanation was more bizarre than the last. No one dared state the truth. In Marxist jargon, it was a classic example of "ultraleftism" when leaders are divorced from reality, confusing it with wishful thinking. It was precisely the kind of thing Mao had opposed during the 1930s, but this time, Mao himself was the ultraleftist.

During the three "difficult years," my wife gave birth to our second child, Ying Da. He was born a healthy 3.6 kilograms, but I didn't know how we would be able to feed him. We were luckier than most of our colleagues, since we had a bit of extra money from my moonlighting as a translator. With those funds, I surreptitiously bought food on the black market. We managed to scrape by thanks to my wife, who spaced out the little food we had to make it last as long as possible. Not every family was so fortunate—many couples split up amid the pressure brought by the shortages.[26]

Plays during that period became political propaganda, and people just got bored, but by 1962–1963, we began to draw people back to the theatre by reviving popular plays like Teahouse.[27] Then the Cultural Revolution began, and we no longer staged plays for the public at all.[28] Artists were shipped off to cadre schools in the countryside, while Wu Shiliang and I were sent to prison. After the Cultural Revolution finally ended, the theatre's most popular pieces were revived because the young people had never seen them. This brought audiences back to the theatre and artists back to the stage, and Teahouse in particular created a huge sensation.[29]

After Lao She's tragic suicide following his interrogation during the Cultural Revolution, the revival of his masterpiece was considered a spiritual triumph.[30] As an actor who had performed in many of his plays, I was elated to see him rediscovered and appreciated. When the new regime had been established in 1949, Lao She was already a well-known novelist, and through his close relationship with the Beijing People's Art Theatre, he developed into a dedicated playwright. He felt that the performing arts were more accessible to the common people than printed literature, which required literacy from readers. In his first collaboration with the theatre, on *Dragon Beard Ditch*, he found in Jiao Juyin the ideal stage director for his plays. Most of the actors in the brand new theatre company were in their twenties and inexperienced, but guided by Lao She's writing and Jiao Juyin's directing, they became the best interpreters of Lao She's work. Between its founding in 1950 and its staging of *Teahouse* in 1958, the Beijing People's Art Theatre produced more than half a dozen of Lao She's plays, including a stage adaptation of his famous novel *Rickshaw Boy* (also known as *Camel Xiangzi*), in which I played Liu Siye (Fourth Master Liu).[31]

Teahouse came about in a rather interesting way. In the original version of *Dragon Beard Ditch*, there was a scene set in a small teahouse, and this scene became a favorite moment that instigated the idea of a separate play with a similar setting. Lao She was also deeply interested in the idea of constitutional democracy in China (something that had inspired his play *A Family of Delegates*). After the Constitution of the People's Republic of China was created in 1954, Lao She wrote another play about the history of constitutional democracy and its failure under all the regimes before 1949. When he came to the theatre to read his first draft, people were not very enthusiastic and he was prepared to scrap the whole thing. But everyone agreed that there was one scene set in a Beijing teahouse at the end of the nineteenth century that should be expanded into an entire play. The result was *Teahouse*.

The play has more than sixty characters and covers a span of fifty years, from 1898 to 1948, showing daily life in a teahouse during the fall of the Qing dynasty, the establishment of the republic, and the civil war between the Nationalists and the Communists. Lao She's stage directions call for a sign to be plastered on the wall throughout the play that says DO NOT DISCUSS AFFAIRS OF STATE—a move that required quite some courage at the time. Unlike other plays of the time, Lao She never tackles any of the political issues of the day head-on, but provides convincing three-dimensional images of the common (and even the grotesque) that were rarely portrayed on stage up until then. Some of the play's most memorable scenes—such as an aging eunuch buying a young wife—verge on the bizarre and ridiculous, but simultaneously give the play a remarkable inner truth.

Lao She's mastery of Beijing dialect and the language of the man in the street—from coolie and shopkeeper to artisan and petty official—was unsurpassed, and made his work, especially *Teahouse*, almost untranslatable. In 1978, I accepted the challenge and produced an English translation that was published and used for British and other European audiences when we toured the production in 1980.[32]

In the original production and the subsequent revival and tours, I played the role of Pockmark Liu (Liu Mazi) in the first and second acts, and his son (Pockmark Liu Jr.) in the third act. Liu was the worst of the lot. There were retired musicians; there were sellers of cheap cigarettes; there were sellers of peanuts—but he was selling human flesh. He was a pimp who arranged temporary liaisons and also sold young women as wives to the highest bidder.

I still remember vividly Lao She's reaction to my portrayal.

"You brought the play to life," he said. "But some people wished you to be more villainous."

Lao She was a man of great capacities, and what he didn't know was not worth knowing. We actors all loved him, because he was so magnanimous and full of all sorts of humor.

Director Xia Chun was entrusted with the job of starting the rehearsals in 1958, but he didn't really do very much. He kept at it for about three weeks, by the end of which everybody felt hopeless. Xia had no idea how to deal with this. The play is rather unusual to begin with, with so many characters and such vast time coverage. At the time, Jiao Juyin was not immediately given the job for political reasons—he was going through the Anti-Rightist thing. The decision to bring him into the rehearsals had to be made from quite high up. At last, after twenty days of moping around with Xia Chun, Jiao was called in, and the whole scene changed. Xia Chun stayed on, of course—with the kind of social system we had at the time, he couldn't exactly be kicked out. We all had to pretend that he was the director, but nobody took him seriously.

Jiao, on the other hand, was just about the most erudite theatre scholar I have ever met, and an exceptional director. He had spent many years in France, had been a university professor, and had founded the Chinese Traditional Opera School, so in addition to working with so many superb spoken drama actors at the Beijing People's Art Theatre, Jiao also mentored the most famous Beijing Opera actors in the country.[33]

When Jiao Juyin directed me in the role of Pockmark Liu, he often took me aside to work on aspects of my character. Liu has a whole philosophy behind him and felt totally justified in what he was doing. As an actor, it wasn't enough for me just to play a villain. That's what made playing the role so interesting.

Planting Rice after Prison: 1972–1973

When I was released from prison in June 1971, my wife and I mailed a letter to our daughter Xiaole, but it took a long, long time to reach her since she was out on the Mongolian border. As soon as she got the letter, she rushed back—it was sometime around November and it was pretty cold.

In the meantime, I was contacted by the theatre's accountant.

"Lao Ying [Old Ying], you are supposed to come to my office tomorrow with a briefcase—make sure you get a big enough one, because you're going to have to carry some weight."

The government was reimbursing those who had been badly persecuted at the height of the Cultural Revolution. My wife and I collected more than eight thousand yuan, which was a fabulous sum in those days because things were so cheap. I bought a Philips electric record player from a second-hand shop and lots of Western classical music.

Xiaole had only been back for a couple of months when I was sent to a cadre school in the countryside south of the city. Today it would take about an hour and a half to get there by car, but in those days we had to take a train. The place was called Tiantanghe—Heavenly River—rather ironic, since laboring in rough conditions alongside the peasants was not exactly heavenly.

I was kept at the labor camp for one full year. My wife was not sent—she stayed in Beijing. I was permitted to come home once every two weeks, and it was during those visits that Xiaole and I started rebuilding our apartment, and I turned the bedroom into a bridge club.

I remember exactly when I was shipped off: February 1972, just as Nixon was coming to China. I was singled out to be sent to the countryside at precisely that time—because the authorities were feeling that if any Americans were around, it was best to keep Ying Ruocheng away. There was no use trying to convince them that I didn't know Mr. Nixon personally.[34]

Many of my colleagues from the Beijing People's Art Theatre had been sent to Heavenly River cadre school before me, so I was reunited with them when I arrived. Some of them had been there for quite a few years, while others were newer arrivals like myself.

There were certain individuals there who should never have been persecuted—like Jiao Juyin. He was one of the few refused reentry into Beijing. He was already there when I arrived, and remained for quite a long time after I left. Even under those conditions, Jiao was still his polite old self. And we had some fun, too. I was the only one there who could talk to him about Western literature and culture, especially the Comédie Française, of which he had grown fond during his years in Paris. As far as I know, Jiao did not do any reading or writing during his time there, most likely out of personal preference. He planted rice, but not very much. He was in charge of the water pump, and all he had to do was to switch it on and switch it off. I honestly don't know how he kept his mind occupied. I suppose he didn't read because he just lost interest. He didn't live much longer after cadre school—he died in 1975 just before the end of the Cultural Revolution.

Unlike Jiao, I kept very active at the labor camp. While I was there, I built huge plastic sheds in which temperatures were kept high so that the rice seeds could shoot out ten days or two weeks before those of our neighbors. I also set up a little laboratory making bacterial fertilizer.

Compared to prison and the atmosphere in Beijing at the time, cadre school was relatively carefree. There was no one to persecute me anymore. There were no more interrogations, and none of that class struggle thing— because the year before I was sent there, in 1971, a plane carrying Mao's rival Lin Biao crashed in Outer Mongolia, and after that the whole situation relaxed. The army officers who were supposed to be our bosses at the cadre school gradually withdrew back to their barracks. So we were pretty much on our own.

Together with my fellow actor and good friend Zhu Xu, I devised a special system for our personal entertainment. Zhu had gotten hold of glass jars with hermetic lids, and he went to the Chinese pharmacy and purchased two little snakes. We soaked them in *erguotou*, a very strong liquor. Every evening the two of us would hold a little celebration with our libation, and if anybody saw us, of course we pretended we were having our medicine. "You want some?" we'd offer, and they'd see the snakes and run off.

I hate to be idle. I've got to occupy myself with something. And I discovered this was also for my own good, ever since my prison days. I kept myself busy at the cadre school by reading, and I read whatever books I could get hold of from my friends and colleagues. Nobody was really monitoring us, so we could read what we wanted as long as we could find it. On one of my visits to the city, I was in Lilichang just walking around. Lilichang then was not what it looks like now—it was still pretty much in shambles. One day, I ran into a former Qinghua classmate who had been a member of our student drama group. He was happy to see me.

"I've just been rehabilitated," he told me.

"So what are you doing now?" I asked.

"I'm running the Liulichang bookstore," he answered. He had become the restored party secretary of the old bookshop in Liulichang.

"You must do something for me," I implored him. "Take me to your store-rooms so I can choose some books."

"Sure, no problem," he said. He led me to a locked room where regular customers were not allowed, and I bought as many books as I could carry. By that time, I had already received my back pay from the years I had been imprisoned, so even though I was stuck in the labor camp most of the time, I was actually one of the nouveau riche.

I left Liulichang that day with a whole set of Chekhov's plays—I had missed Chekhov very much. At the time, Ying Da was eleven years old. The little brat was so clever—he had taught himself how to read during his childhood even though the schools were closed. When I brought the books home, he started reading Chekhov.

The next day he came to me saying, "I never knew there were such interesting books!"

At about the same time, I also dug out all my favorite music records and listened to them on my new Philips record player. I started with Beethoven because I wanted to introduce Ying Da to him. First I told my son the story of Beethoven's life—how he had been deaf but had achieved so much with music. I still remember I had a recording of Beethoven's Third Symphony with Irish dancing music in it that was not easy to find in Beijing then. When I listened to it, I couldn't hold back my tears. I knew what a great feat it was to be able to listen to Beethoven and read Chekhov at that moment in China.

On the Road with Yu Shizhi: 1974

Zhao Qiyang was the soul of the Communist Party for the Beijing People's Art Theatre—serving as the theatre company's party secretary from its founding in 1950 until 1977—so he knew all the ropes, and all the people there, and it was his idea to bring me back from the cadre school to write a new play. That's why I was able to get out so early, while others from the theatre had to stay at Heavenly River for several more years. While they continued to plant rice, I joined up with Yu Shizhi—the theatre company's most prestigious actor—and the two of us were given the task of writing a new play. We were only vaguely told what it should be about, so basically it was left for us to decide. We were supposed to investigate the daily life and struggles of the masses to find material, and this gave us an opportunity to run around the whole country. The two of us really had a wonderful time. While everyone else was being confined, we were set loose and could travel anywhere we wanted. Of course, I felt a little guilty knowing that all my peers were working in labor camps, but I enjoyed the experience nonetheless. Yu Shizhi and I did create a play—because ultimately we had to hand something in when we returned to Beijing—but we also explored the state of things in China, and we drank quite a bit too.

Everything was paid for by the theatre company, and we had an official letter of introduction from Zhao Qiyang. Since Zhao was a party secretary from the municipality of Beijing, everyone treated us very kindly.

I had been working with Zhao Qiyang and Yu Shizhi for years, long before I went to prison. We were all good friends. I was two years younger than Yu and about twelve years younger than Zhao. One day, Zhao called us together, telling us that he had to fight very hard to get us this assignment because there were several people aligned against the two of us. As an experienced leader of the theater, he said he knew the importance of a playwright who could write a good play.

"As to what kind of play you should write," he advised us, "I will tell you. Read the newspapers and see what the current propaganda line is. . . . "

My wife, Wu Shiliang, was very happy when I told her about the assignment.

"Try to find out what the country is like now," she implored. "We are both so out of touch—we don't really know what is happening."

Fortunately, I was able to telephone her long-distance during the trip—at the theatre company's expense.

Yu Shizhi and I didn't take much on our journey—just a small bag of clothing with a change of shirts and underwear. And of course it was compulsory to bring along a copy of *Chairman Mao's Selected Works.*

The only thing that really was irritating was that there was a high-ranking official at the theatre, the army man Peng, who was reluctant to let the two of us go off unsupervised, so he sent along a young graduate from the Chinese literature department of Nankai University. His name was Wang, so we called him Xiao Wang (Little Wang), and he was forced on the two of us as the third member of our travel party.[35]

We could go virtually anywhere we wanted, and we decided to go to the Yangtze River valley for our research, because we thought we should write about the steel industry. Mao believed that steel was the key to construction in industry, whereas in agriculture it was grain. Our destination to visit the steel workers was a place called *Ma'en Shan* (Horse Saddle Mountain)—a hilltop shaped like the saddle of a horse.

But first we concocted a little conspiracy to visit Yu Shizhi's cousin in Tianjin. We had no definite schedule, and one city is as good as another, so we went off to Tianjin with Little Wang trailing behind, trying to write down in his little notebook what we were saying, and recording whatever suspicious behavior he thought we displayed. I forget now how we did it, but we did throw him off our scent once we arrived in Tianjin. Since he had just graduated from Nankai, which was right there in Tianjin, Little Wang knew some people there. He didn't speak English, but neither did Yu Shizhi—Yu spoke French, though, and I could speak a little French when necessary to keep Wang in the dark.

Yu's cousin entertained us with some very good, very strong drink. I had a rather notorious reputation for my capabilities as a taster, so she presented a bottle and said, "You have to identify the name of this liquor from just a small taste before you can drink it."

So I sipped it and said, "This is not a pure drink—this is a blend of *Gu jing* and the Sichuan libation *Luzhou daqi*," and she nearly fell to the ground.

Luzhou is the name of a place in Sichuan and *daqi* is the kind of drink.

I went on to say, "It's difficult to tell by what proportion these two drinks have been mixed or blended, but I don't think that was required in the challenge."

By that time, Yu's cousin was on the floor in surprise.

I was right, of course. We finished the whole bottle before Yu and I went back to the hotel that was booked for us.

The days we passed in Tianjin weren't all so lighthearted, however. My youngest brother was living there and had been cruelly persecuted.

Ying Ruozhi was born in 1935 (the younger twin of my brother Ying Ruoshi) and had attended Tianjin University. While he was a student there, he contracted tuberculosis and came to live with me and Wu Shiliang in our home in Beijing during his recuperation. Now he was living in an area outside Tianjin, in a desolate part of a dried-up riverbed where he shared a hovel with his wife. They had two young children whom they had sent away temporarily to live in Tianjin in hopes conditions would be better for them there. When I arrived, my brother had already been there for a few years, but our family had heard no news of him. It turned out he was living out there working as an engineer on a project at Haihe. Coincidentally, Yu Shizhi's cousin had worked with him on the project, and that's how I was able to find him.

My brother had gotten into serious trouble quite by accident.

One incident came about during the celebration of a holiday Mao had declared. A procession was being organized on the banks of Haihe, along a road with an arch decorated with flowers. As was typical of my youngest brother—who, even with everything he has suffered, is still today a happy-go-lucky man—he said to the others, "You guys all go home, and I'll finish the work on the arch." I suppose people were only too glad for a chance to go home, and my brother stayed behind. A little later, he finished the work and went home too. But there was a rainstorm during the night, and by morning when people arrived, a piece of one of the five characters on top of the arch had been blown away by the wind. Instead of saying *Mao zhuxi wansui*, meaning "Long Live Chairman Mao," half of the last character was missing and it said *Mao zhuxi wanxi*, implying that Mao's days might be numbered.[36]

The next day, this was seized upon as a serious counterrevolutionary incident. People in remote places made a big case out of such things.

Ying Ruozhi had been in trouble before, too, for drawing an innocent cartoon. He was living with the others in camps not far from this dry riverbed while working on the Haihe project, and he sketched a satirical cartoon depicting a moon that could be seen through a window, and a cat perched on the windowsill. Someone said that since the word for cat was *mao*, he must have been drawing this cat on purpose as an attack on Chairman Mao. In reality, he was probably just satirizing comrades who were spending their work hours sleeping, or something as innocent as that.

For these two crimes, he was arrested and jailed for three months. By the time Yu Shizhi and I went to see him, he had been released, but his pay had been severed—he had no wages, but only a monthly stipend of eighteen yuan from the police. The family had to live on his wife's wages and this meager stipend. When I found him, he had been in this situation for about a year, and he was dressed in rags. Yu Shizhi was with me, and so was Little Wang, who was writing everything down in his notebook. I didn't worry about that at the time, because I didn't think anyone would sink so low as to use the suffering of my brother against me.

When I first saw Ying Ruozhi, I just thought he was trying to dress as poorly as possible because it was considered counterrevolutionary to dress nicely during the Cultural Revolution. There was a funny saying about this at our cadre school, where we were referred to as *wenhua ganbu* (cultural cadres), or *wengan* for short. The ditty went like this: "*Yuankan shi yaofan, jinkan shi taonan, yiwen shi wengan*," meaning, "From a distance, they look like beggars; from up close, they look like refugees; upon asking, they are *wengan*."

So as soon as I saw him, I said to Ying Ruozhi, "Can't you wear more decent clothes?"

"No, no, no—not so loud," he replied in a whisper. "*Wo xianzai fanle cuowu le*—I've made a mistake."

I had no idea all this had happened. My mother didn't know, and our brothers didn't know—none of us knew he was in this plight, though everybody seemed to be in trouble for something in those days. I was only able to spend about an hour with him, and I gave him some money, but he handed most of it back to me, saying he had no use for it.

Eventually, Yu Shizhi and I moved on to Ma'en Shan to do our research for the play, which we titled *Workers and Peasants (Gongnong yijia).*[37] In a nutshell, our play was about how the industry of a country is of course important, but that the benefits of the peasant mustn't be sacrificed to pay for it. The story unfolds near one of those new steel centers, which was planning to annex a lot of land from the rural communes in order to build an industrial base. Our play was arguing against that. It is a real problem in China, even now, because our per capita land distribution is among the lowest in the world and with that limited space we have to feed one-fifth of the global population. Those are the kinds of issues our play addressed.

Unfortunately for us, our dress rehearsal was scheduled for the night that Jiang Qing mounted the "Criticize Lin Biao and Confucius" campaign. Jiang Qing, Mao's wife, had been making a gradual comeback for about three years, ever since Lin Biao's plane had crashed mysteriously in 1971 after the alleged coup attempt. The essence of the campaign criticizing Lin Biao and Confucius was that both Lin and Kong were trying to restore the old social order. In China, every movement or campaign must have a target, and the target must be the wrongdoer. In this case, the man who had to bear the blame was Zhao Qiyang himself. One of those big character posters was displayed with a detailed account of what Zhao did before the campaign started. Among other things, he was accused of using undesirable elements to perpetuate his pet projects—and his number one pet was identified as Ying Ruocheng.

Apparently some people at the Beijing People's Art Theatre had asked, "Why should we keep Ying Ruocheng at the theatre at all? He's a jailbird. He's just been released from prison. How can we trust him?"

That was when Zhao Qiyang responded, "But he's a rare talent. He's a good actor, and he could direct. He also wrote several plays for the theatre, and he knows foreign languages. Of course we should keep him."

So he protected me and then he got criticized for it. Yu Shizhi was also mentioned at the time, because his name had been found on a KMT list. But it was mainly Zhao Qiyang who was faulted for restoring the old social order using people like me and Yu Shizhi.

Our comrade Little Wang emerged during the campaign, too. He wrote a *dazibao* supporting the one I referred to just now.[38] The original one was written by Peng, the army man at the theatre who had sent Wang along with us on our journey in the first place. Since arriving at the theatre, Peng always thought of himself as its future leader, so he probably wanted to get Zhao

Qiyang out of the way. He saw the job slipping through his hands during the previous couple of years and knew he had to fight for it.

In his follow-up poster, Wang declared, "The three of us were supposed to be in the same group creating the same play, but Yu and Ying spoke a language I could not understand."

Looking back on it now, it is rather funny.

"They used all sorts of quaint terms," Wang wrote on the poster.

And of course we had to defend ourselves.

"The only thing we said that he couldn't understand," we explained, "was 'such-and-such a passage won't do—that's a typical coughing scene,' meaning that during this part of the play, the audience would feel restless and start coughing." It made Little Wang angry when Yu and I used theatre terms like "coughing scene" that he didn't recognize. Perhaps he was also referring to our occasional use of French.

In the end, after all that, the play was never performed in public. The only performance was the dress rehearsal.

Yu Shizhi and I weathered the campaign against Zhao Qiyang without any visible wounds. But Zhao lost his job at the theatre.[39]

If You Can't Stand the Heat . . .

The big character posters against Zhao Qiyang that implicated me—along with everything else that had been happening during the Cultural Revolution—changed my mind about being an actor. Jiang Qing was ready to attack any new play that was not prescribed by her or didn't fit in with her ideas of theatrical art. Such plays were considered a challenge to her model revolutionary plays. By then, of course, she had the last word on everything, especially in the arts—she had become a kind of super producer on the mainland. During that time, I had discussions with my close friends, and we felt that all our efforts to revive the theatre were hopeless—because with Jiang Qing in charge, theatre in China had no future. I began to think about leaving the theatre altogether.

The play that Yu Shizhi and I had created died an early death—but another play in 1974, *Taoyuan*, suffered an even worse fate. Jiang Qing was organizing a festival and this play had been chosen by the province of Hebei to take to Beijing as their bid for first prize. It was all ready to be performed when Jiang Qing came down on it with a vengeance, saying something like, "This is typical! The moment I turn my back people are trying to sneak in these reactionary, bad works!"

The play was written by a group of writers. No one wanted to put their names to plays anymore for fear of the repercussions, so who knows who really wrote this play? It became quite a joke. For instance, the newspaper *People's Daily* devoted at least four full pages to this new play, but the name of the author was deliberately left out. In the place of the name of the playwright, it said *Taoyuan chuangzuo zu*: "*Taoyuan* creative team," indicating it was an anonymous group of people who created it.[40]

After this incident, I made the decision to leave the theatre and surrender this dream that I had had since I was seventeen years old. I had spent all my life on the stage and on the screen, but now the time had come to abandon it. Jiang Qing obviously was quite a bit younger than Mao himself and would survive him, so no end to her policies was in sight. It was a very difficult decision, but I left the Beijing People's Art Theatre in 1975.

I turned to my friends in my other world—that of foreign languages—and asked if I could join the magazine *China Reconstructs*, published by the Foreign Languages Press.

"Of course," they said.

They were delighted that I was interested and available, because their original English-language staff had more or less dwindled down to nothing. *China Reconstructs* had been started by Sun Yat-sen's widow, Soong Ch'ingling (Song Qingling)—but during the Cultural Revolution the staff all came under suspicion because of some blemish in their history or because they were wrongly accused by their colleagues as having incorrect ideology. So, by the time I arrived, the entire editorial board of *China Reconstructs* consisted of only a few people who could manage (with difficulty) to write anything in English. Due to their linguistic limitations, they needed to recruit people, and they also restructured by combining the two departments of editors and journalists.

Changing jobs was not easy. The Beijing People's Art Theatre belonged to the Municipality of Beijing, whereas the Foreign Languages Press belonged to the Central Liaison Ministry (*zhonglian bu*), so they were two distinct organizations. But the press was very keen on getting me, so the transfer finally went through.

In changing work units, I also changed housing, because my housing until then had been provided by the theatre. Wu Shiliang still worked for Cao Yu as his creative secretary.[41] He was quite ill at the time, but she helped him write his final play, *Wang Zhaojun*, about a famous beauty in ancient China who was given in marriage to a Mongol chief. Even though Wu Shiliang still worked at the theatre, we were given housing by the press, and we were happy to move to a newer building. The only problem was that it was at the other end of Beijing on the western edge of the city.

The building we moved to was more modern, and the apartment was larger and nicer. We were on the top floor of the building (the fifth floor, which made it quite a tall building at the time) and I hated climbing those stairs every day. The only telephone was one installed in a separate building for use by the entire residential community. I rode my bicycle the long distance to work, even in winter, riding about an hour against the Beijing wind in very cold temperatures. When I came home, I would climb the five flights of stairs and then remove my many layers of clothing because the temperature inside was always so hot. In the dead of winter we still opened all the windows to let in some cool air. This was unusual, because most Beijing residences did not have much heat. What I hated most was that I would come home, and no sooner had I stripped off all my woolen clothing when someone would shout up at my window from way down below, "Comrade Ying, telephone!"—and I would have to put on my overcoat again and rush down all the stairs and into the other building to answer the call.

China Reconstructs was produced in various languages, and I worked for the English-language version. There were also editions in French, Spanish, Russian, Japanese, and German, among others.

I found out soon after my arrival at the magazine that it was up to me to find my own sources for news. Luckily, I still had some friends in the right places. Through one of these connections, I managed to travel to Tibet to interview the Panchen Lama. I also interviewed another living Buddha in Qinghai who was rather young to be a living Buddha, but was a very intelligent boy. Much later, I would draw on the knowledge I gained in these two interviews when I played the Buddhist monk in Bertolucci's film *Little Buddha*. I had learned about the way the monks dressed—in a piece of high-quality saffron-colored material imported from India, with one arm bared. I also learned how to resist the smell of stale butter, which can be pretty horrible. In Tibet, making little figures of various heavenly deities out of cream or white cheese is a treasured art form. And of course, by the time I visited Tibet, these figures had all been changed into the leader of these heavenly hosts himself—Mao Zedong—along with his faithful assistants Zhou Enlai and Zhu De standing beside him, all made of butter. But after a few days, this type of butter goes sour, and the smell of Mao and his friends became horrendous.

As a journalist, I tried to interview people I was interested in meeting, and I could always convince the publishers that the world was anxious to know about them. And I did try to choose subjects that I guessed the government wanted. Once I interviewed a ballet dancer named Dai Ailian who came originally from the West Indies, where there were quite a number of overseas Chinese. She couldn't speak a word of Mandarin, so I was the only one capable of interviewing her about her early life and her studies of the art of ballet in London. Another time I interviewed Chiang Kai-shek's number one economic advisor. When Chiang collapsed on the mainland and fled to Taiwan, this man was sent to Europe on some anti-Communist mission, but instead of doing what Chiang wanted him to, he came back to China via the Soviet Union.

I interviewed an interesting assortment of people and wrote articles intended for foreigners to read. The magazine was circulated among expatriates in China and also exported abroad; the average Chinese couldn't read English in those days. When I first arrived at the Foreign Languages Press, the playwright and novelist Gao Xingjian was already there, working on the French version of *China Reconstructs*. Since winning the Nobel Prize in 2000, Gao Xingjian has been a whispered name in China and he has aroused the curiosity of a lot of people.[42] Soon after we met—perhaps even the first week I arrived—he came clean about how he felt about working there, lamenting that it was terribly uninteresting and saying he had great admiration for the People's Art Theatre. He was mystified why I should want to leave there and come to this hole of holes, *China Reconstructs*.

I told him the truth.

"That world is hopeless," I said. "We are only allowed to produce propaganda pieces. If I want to create propaganda, I might as well come to *China Reconstructs*. Why stay at the People's Art Theatre and pretend to be an artist?"

"I want to be an artist," he told me. "Can you get me into the People's Art Theatre?"

"I can always try," I replied. Eventually, Yu Shizhi and I helped him get hired there.

The theatre was short of writers then, so his timing was good. And after he arrived at the theatre, he wrote several good plays.[43]

When Gao Xingjian won the Nobel Prize, opinions in Beijing circulated in what I would call a whispering campaign. No one wanted to look too prominent in this Nobel Prize business, either by showing approval or disapproval. It has become a rather knotty problem. Roughly speaking, there were two schools of thought. One was that it was high time that someone Chinese won the prize, and the second was that it was a total distortion of reality because many had never heard of Gao. Time will tell how it gets received in another quarter of a century.

My Return to the Theatre

If I had stayed one more year at the theatre, I wouldn't have had to move, because the Gang of Four collapsed in 1976. They were arrested and imprisoned, and the atmosphere began to change, but I chose to remain at the Foreign Languages Press for two more years.

Eventually, my return to the Beijing People's Art Theatre was prompted by the fact that the theatre was always coming to the press to "borrow" me for various projects. Our editor-in-chief finally got fed up and said, "You constantly come and try to borrow him. It's like the tiger borrowing the pig. I'll never see the pig again."

At the time, I did not wish to go back to the theatre. I thought that was a page in my history that had been turned for good. But several things happened that led me to change my mind. For one thing, there was a group of "foreign experts" who were invited to China to assist with the editing of publications into foreign languages in China. These language experts were unanimous in their praise for Lao She's *Teahouse*—the play was a phenomenon unto itself. Some of the foreign experts were longtime China hands who had seen *Teahouse* when it was first staged in 1958, and they enthusiastically recommended the play to other Westerners. I was persuaded by the Foreign Languages Press to translate it into English, which I did in 1978, and the play then enjoyed a second hit run in Beijing and was also well received when it toured abroad. As soon as I finished the translation, it was published by the magazine *Chinese Literature*, a publication of the Foreign Languages Press.

Amid this renewed interest in *Teahouse*, I was approached by the theatre. At that time Cao Yu was quite ill and Jiao Juyin had already passed away. I suddenly found myself one of the senior members of the theatre company. The administrators at the theatre all realized that without me it would be difficult—perhaps nearly impossible—to restore the play. I was one of the few people who could still remember the last time we produced it, which was in 1963, three years before the Cultural Revolution. Records hadn't been carefully kept and the notes weren't complete, or in some parts were even wrong.

So it was the revival of the play *Teahouse* in 1979 that brought me back to the People's Art Theatre for good. In addition to translating the script into English preceding the revival, I also reprised my role as Pockmark Liu. *Teahouse* became the first modern Chinese play ever sent to be performed abroad. In 1980, we toured Germany, France, and Switzerland. That same year, I accompanied our theatre president, Cao Yu, to England and the United States.

After Lao She's death in 1966, *Teahouse* became a prime target of calumny, and the amount of slanderous attacks on both the play and its production could fill a fair-sized volume. In that respect, *Teahouse* is but one of the numerous examples of good plays unjustly suppressed and banned during that period. Its rehabilitation and revival in 1979 helped people rediscover Lao She and reappraise some of the criteria by which *Teahouse* and other theatrical productions had been judged—or misjudged. As a literary critic phrased it during one of the symposia on *Teahouse*: "We have not done sufficient justice to Lao She's writing in the past. It took the upheaval of the last ten to twelve years to make us realize that. There is much we can learn from Lao She."

Having performed in many of Lao She's plays and in all performances of *Teahouse* from 1958 through 1979, I fully agreed with this assessment. *Teahouse* had always been a popular play and the audience reaction had always been strong—but we were not prepared for the rapt attention and outbursts of spontaneous laughter during the 1979 performances. Was it due to the nostalgia and goodwill of our old fans? Not entirely. For one thing, a large part of the 1979 audience consisted of young people under age thirty who had never seen any modern spoken drama, let alone *Teahouse*. The truth is that the revival of *Teahouse* served as a timely antidote to the kind of stereotyped ultraleftist fare crammed down people's throats in the previous ten to twelve years. For a large number of people, to see life truthfully portrayed and to hear the everyday speech of Beijing turned into pithy, expressive dialogue were in themselves exciting experiences. Even more significant was the fact that after so many years of turmoil, people were beginning to realize that the evils of the old social order die very hard indeed and that the phenomena Lao She depicted in *Teahouse* as an indictment of past social injustices had reappeared in uncanny and devious ways. The result was that not only the audience but also the actors were reading new meanings into the text. Scenes like the arrest of Master Chang for worrying aloud about the future of the Qing Empire or the illiterate thug being turned into a college student overnight in order to suppress student demonstrations forcefully reminded people of what had been happening in their midst only a few years before.

In writing such incidents into the script, Lao She had been careful to heed his own warning that appears throughout the play in the form of signs plastered onto the walls of the teahouse: DO NOT DISCUSS AFFAIRS OF STATE. Lao She cleverly avoided specific references to politics, but merely depicted their impact on the lives of ordinary people during three periods (1898, 1918, and 1948) spanning fifty years—thereby creating a classic that remained as relevant in 1979 as it had been in 1958. It remains so today.

From Despair to Hope

Aside from the revival of *Teahouse* and other plays, something else very interesting happened at the Beijing People's Art Theatre in 1979. Bob Hope came to visit. He was making his famous television special *The Road to China*. At the time, there were few Americans living in Beijing—the entire American community at the time could fill only half the seats in the theatre. The other half of the seats were filled with Chinese. The show was getting ready to open, and I was supposed to be there merely as a representative of the People's Art Theatre. But then they discovered that I was an actor and that I could speak English, so they asked me to interpret. Bob Hope himself said that he had never before experienced someone translating his jokes to an audience. It was a full house, with me interpreting Hope's comic monologues, something I don't ever want to try again. They say that poetry by definition is untranslatable, and I think jokes are the same way. Fortunately my performance was well received.[44]

I faced a similar challenge when I managed an international collaboration with London's Old Vic, for which Derek Jacobi performed as Hamlet in China. A lot of Chinese had seen Lawrence Olivier's movie, but none of them had seen the stage version of *Hamlet* before. So I was responsible for organizing a group of actors to say the lines simultaneously in Chinese while the British actors performed the roles on stage, with the Chinese audience members listening to the backstage translation through headphones.

During my visit to the United Kingdom in 1980—my first travel ever outside of China, at age fifty-one—I saw Peter Shaffer's play *Amadeus*, about the rivalry between Mozart and Salieri. I liked the play because it is so unusual. In it, Mozart is portrayed to the public for the first time as a kinky little boy instead of an ethereal genius. Things like that always attract me, so I was eager to translate the play and stage it in China. I did so in 1986, and it was very well received.

Amadeus could be relevant anywhere in the world, not only because it is about Mozart, but also because it dismantles the image of Mozart to an incredible degree—I don't know how true it is, but it can't be all false. We had a streak of artists in China who behaved in such an outlandish way. One was Su Dongpo, a great court poet of the Song dynasty. Another was the great reformist Wang Anshi.[45] It has always been the dream of Chinese intellectuals on the left to push the image of such a character to its acceptable limits.

The young actor I cast to play Mozart was Zhang Yongqiang. At age twenty-three, it was his first major role onstage, and he had to learn how to play the piano to master the part.[46]

I directed *Amadeus* just before taking my post as vice minister of culture in the central government. At the time, I was in charge of all the playwrights at the theatre, serving as a sort of literary manager. When I returned to the theatre in 1990, I directed a play that had been a dream of mine since my days at Qinghua—George Bernard Shaw's *Major Barbara*.

I wanted to translate and direct *Major Barbara* because my time in the ministry had proven to me that the term "politics in command" had become a password for many of the people who should know better. I was dead against putting politics in command of the theatre and had done what I could as vice minister of culture to institute reforms that might change that. I found that Shaw could express my feelings best. There is a whole scene in the play in which Undershaft is having a heart-to-heart talk with his son, who is a typical product of the universities in London at the time. His father asks him, "Are you adept at this? Are you good at that?" and finds out he is good at nothing except politics. So he concludes, "Well, in that case, I think perhaps being a politician is your best way out."[47]

Now, you can imagine how this scene, which appears in Act III, just before the family's visit to their inherited business—an armory, a munitions factory—really brought the house down. There were rumors going around, with people saying, "George Bernard Shaw couldn't have written that line about taking up politics." The line implies that it is the most useless kind of theatre person who would make it the theatre's job to support political theatre—and yet this is precisely what we artists in China had been doing since 1942 at least.[48]

In 1991, it was a pretty risky thing to say onstage, especially so soon after June Fourth.[49] The audience more than caught on to the meaning of the scene, and that line in particular. The whole theatre was full of applause when it was said, and I knew it would have that effect. Audiences actually cheered, believe it or not. And many wanted to meet the translator of the play. That had never happened before.[50] Rumors continued to spread: "Did you know that line was not Bernard Shaw, but Ying Ruocheng?" Of course I didn't add the line—it was one hundred percent Shaw.

The government censors never bothered me about it. They were in a very precarious position, because some of the brighter leaders had long seen that the rigorous interpretation of art—or misinterpretation of art—as promulgated by the likes of the Gang of Four was hurting the country and was losing us friends overseas. And the propaganda department was going through an overhaul: four vice ministers of propaganda lost their jobs, one by one, after *Major Barbara* opened. Reformist government leaders like Zhao Ziyang caught on to the meaning behind the line—and they would have loved to have added a few lines to it—but, of course, they had to restrain themselves.

Part of what allowed me to be so bold in choosing to produce this play was that I had just served the government as vice minister of culture and I knew these people. Rather than warnings from them, I received friendly pats on the back. Some of the old-timers even came up to me after the show saying, "That was really well put." So you can see from this example that theatre in a totalitarian country can be very powerful. In some cases, it can help bring down a government, as we saw in Poland. The example of Polish theatre was certainly an inspiration to me.[51]

Now, when we were rehearsing *Major Barbara*, most of the actors did not realize how significant the production was going to be or what the content could reflect politically. Even Song Dandan, playing the lead role, did not recognize the subversive element in the play. I never discussed any of that with the actors. I directed the play just as I would direct any play, staying within the text and within the world of the play. But I knew what the results might be. And some of the actors, like Ren Baoxian and Yan Yansheng, caught on very early in the rehearsals. I had to restrain them, instructing them not to overemphasize certain lines.[52]

Zhu Xu played the role of Undershaft—he was the most brilliant actor in the group—while Zhu Lin played Lady Britomart. Zhu Lin had been cast as my wife Linda when I was Willy Loman in *Death of a Salesman* in 1983, and Zhu Xu had played Charley. Our collaboration with Arthur Miller was undoubtedly the peak of our professional careers up until that point—and it still remains, for each of us, one of our greatest moments in the theatre.

CHAPTER SIX

~

Cultural Diplomacy

At the end of the first night, we [actors] were waiting in the wings. We were not sure what the reaction would be. There was a long pause—and then the applause burst forth. And in the audience were a number of Americans and most of them did not understand a word of Chinese, yet even they were moved. You could see the tears streaming down their faces. And I saw the future of mankind—that we can communicate—not only intellectually, but emotionally. What we proved was that as far apart geographically and historically and in so many other ways as are the Chinese and the Americans, we are one humanity. We laugh at the same jokes; we cry the same tears; and we all love Arthur Miller.[1]

An Unexpected Visitor

It was the chance of a lifetime to have an opportunity to work with Arthur Miller. I consider myself very lucky.

My first encounter with Arthur was in 1978 when he came to China incognito. China was just beginning to open that year, after the decade-long isolation of the Cultural Revolution. At that time, an ordinary foreign citizen could come to China as part of a tourist group, but otherwise one had to be invited by an official organization in China and a special visa had to be issued—along with special attention to one's application, and special surveillance during one's visit.[2]

One of my friends who worked in the Friendship Association told me, "We have a traveler, a tourist, who has the same name as that playwright you always mention—Arthur Miller."

"He wouldn't come as a tourist," I replied. And we left it at that.

It so happened that a few days later I met with colleagues to discuss preparations for my upcoming visit to the University of Missouri, which was scheduled to happen a year or two later—and at that meeting, I found out that it was indeed *the* Arthur Miller who happened to be visiting China. I was very excited.

I told my friend at the Friendship Association, "Get hold of him and don't let him out of your sight."

Then I immediately informed Cao Yu—he had heard of Arthur Miller too, of course. Cao Yu and I traced his whereabouts and caught up with him in the hotel where he was staying. We went to meet Arthur, who was feeling quite lost in the huge city of Beijing (which had more than ten million residents at the time). He didn't know anybody, didn't know what was happening, and didn't know the social structure or what had really taken place in China in the past ten years. So Cao Yu and I felt we could help him quite a bit. We introduced him to a number of writers—artists who had all suffered to different degrees during the Cultural Revolution. And of course it was a revelation to him to learn what China had just been through.

Arthur was excited to meet Cao Yu and me, because he didn't expect that he'd have a chance to observe any modern Chinese theatre. Like me, Cao Yu was a Qinghua University graduate, but his English was a bit rusty because he hadn't spoken it in many years.

When I arrived at the hotel to meet Arthur, he didn't know who I was, of course. I carried with me an invitation for him to come to our theatre and watch our production of *Cai Wenji*.[3]

He was so surprised. "How did you find out I was with this group?" he asked.

"Your name itself is advertising enough," I answered.

He laughed and said, "I'd be happy to come."

"If you find this interesting, I can arrange further meetings so that you can talk to a number of Chinese people of the theatre," I offered. "We can get you away from this tourist group. You don't have to stay with them." He liked that idea.

That first encounter was the beginning of a deep friendship. I was really impressed by this humorous man. He was a head taller than I was, and Cao Yu was a head shorter than I was, so you can imagine the sight of the three of us together.

Arthur attended the performance of *Cai Wenji* and we were honored to have such an accomplished international playwright in the audience. He offered some interesting remarks in his critique after the show. Cao Yu accompanied our distinguished guest, and after seeing the performance, he was welcomed by the actors backstage—they used the star makeup room to hold a brief discussion, asking Arthur his impressions of what he had just seen. He was trying to be polite, of course, but Cao Yu wouldn't let him go that easily.

"You haven't spoken the truth—you haven't said everything that is on your mind and we want to hear it," Cao Yu urged.

Cai Wenji was written by Guo Moruo when he was the top-ranking Chinese intellectual (undeservedly, if you ask me—I never liked the man).

When Cao Yu literally forced Arthur to say what was on his mind, he finally said, "The production was superb. The director is one of the best I have seen in terms of his artistic direction. But as a playwright, I can't help feeling that there are many places that ought to be revised."

Everyone was shocked, because no one was supposed to criticize Guo Moruo—it was like criticizing Mao Zedong himself.

Nobody dared show any reaction since this was a world-renowned playwright speaking. I don't think he had any idea that he had just crossed a line.

He continued, "The playwright made a mistake with this play, which a lot of beginners are likely to make." He called Guo Moruo a beginner!

And there was more. "The whole story—the plot of the play—has been fully developed in Act I, so he has nothing left for the rest of the play—no more suspense. The remainder of the play is just a repetition of the same old story, and that's something a playwright should never do."

An awkward silence ensued.

At last, Cao Yu broke the silence, applauding, "Bravo! Bravo!"

Thank God that Guo Moruo was not there. He had died a few months earlier.

At that time, tourists to China were supposed to stay only one week, but Arthur stayed for almost a month, and he interviewed a lot of people. His wife Inge Morath, a professional photographer, took innumerable pictures, and during the interval between their stay in China in 1978 and when I saw them in the United States in 1980, they published a book about their visit.[4]

Bringing *Salesman* to Beijing

During the time Arthur spent with us in Beijing in 1978, we only vaguely discussed the idea of collaborating on a production one day—we didn't decide which play to choose or when to produce it and so on. That conversation had to wait until I was in the United States in 1982 for my visiting faculty post at the University of Missouri in Kansas City (UMKC).

We did share initial ideas about it in 1980 when Cao Yu and I visited the United States to attempt to make arrangements for a touring production of *Teahouse*.[5] Arthur was the representative who welcomed us when we arrived on that visit, but he was busy with a production of one of his plays and couldn't really run around with us. He did, however, devote a lot of time to us during our stay in New York. He was pretty old by then—about sixty-five—but he drove us all the way from New York to his home in Connecticut. He was driving a German Mercedes Benz with a diesel engine, quite a powerful little car. I think it was at his home where I first met Inge. She did some of the cooking—European cooking—and she was already learning Chinese at the time.

It was in 1982 while I was living in Kansas City that Arthur and I discussed in earnest the possibility of one of his plays being staged at the Beijing People's Art Theatre. He suggested *The Crucible* because he had heard so much about persecution during his visit in 1978—laments of intellectuals who were wrongly accused during the Cultural Revolution and so forth. I had to convince him to choose another play.

"Actually, that is over," I said—because by this time in the early 1980s we were already several years past the Cultural Revolution. There had been so many rehabilitations. Thus, if merely for the theme of unjust persecution, I felt *The Crucible* was an uninteresting choice. Arthur became very serious; he believed he owed the Chinese people something in the choice of the play. I had my own ideas.

Remember, I had been dreaming about the play *Death of a Salesman*—about putting it on in China—since I first read it in 1950 before I left Qinghua University to join the Beijing People's Art Theatre. If I could help it, I wouldn't allow that dream to be shattered, so I tried my best to convince Arthur that a story of persecution wasn't enough anymore. China's trauma had gone much deeper than the persecution of intellectuals.

There would not have been any particular danger in producing *The Crucible* in the early 1980s, contrary to Miller's perception. Such tales were common—in fact, they were the fashion at the time. It was the period of *shanghen wenxue* (scar literature), with so many works of literature exposing the persecutions suffered during the Cultural Revolution.[6] So in that respect *The Crucible* would not have been something new—whereas *Death of a Salesman* was truly a breath of fresh air, especially because of the way it was staged. Few people realize it now, but at the time that Miller wrote the play he was rather keen on trying out new forms. For instance, the walls didn't exist for the people in the play anymore, especially for the central character, Willy Loman. He could walk through any wall and could communicate with whomever he was in the mood to. And Arthur created the necessary ambience for such things to be believable. People were shocked—especially Chinese audiences, who were not accustomed to this kind of surrealistic style— but after a scene or two, it was absorbed very easily, without any hitches. This was something quite new.

I was overseeing the playwrights at the theatre during the period following our production of *Salesman*, and I tried to encourage our writers to experiment with ideas like that—to break out of the old frameworks and stereotypes—and several writers were willing to try. Jin Yun, for example, wrote *Uncle Doggie's Nirvana* (*Gou'er ye niepan*) shortly after *Death of a Salesman* was produced in Beijing. The play's structure, the characters, even the story—and the passage of time back and forth—were definitely influenced by *Salesman*. Even the ending of *Uncle Doggie's Nirvana* hints at a suicide, though it's not quite as clear as Willy Loman's. The play ends with destruction—Doggie throws himself in front of the fire. In *Salesman*, instead of burning down an arch, Willy crashes his car, but the message is the same. Several other plays written in Beijing during that period were influenced by *Salesman* as well.

So when Arthur and I were choosing a play to produce in Beijing in 1983, I still had my eyes on *Death of a Salesman*, which had impacted me so strongly in my youth, and which was, after all, the beginning of Arthur's career as one of the great playwrights of the United States. I also felt it was his most representative work.

Finally he was convinced, but he said, "I have one condition—*you* must play Willy Loman."

Under the circumstances, I of course had to agree.

He had seen my performance as Kublai Khan in the television miniseries *Marco Polo*, and knew of my stage roles at the People's Art Theatre.

"And you will also do the translation," he added.

When Arthur arrived in Beijing at the beginning of 1983, I had just finished translating the script.

One thing that made him very nice to work with was his rich sense of humor. The two of us always loved getting together. There was no challenge, it seemed, that couldn't be solved with a joke. During one rehearsal, I was feeling somewhat prudish about Willy's affair, and the fact that he was being unfaithful to his wife.

Arthur cornered me and said, "Now I want to hear the truth. What do you really think? Do you think this is something criminal? Do you think it doesn't happen to the Chinese?"

"Well, of course it happens to the Chinese," I said with a smile. "But we don't show it on the stage."

"That's hypocritical," he said.

That moment was, in a way, my liberation from the shackles of ideology.

When we first performed the play in Hong Kong a few years later, I had already directed two plays for the Hong Kong Repertory Theatre, so I knew the local actors pretty well. They all seemed to be very excited after the performance, but they were giggling, so I asked them what they were giggling about.

Finally they said, "We all watched this extramarital scene between you and the woman from Boston to see if you really kissed onstage."

"And what did you conclude?" I asked.

"You did!" they replied. They considered this a great victory of art imitating life. Even in a place like Hong Kong, Chinese are still Chinese. It took them some effort to break through the taboos.

We toured the play to quite a few places, including Hong Kong, Singapore, Japan, and Canada.

Another nice thing about collaborating with Arthur was that no one felt he was tyrannical or unsympathetic. We could not change anything in the text he had written—I translated it very faithfully—even though the play ran longer than any play our theatre had ever produced. We were concerned about that, but there was nothing we could do.

Arthur couldn't understand a word of Chinese, of course, but he timed the play with a stopwatch and he was very satisfied with the results. One of his happiest moments during the rehearsal process was when he timed the play all the way through for the first time.

"Congratulations!" he said. "To the minute, the play in Chinese is the same as the play in English." Then, turning to me, he said, "Thanks to your translation."

It was a nice tribute to me for my linguistic powers, but I wanted to tell him, "That's the easy part."

In translating the play, I tried to reconstruct the kind of language that would have been spoken in a crowded Chinese city at the end of the 1940s, which to me would be the closest equivalent to the playwright's intentions. Most translators don't use that approach, however, because it makes the work far more difficult.

The original language of the play is very colloquial English. In translating it into Chinese, I tried hard to avoid literary language, because I didn't want it to sound like a stiff translation. Because our cast was from the Beijing People's Art Theatre, my translation is heavily salted with Beijing dialect and slang. I also paid a lot of attention to maintaining the original tempo of the dialogue, because I think that's important to the feeling of the play.

One has to take a middle way in translating a play like *Death of a Salesman*—the translator can't be completely faithful, but I don't think one should go too far into adaptation. With Willy Loman, for instance, the translator should not remove references to place names like Brooklyn and Yonkers—and, on the other hand, there is no need for actors to put on false noses and blond wigs. The best result is when the play is performed and after five minutes the audience forgets about the actors' appearance and ethnicity, and buys into the belief that they're watching Americans—even if the characters don't look American. In terms of the actors' internal characterization of the parts they play, the challenge differs from play to play. For our production, Arthur's verdict was that the Lomans were a second-generation Chinese family in Brooklyn.

One day he said to the cast, "You've done what I wanted. You look like a family, but a Chinese family in Brooklyn," which we thought was a funny way of putting it at the time. In 1983, none of us knew any Chinese families in Brooklyn, but we supposed it could happen.

As a director, Arthur was not very versatile in the positioning of the actors, so I actually stepped in quite a bit in that regard. I was serving as his interpreter, but at times I usurped his role and nobody really knew Arthur Miller's ideas from Ying Ruocheng's ideas.

The fact that Arthur was a playwright rather than a director—and that he was directing a play he himself had written—certainly affected his directing style. Obviously, he paid great attention to the lines. And during discussions at rehearsals, he was able to tell us a lot of things that we certainly couldn't imagine for ourselves. The background and activities of the Loman family is a good example. The play does make mention of some of it, saying that Willy's father used to make simple musical instruments (flutes) and that they roamed the plains of North America—but when Arthur told that story to us directly, it came alive.

Chinese are very much tempted to think of Americans as just another bunch of Europeans, but they're not. Americans have a different past—for want of a better word, a revolutionary past. They really had to struggle to finally emerge as a prosperous and strong nation. They embody the dream, the American dream . . . just like Uncle Ben in the play.

I wouldn't say Arthur is a very lyrical playwright—and I don't think he thought so himself—but one could feel his mind seething with ideas. And he knew exactly what he wanted. And what he didn't want. And one thing he didn't want was wigs and noses.

We Chinese have been producing Western plays for a very long time and we have been using the most modern techniques to make up the Chinese face into a Caucasian face with great verisimilitude.[7] When it is badly done, we make ourselves laughingstocks. But even when it is successful, the audience might start thinking about our wonderful makeup jobs—what the noses are made of, and what would happen if one were to fall off—and forget to concentrate on the play itself. So Arthur did not want any blond wigs or big noses for this play, and this became one battle we had to fight. His decision greatly disappointed our makeup staff at the Beijing People's Art Theatre. One day they held a costume parade, exhibiting a variety of wonderful wigs for Arthur, everything from platinum blond to red.

"How do we get rid of this?" he asked me sotto voce, not wishing to hurt their feelings.

Eventually, we found a way—and finally all of us actors had our own hair. True, the characters in the play live in Brooklyn, New York, and not in downtown Beijing, but we wanted audiences to know the pulse of their hearts, not the color of their hair.[8]

We actors deliberately avoided seeing a film version or listening to recordings of the play in English. Sometimes in the past, when we performed Shakespeare, we did watch films of the work, but it turned out to be a hindrance because we had preconceptions and tended to unconsciously imitate the other performances. Of course we did a lot of research in preparation for *Death of a Salesman* and watched American films of the period, but this was to get some background information on lifestyles, relationships, and even dress styles.

Frankly, some playwrights are good at writing plays but know nothing about directing. Arthur Miller was extremely competent at both. He was able to give us a much deeper understanding of the play and its characters. Once, when Zhu Lin (the actress playing Linda) and I were having trouble concerning the relationship between Willy and Linda, Arthur told us he thought of Linda as having run away from home to marry Willy over her parents' objections. The audience knows nothing of this, but it helped immeasurably in our interpretation.

The most interesting moments in acting often come when least expected. This happened for me while playing Willy Loman. Willy was certainly a tragic figure—if you just put him there as a neutral object to study, he's a tragic figure. But I had this incredible experience regarding his final realization that he had found a way to leave something behind for his son, Biff, to build a career on. Willy never lost sight of that career, and he came up with a plan to commit suicide in order to get the life insurance money. I remember I was on the stage by then toward the end of the play, when Willy appears with his brother's ghost, who is giving him advice. He is exchanging ideas with this dead brother of his, and the more he describes his plan the more excited he gets. He becomes increasingly convinced that he can achieve this—that, thanks to him, his son will soon be holding twenty thousand American dollars and will begin a new career.

While onstage playing the role of Willy at this moment, I could hear the audience sniffling. The happier I got, the stronger the sniffling of the audience became. So in this case, we—the actor and the audience—were playing against each other.

I was trying to convince them: "Don't you see what a bloody good idea this is?" But somehow they just didn't understand.

In this instance, the representation—that is, the future that Willy paints for his son—becomes very real, very true to life, and the more Willy thinks about it, the happier he becomes. But the audience went the other way, totally the other way.

I never discussed this with Arthur. I didn't think it was necessary. And by that point in the production process, he was being very careful, like a sensitive conductor trying to mold me, trying to lead me on in my fantasy and encouraging it in a way. So I suppose we two were in league against the audience.

At the time, it was tricky to put on a play by a living American. The relationship between China and the United States was still awkward. Well, even today it is awkward. When I tried to convince the theatre company to produce *Death of a Salesman*, I was still among the younger generation of the leaders in the theatre, so many who had seniority were pretty arrogant. I translated the play orally to them, hoping that none of them would object to it.

The final scene of the play is called the Requiem. Willy Loman is already dead, so it is supposed to be at his burial and there are only five people present: his wife, Linda; his two sons, Biff and Happy; his neighbor Charlie; and Charlie's son.

The theatre administrators said, "This might do for an American audience, but in China this won't work. When the story ends, Willy Loman is dead. His family and friends should say, 'He was a nice chap' and that's about it. No Chinese audience will have the patience to stay for that scene. And we must think of the transportation problem: the buses will stop running. People will start rushing out of the theatre before the end. When Willy dies, they will feel that's the end of the story and they will want to go home." I was a bit doubtful myself. I knew Chinese audiences could be unruly and impolite.

"It's a long play," they continued. "What time will it end? Something like ten o'clock?"

"Probably later than that," I replied.

"Then we're in trouble," they said.

They had a point actually. In Beijing in those days very few people had private cars and all citizens depended on public buses. The bus drivers were generally very kind and would wait for the audience to come out of the theatre, but their patience wasn't endless—if the play went on for too long, the bus drivers might feel that it was not worth their while and just go home.

"And then what?" people argued. "Then we're stuck with more than a thousand people on our hands and we won't know what to do."

"I am sure that won't happen," I said.

But, to tell the truth, I was just as worried as they were. We didn't want to have hundreds of people lingering in the theatre without transportation and we would probably have to feed them.

"We'll just have to hope for the best," I said—trying to convince myself as much as everyone else.

But the authorities persisted.

"This is a very strange play," they said. "By the end, the main character has died. He isn't there anymore. He has no more story to tell. There is no more suspense. And all that happens is that a few family, friends, and neighbors stand there on the stage saying something about this dead man. Who would want to listen to that?"

"Oh, I am sure they'll be willing to," I said. "The play is so powerful. Everyone will have been receiving the emotional impact. I'm sure the audience will have the patience to wait."

"Want to make a bet?" someone asked.

"Let's stop joking," I replied. "I am not into this betting business. We'll just have to trust our luck, cross our fingers, and see what happens."

And here's what happened. When the time came—after the car crash, which the audience recognized by the sound of it—I told the actors not to hurry, but to make their way onto the stage to the designated place (which was indicated by the lighting as Willy's tomb), and act out the scene seriously. And that's what we did. Miraculously, it worked. Nobody left the theatre. Nobody was even showing any impatience. In fact quite a number of spectators—a large fraction of the people there—were blubbering into their hankies. In other words, the play was a total success. In the audience were quite a few foreign journalists and correspondents—as well as the more prominent media and theatre critics of Beijing.

On opening night, Arthur Miller was very nervous. We couldn't keep him in his seat. He was running around the theatre trying to listen from all angles, gauging the reaction of the audience—to discern whether they were laughing at the right places and silent at the right places. The whole evening he was try-ing to observe the audience and sense what they were feeling—but the Chi-nese are not usually very demonstrative of their feelings, so I don't know how much he got from it. Finally, after the play's final moment, he breathed a deep sigh of relief and came toward the stage to receive his curtain call.

I was waiting in the wings, while the other actors came off the stage one by one after paying tribute to Willy Loman. As the curtain came down, there was absolute silence from the audience for what seemed to us like a long time. One of our actresses started sniffling, thinking that the show was a to-tal failure. And then, all of a sudden, I don't know who started it, but it came like an avalanche: the applause came forth and it didn't end. Everyone was cheering. I was relieved and excited—all of that effort had not been in vain. Nobody in the audience was concerned about the last bus. Instead of running out of the theatre as some of my colleagues had predicted, the audience rushed forward to the edge of the stage, shouting and pointing.

This was the first truly successful new play since the end of the Cultural Rev-olution. There was still so much controversy at the time about how to assess in hindsight the productions during the Cultural Revolution. Some people, though they hated Jiang Qing and hated all the practices of the Cultural Revo-lution, couldn't help remembering her model plays and their various produc-tions. At the height of her power, Jiang Qing gave orders that everyone in China should be capable of singing an aria from one of her model operas. That still lingered. Sometimes, revivals of modern plays we had produced before the Cultural Revolution would be met at best with grudging approval, and our re-vival of *Teahouse* had been wildly popular. But this new play was totally differ-ent. This was a success with a capital S. The applause was unlike anything I had ever experienced as an actor. It was like a tidal wave. For an actor, this is the moment one lives for. As the curtain call continued, Arthur was helped onto the stage and received the appreciation he deserved.[9]

Unlike other performances, nobody bothered about washing off their makeup afterward. We had a party, of course, with strong drink—even the teetotalers among the actors shared the bottles that night. By that time we all knew we had a hit on our hands.

Wu Shiliang joined Arthur and Inge and myself to celebrate. She was pulled in as part of the team early on because she spoke excellent English. She was also instrumental in arranging for Arthur something he had always wanted—to live in a Chinese-style old-fashioned courtyard instead of a modern hotel. It wasn't easy at the time, but my wife managed it. We got Arthur and Inge a car, a driver, and his dream hotel. We even gave them a few days to run around a bit so they could see some of the sights.

The place to live that we found them was one of the more luxurious old-styled hotels in Beijing, a palatial home originally inhabited by Kang Sheng, China's security chief and the number one villain who was supposedly behind the Gang of Four. He was educated in Russia at the Kremlin, and was from Shandong province, just like Jiang Qing, so of course people made up stories about their relationship. His residence was on a street near the bell tower and the drum tower. I never could get rid of the feeling of something sinister in that place, but I still arranged for Arthur to live there because he wanted an old Chinese-style hotel, and all the other hotels by that time were already carpeted, had elevators, and were at least thirty stories high. This place was traditional, but elegant—Kang Sheng, whatever his sins, had very good taste.

We entertained Arthur and Inge in our home several times, and Arthur seemed to like my little house very much. At the time, I was living in what could be called—with a stretch of the imagination—a three-room flat. It was a single-story residence inside a *hutong* and I spent a lot of time trying to fix it up, doing carpentry, stopping leaks. My wife was a superb cook, so she did the cooking and I did the eating, which I am very good at. We had been forced to move out of this same house during the Cultural Revolution, when we were pushed into the neighboring *hutong* with even smaller accommodations. When we returned from prison, we were asked by the housing authorities which living quarters we preferred. It was our son, Ying Da, who insisted on returning to the home where he was brought up. Shortly after, he took the entrance exams for Peking University. His older sister could never go to college. First we were told she was too old and then we were told she was too young.[10]

Our home had a little courtyard where we could entertain friends, and that is where we sat with Arthur Miller and his wife Inge. She was a very interesting woman, an Austrian aristocrat. She told us all about her life in Europe. She was a wonderful photographer too, who had quite a few exhibitions, including several of photos of Arthur's trips to China. Inge studied Chinese. I wouldn't say she was fluent or anything like that, but she could get by. She was determined to learn about China, which was rather touching.

I was also very moved by the things that Arthur wrote about me in his books "*Salesman*" *in Beijing* and *Timebends*. *Salesman* is a detailed account of his work on our production and our collaboration, so I wasn't surprised that he talked about me in that book. But I was very flattered by his comment about my acting in his autobiography, *Timebends*. He included a photograph of me in rehearsal and called me a "brilliant Willy Loman." I will try to live up to that for the rest of my life.

Bertolucci Beckons

It was indirectly through Arthur Miller that I ended up with a featured role in Bernardo Bertolucci's 1987 film *The Last Emperor*, because Arthur had recommended me to the producer of the 1982 television miniseries *Marco Polo*, in which I played Kublai Khan, and Bertolucci saw it.[11] During the Sino-Italian joint production of *Marco Polo*, filming proceeded for many months without a Kublai Khan, and producer Vincenzo LaBella was beginning to get a little desperate. Suddenly one day the Beijing studio called him up, saying, "We think we have found the ideal Kublai Khan."

Meanwhile, LaBella had met with Arthur Miller and explained to him, "I need a Chinese actor who speaks English and also must be knowledgeable about this period of history."

"I have just the person you need," Miller said, writing down my name and handing it to LaBella.

The next time LaBella came back to Beijing, he had a meeting with the Chinese producer from the Beijing Film Studio, and both sides were very excited, saying, "We think we found Kublai Khan!"

LaBella suggested, "Let's each of us write the name on the palm of our hand."

This is exactly like a scene in the classic Chinese novel *The Romance of the Three Kingdoms* when Zhu Geliang is resisting Cao Cao and two generals are discussing a tricky problem. One says, "I have the answer," and the other says, "I do, too," and adds, "Let's both write it on the palm of our hands"— and of course when they compare it, it is the same Chinese character.[12]

The two film producers did the same thing and wrote the name on the palms of their hands and compared them, and it turned out both of them had written Ying Ruocheng. So that's how I got the part of Kublai Khan in *Marco Polo*.

And that led to my role as the governor of the prison in *The Last Emperor*.[13] By the time Bertolucci was ready to shoot the film, I was already vice minister of culture, and I was invited to the shooting location at the Forbidden City as a spectator.

When I was introduced to Bertolucci on the set, his eyes suddenly became bright and he said, "I know you—I've seen you in *Marco Polo*!"

I was flattered that he remembered me, and even more flattered when he explained the role he had in mind for me and asked if I could help.

"Well, I am now a government official," I said. "I have to attend to my duties."

"I will move heaven and earth to get this done," he assured me. I wasn't sure what he meant, but he ended up going all the way to the very top. It was Party Secretary Hu Yaobang himself who suddenly informed me one day that I would be permitted to take part in this Bertolucci film, even though I had never applied for it.

By the time I returned to the set as a member of the cast, they had already built replicas of the Imperial Palace rooms at the studio. The wedding chamber of the last emperor and the gate of the palace looked very authentic. I was given a tour of the sets, and then Bertolucci met with me.

"This film will begin with you and end with you," he said.

It begins with me because I am on the railway station platform receiving all the prisoners of war handed over by the Russians in 1950, including the Manchu dynasty's last emperor, Pu Yi. The location was supposed to be Dalian, but the original Dalian railroad station had been demolished by that time. Since the Japanese had built all these stations to look exactly the same, we used the station in Changchun. It was bitterly cold when we started shooting there. The film *The Last Emperor* opens with that scene—with me walking through rows of prisoners of war, and then shortly after I discover the emperor trying to commit suicide by cutting his wrists. So the film starts with me saving his life. I also appear in prison sequences that occur between the flashbacks telling the story of Pu Yi's life.

And the film ends with me, too, because the last thing the former emperor sees is the beginning of the Cultural Revolution, when all these people with questionable pasts are led through the streets wearing high dunce caps. My character is one of them, and Pu Yi tries to save me, telling the young Red Guards, "He's a good man—a good teacher." He is thrust aside, of course, and I am taken away by the Red Guards near the end of the film.

Bertolucci was younger than I. Physically he was a little overweight, but apart from that he looked very typically Italian, with a profile like a Roman sculpture. He was once an Italian Communist—many Americans do not know that. I think he got on the wrong side of the Italian Communist Party with his film *Last Tango in Paris*.

I respected him because he was never hesitant about correcting himself. So many directors hate to correct themselves. They get this mentality of a prophet, and if you doubt their words, they fly into a rage and think very hard about how to refute you—if not today then tomorrow. But Bertolucci was never like that. I liked working with him very much. He was always humorous, always seeing the funny side of things.

Our collaboration on the film *Little Buddha* came later. We didn't discuss it at the time of *The Last Emperor*, because his head was full of Malraux's *La Condition Humaine*. It was part of a trilogy on China that he said he wanted to make. His producers bought the rights to *La Condition Humaine*, but he never got around to filming it. It is a story set in 1920s Shanghai when the Communists were rising and Chiang Kai-shek staged a bloody coup to defeat them.

In *Little Buddha*, I play the old Lama, and I sort of carry the story through.[14] We filmed parts of *Little Buddha* in Bhutan and Nepal in September and October 1992, and then filmed for another month and a half in Seattle. In the summer I had some postproduction work—looping and so on—in London.

While we were filming in Nepal, our backdrop was the Himalayas and there was a huge temple near our location that is one of the holy places for Tibetan Buddhism, with pilgrims visiting all day long. There were no facilities on the set for makeup and costume changes, so I had to change at our hotel and then get into a car, which would take me to the *dagoba* temple where the faithful were gathered. They thought I was a real holy man, so I was always surrounded by pilgrims. All they actually wanted was for me to touch their heads, so I did, as if I were indeed a real monk.

By the time Bertolucci called in 1992 and asked me to join the cast of *Little Buddha*, I had the freedom to choose my own creative projects—but that had not always been the case. It was a rather recent reform, in fact. Before that, when I belonged to the theatre, they owned me. So when I was borrowed by others to make a film, at least forty percent of my salary for that project went directly to my Chinese work units. For instance, when I played the role of Kublai Khan in *Marco Polo*, I only received ten percent of my pay—given to me by the Italian production company R.I.E. The other ninety percent went to the Beijing Film Studio and the Beijing People's Art Theatre. That year, the theatre paid everyone their annual bonuses out of my money.

Highs and Lows as Vice Minister of Culture

I served as vice minister of culture for three years, from 1986 to 1989, but my term did not ultimately come to an end until 1990.[15] When political events of 1989 in Beijing unfolded before the eyes of the entire world, it became impossible to extricate myself from my post—but I became more determined than ever to do so.

At the time I was appointed, the secretariat of the party center made the choice of any appointment equal or beyond the rank of vice minister. In my case, it was Hu Yaobang who had chosen me. I had never met him before that, and he hadn't often shown up at theatre events or in cultural circles. Once I became vice minister, I had considerable contact with Hu, and I must say I really liked the guy. He was an honest man, and did not refrain from unpopular decisions for fear of embarrassment. During the mid-1980s, his word was law. He gave the impression of being a rather happy-go-lucky man, but of course he was much deeper than that. And he never refrained from saying what was on his mind.

I found out later how Hu had selected me: he gathered a group of experts from the theatre world, told them he was thinking of appointing me, and solicited their opinions. He must have consulted about twenty people, including Cao Yu, and also Zhou Yishi, the former minister of culture. Such a process was very unusual at the time.

As vice minister, I reported directly to Wang Meng, the minister of culture, who had also been appointed by Hu. I knew Wang Meng, but not very well. We were not close friends. With his permission, I began organizing large biannual international arts festivals, and they were very successful. Usually they were held for a month, beginning in September and winding down just as National Day approached on October 1. When I agreed to stay one extra year after 1989, it was mainly because Hu and Wang convinced me that no one else could properly supervise the arts festival that year. Before Hu Yaobang died in April 1989, he had already assigned me the task of organizing a better festival than the previous one. His death was unexpected for me, and quite a loss. Despite the political unrest and its aftermath, the 1989 festival that September was a success, and the only foreign participant I recall pulling out was the Joffrey Ballet.

Under Wang Meng, there were a handful of vice ministers besides myself. One was Liu Deyou, concentrating on foreign relations; he was kept very busy deploying and checking on cultural attachés and relations with embassies. Gao Zhanxiang was a general factotum, handling all the odd jobs that were inevitably swept to his door. Another vice minister, Wang Jifu, was a fiasco. The leftists still had quite a lot of power at the time, and so their camp sent Wang from Shandong. He was supposed to be in charge of the libraries and the Forbidden City, and museums in general. The left-wingers sent him over to counterbalance what they felt was a group of rightists, headed by Wang Meng and myself. Among the vice ministers, I was perceived as having more influence than Gao and Wang, but I think it was purely because more people knew me.

My responsibilities fell under three areas. First, I was in charge of all performing arts troupes, such as ballets, theatres, operas, folk dance troupes, and so on. Second, I oversaw the training academies for these various arts. And third was a new branch called the Cultural Market (*wenhua shichang*). I developed this branch because I saw that we could generate significant income by introducing reforms that would partially privatize these companies while also adopting market techniques. For example, people were always complaining that museums didn't have enough funds. Well, we could sell one terra cotta soldier on the international market and build a whole museum with the income. Why should we go begging for money when we were sitting on a treasure trove?

The situation looked promising during the first two years of my post, when performing arts and education were on the threshold of fundamental reforms. Surprisingly, my official duties were quite exciting. In a sense, though this may sound grandiose, I had the feeling that I was picking up the thread left by my grandfather and my father in their efforts to modernize China.

This feeling did not last long, however. Overall, after my appointment as a government official, life definitely took a turn for the worse. I was kept busy most of the time doing things that I disliked or that I did not understand, and I was barred from doing things I was good at. As 1988 progressed, things became worse and I knew I needed to find a way out of the ministry. In addition, my wife had died in January 1987, and a year later I found myself a busy but lonely man.[16] In contrast to my involvement with genuine reforms during the first half of my post—and experiences like shooting *The Last Emperor* and attending its premiere in London in February 1988—one of the only satisfying experiences during the year leading up to the events in Tiananmen Square was when I was permitted to leave the ministry briefly to act on stage again for the revival and Shanghai tour of *Death of a Salesman* and *Teahouse*. The performances were exhausting but spiritually satisfying.

The year 1989 marked my sixtieth birthday, and I became determined to get out of my rut in the ministry and spend my life more meaningfully. My boss sympathized with me, but he insisted that I find a suitable replacement. This was more difficult than it sounds. I am not trying to show off, but the fact remains that it is a job that requires specialized skills and also acceptance by the Chinese artistic community. I told him that I would see him through the Second China Arts Festival (September 15–October 5, 1989), but after that it was good-bye. I had done my bit. So, my three-year term was extended to four years, and I retired from the ministry in 1990.

I had planned to go to the United States in March of that year, but was not able to pull it off because those in power placed several restrictions on senior officials concerning foreign visits. As vice minister of culture, and particularly in the months following June Fourth, I was not able to speak freely on the telephone and had to scribble notes and send them back through departing acquaintances in order to communicate with a few select friends abroad. I could not make international calls on my telephone, although I could receive them—but any discussion of politics was off limits. At that time, every long-distance call was paid for by the ministry and duly recorded. I was once at a meeting where these calls were minutely examined, and I did not want that to happen to me.

In extricating myself from my post, I wanted a "soft landing," so I knew it would take me a few months in order to be above suspicion. I was eager to go abroad again and didn't want to spoil that chance. By December 1989, we in the upper levels of the government had gone through a careful sifting of all high-ranking officials, and it was of the utmost importance that I come out of the process unblemished. I had close relations abroad—including my sister Ruoxian, my daughter Xiaole, and my adopted sister Stella, all in the United States—and also many close friends, two of whom decided to stay away out of concern for me. This was in fact necessary for my survival. Stella was eager to communicate with me and for me to visit her in Massachusetts, but I wrote to her and asked her to keep her distance, adding, "Don't worry about me, I am pretty good at taking care of myself."

I had others looking after me, too. My son, Ying Da, married Song Dandan in July 1989, and they moved in with me and treated me well. My health was fine aside from the heavy feeling of aging. Ying Da had rushed back from Kansas City when his mother was dying, and had completed his master's thesis project for UMKC from Beijing. He went back to the United States in the summer of 1989 with a film crew and returned by Chinese New Year 1990, and his first son, Batu (Ying Rubin), was born in March. My daughter Xiaole, living in Chicago with her husband and son, reluctantly resigned herself to her new sister-in-law.

Wu Shiliang's last literary work was her translation of Bette Bao Lord's novel *Spring Moon* into Chinese. She died leaving it unfinished, so I completed it in her memory. And, somehow, life seemed to go on without her.

The Greatest Loss

After Wu Shiliang died, every now and again I would suddenly stop doing something midstream and think, "Oh my God, she died—how could I let her die?" I still have these thoughts from time to time. Almost anything can suddenly make me think of her: references to poetry, or a reminder of some episode in our lives. I don't think I will ever be able to fold her up and tuck her away—that will never happen. I have thought about her every day since her death.[17]

Shiliang was an amazing person. It was not only I, as her husband, who loved her—but she was also the ideal woman in the eyes of all my younger brothers. To this day, my siblings and their spouses talk about her with a kind of awe and respect. When Shiliang was still around, everyone knew who to go to if they were in trouble. My younger brother Ruozhi (the younger of the twins) was diagnosed with tuberculosis in 1957, and he didn't want to stay with anybody else but our family—so he came and lived with us, and Shiliang helped nurse him back to health. Her mother was living with us, too.

Shiliang's death was the culmination of a lifetime of deteriorating health, influenced most of all by a disease in her youth which was exacerbated during her three years in the harsh conditions of prison. She never fully recovered from that.[18]

Back when she lived in Chongqing with her family as a patriotic young teenaged girl trying to save China, she had a severe case of malaria. That illness affected her for the remainder of her life, but she always took care not to show it. She was one of those stereotypical noble Chinese women who never showed an ounce of self-pity. Although she had a full Western education, it didn't change her Chinese heart.

Shiliang was alone during the worst stage of her illness. I was filming *The Last Emperor*. Our daughter Xiaole was living in Chicago, and our son Ying Da was in graduate school at the University of Missouri in Kansas City. We all rushed back when we realized the end was near. Xiaole arrived one week before me and Ying Da one day before me.

I was in Italy and it was not a good stage of the shoot for me to go missing, so I wanted to stay a little longer. But Shiliang's doctor sent me an urgent message saying, "We cannot guarantee that she will be up and about when you come back from that stage of filming."

I requested permission to leave and a ticket to Beijing. I didn't believe I could go on with the film, but in the end I did go back and finish it. It was Shiliang's last wish. She knew that the chance for an actor to get a part like that happened only once in a lifetime.

I had purchased something wonderful for our home while I was in Italy and I brought it back with me. It was a unit that I could install in our bathroom to heat plenty of hot water for a bath. Ordinarily, Chinese could never afford to have such a thing—they would just boil water and pour it in a basin, and it was never plentiful enough.

I had brought the water heater as a piece of checked luggage from Italy. When I arrived at the airport in Beijing, I informed the man responsible for special luggage that we were in a hurry. He shrugged and made a face and said he couldn't find the piece. I was furious, but there was nothing I could do about it at that moment, and in those days the Beijing airport was in much worse disorder than it is today.

He thrust a piece of paper toward me and said, "Sign here. I will notify you if it arrives." So I just signed my name and hoped it hadn't been stolen.

My son's father-in-law was waiting for me at the airport.[19] He had hired a car and he drove me directly to the hospital. Xiaole was already there. As we rushed down the hallway, we could hear my wife's heavy breathing before we entered the room—she was in a room reserved for high-ranking cadres, and they had brought in various machines and instruments. The doctors and nurses were keeping her in a sitting position as they prepared to perform some kind of procedure on her. I asked Shiliang if she wanted to say anything, and she motioned with her hand, lifting it and brushing away the air with the back of fingers as if to tell me not to cry. She knew she was dying and she didn't want her departure from this life to be full of sadness. I don't remember exactly what I said to her, but I tried to utter comforting phrases like, "Don't worry, I'm here."

I asked to remain in the room for the procedure. She never really regained full consciousness after that, but I think she knew I was there. Xiaole and Ying Da were there, too—we were all in the room.

After I rushed directly from the airport, my vigil over my wife lasted only an hour and a half.

One of her two doctors approached me and said, "We did our best, but there's no hope, I'm afraid. It is only the breathing machine that has been keeping her alive. She is not conscious anymore. Do you want us to stop the machine?"

I don't think I gave a coherent answer. "No, no, no . . . yes, yes," I muttered, contradicting myself.

Eventually they confirmed that I agreed to stop the breathing machine, and they turned it off. It was very emotional for all of us. I was holding my wife's hand at the time, and I could hear her last breath.

Forsaken Children

During the hours that followed Shiliang's death, I flashed back to an earlier memory of holding her hand as she lay in the hospital.

It was 1958 and I was cast in the role of an evil Daoist in a play about the adventures of a PLA detachment in north China called *Tiger Mountain*.[20]

Our daughter Xiaole had just turned seven, and Shiliang was carrying our second child; her pregnancy had been unusually long, but finally the baby was coming. It was August, and very hot in Beijing, and I knew as I walked over to the theatre that I would have to leave in the middle of the performance to see the birth of our child. Since I only had a few scenes at the beginning and at the end, I pulled off my beard and rushed over to the hospital, full of excitement. But when I got there, I found the hospital staff gathered and waiting for me. They told me they had found an excessive amount of *jinji nashuang* in the fluid around the baby, and that the baby—a girl—was dead. Poor Shiliang was full of remorse.[21]

When she became pregnant again the following year, we were extra careful. We didn't even want her to ride in a car.

"Should we have it?" I asked her. "We are running a risk."

Shiliang was in hysterics. "I won't deprive myself of another child. I want this baby."

So we had the baby, and that was Ying Da. He was born on July 7, 1960.

After he was born, I was quite determined to have another child, because both Xiaole and Ying Da showed such obvious signs of talent. I saw that Ying Da was gifted—it was unmistakable—and, after having left him orphaned for three years while Shiliang and I were in prison, I made up my mind that I would try my damnedest to improve the quality of his upbringing. And I must say that his mother and I succeeded. Ying Da now has a thriving career in film and television. I have always had a dream that film and theatre would merge their ways and, if this is indeed possible, I think Ying Da would be a very good candidate to lead the way.

Before Ying Da was born, when we were still permitted to purchase housing, I bought a courtyard residence in a little *hutong* just to the right of the People's Art Theatre. It was actually closer to the stage than the dormitory housing of actors like Yu Shizhi, who had to descend four flights of stairs to the ground level and then cross a long corridor to get to the dressing room. Yu and I once made a bet and compared the distances from our doorways to our dressing rooms, and my commute was shorter even though he lived in the actual building that housed the theatre.

By the time of the Cultural Revolution, the Red Guards had sent out notices demanding that homeowners voluntarily hand in their house deeds because all property belonged to the state. My mother-in-law lived with us, and she was scared to death, so she foolishly went and stood in line to hand in the deeds. Since technically it was required, there was nothing I could do to stop her. I received no compensation for the money I had spent purchasing the house, but on the other hand nobody was chasing us out. We still lived there, and we didn't pay any rent. It wasn't until after they arrested me that our housing assignment was changed, so while Shiliang and I were in prison, her mother and Ying Da had to relocate to a smaller unit.

I was able to tolerate my mother-in-law for the most part, but there is one thing that I could never really forgive her for—and that was what she did to Ying Da after I was taken to prison. It still hurts now to think about it.

My mother-in-law's name was Ying Lingyan: her surname was pronounced "Ying," but it was written with a different Chinese character than our Ying. She was quite a bit younger than my own mother, who was in her late sixties at the time. After Shiliang and I were taken off to prison and eight-year-old Ying Da was left in Ying Lingyan's care, she sent him to his other grand-mother with a slip of paper. When he arrived at my mother's home, he handed her the note, which said, "I really can't handle this boy, so I'm going off to live with my own son's family. Sorry for all the trouble. Good-bye."[22]

After we were released from prison, Shiliang became pregnant again, and she wanted another son. But she was in poor health as a result of her incar-ceration, and early in her pregnancy blood appeared. There were long dis-cussions between the two of us and with the doctors, and we all decided she should have an abortion. It was a very difficult decision. And so, you see, we lost two of our four children.[23]

Exploring the New World

People often refer to me as a "cultural ambassador" between China and the West, especially between China and the United Kingdom and the United States. I suppose that began with my travels abroad in the early 1980s and then continued with my efforts as vice minister of culture and beyond.

After Wu Shiliang's death, I was able to travel overseas more frequently, though I didn't have the pleasure of her company as before.

I went abroad for the first time in my life in 1980. I had always been looked upon by my friends and my colleagues as someone well versed in world affairs, but that was actually a fallacy as I had never been out of the country until I was fifty-one years old. I went to London and immediately after that toured various prestigious universities in the United States. I felt it was all rather unreal and that I didn't deserve it. I couldn't help having a guilty conscience because I knew most Chinese had no prospect of ever seeing the world outside of China. Those of us on the trip were living in hotels—where the prices were always a shock to us—and we felt uncom-fortable spending so much money, knowing it was the hard-won earnings of our countrymen.

Cao Yu and I both loved to drink, but we couldn't even afford a jug of beer. I went out and bought some cider one evening and came back pretending it was liquor. We were not supposed to have alcohol, and were not supposed to spend any money that could otherwise be spared.

Luckily the British Council, as our host in the United Kingdom, provided for our transportation and essentials. The purpose of our visit to London was to make preparations for a tour of the Old Vic's production of *Hamlet* to China. I was responsible for providing the simultaneous translation at performances. There were four of us on that trip: Cao Yu, my wife, myself, and a comrade from our theatre company who couldn't speak a word of English— he knew very little about the West, but we had to take him along because he was in charge of the Chinese Communist Party machine in the dramatists' association to which we belonged.

We were generously treated to plenty of wonderful entertainment in London. We saw plays like *Amadeus* and musicals like *My Fair Lady*, *Jesus Christ Superstar*, and *Evita*, and couldn't believe their budgets. The first one we saw was *Evita*: the theatre had been totally redecorated to provide space for the chorus, with the acting area in the middle. To be honest, we had never seen stage performances of that scale and caliber. I was especially impressed by *Amadeus*—the acting was superb. Then and there, I decided that I would stage the play when I returned to China. I wanted to stage *Evita*, too, but it cost too much.

We arrived in the United States after our trip to London during the same year, 1980. What I remember most vividly is taking a taxi to go someplace and not being able to keep my eyes off the meter. I would just watch that needle race against time while calculating in my head and thinking, "My God, that's another five dollars gone!" The exchange rate was quite ridiculous, something like 1.7 RMB to each American dollar. The pocket money we were given was only a miserable little sum—about one dollar a day. Try surviving on that. That's why taxi rides were devastating. Whenever we could find someone to take us somewhere in a private car, it saved us a great deal of money. The Sino-U.S. Arts Exchange Committee sponsored our trip to the United States, through the efforts of a professor at Columbia University. The committee covered some expenses, but not all.

When we arrived at the University of Indiana, our hosts realized that we were in obvious financial need and having a very difficult time, so they offered us the best accommodations in the university. Cao Yu was asked to give a speech, and since they wanted the speech to be in English, I was paid a thousand dollars by the university to translate it. I bought a German-made color television set in the United States and carried it back myself, and Cao

Yu bought a whole sound system, so I helped him bring that back, too. In addition to Indiana and East Coast schools like Harvard and Princeton, we also visited Northwestern and Berkeley. I made a speech at the American Conservatory Theater in San Francisco while we were there.

My next trip abroad was to Los Angeles in 1981 for postproduction work on the *Marco Polo* television movie, in which I played Kublai Khan.[24] The film company gave me a per diem of three hundred dollars—which was a lot at that time, especially for me. I banked almost all of it. The Chinese state wanted every kind of foreign currency it could get its hands on. We were told that our country depended on us to hand in all foreign money we earned abroad, and that this would be considered an act of patriotism. I was the only one in the entire theatre company that earned any sizable amount of American money, which at that time totaled something like forty thousand dollars. I had no choice but to hand it over to be converted to Chinese RMB at the official exchange rate of 1.7 dollars to the yuan. After the exchange, my earnings had dwindled to a much smaller sum, and then everyone tried to share it. I didn't even see most of my salary, though I was allowed to keep the per diem. Since it was the Beijing studio that had signed a contract with the Italian company, they felt they had a right to half of my salary. The remaining half went to the Beijing municipality, which claimed it was rightfully theirs because they would be responsible for my medical bills in my old age. I think in the end I got something like three thousand dollars, which was very little after being converted to RMB. We were all very patriotic back then, thinking it our duty to bring back every cent we earned. With the bit of surplus money I had, I even bought a photocopier for the Beijing People's Art Theatre, which didn't have one. Such a machine is an absolute necessity for a theatre company, because without it, actors have to copy scripts by hand. So that was my donation. Due to the back pay I received after I got out of prison, Wu Shiliang and I became the richest couple in the theatre.

But I had never seen wealth anything like what I witnessed in Los Angeles in 1981. It was a beautiful place. I was taken around Beverly Hills just to have a look and thought, "How can these people spend that much money in one lifetime?"

I was housed in West Hollywood, where the best hotels were located. A car was provided to drive me every day to the Hollywood studio where we were doing the postproduction work. At that time, our voice dubbing in China was done on the old reels, so when I entered the studio in LA, I marveled to see a huge machine that was fully electronic: by just pressing a few buttons, the desired scene could instantly be located. Nothing in Chinese motion pictures was computerized in those days, so this was remarkable to me.

There were also some curious facts about Los Angeles dining establishments. Every day I had lunch with the producer of the film, who took care to bring me to the finest restaurants. There was always full sunshine outside, and when the hostess would lead us into the dining room, it was so dark I could hardly see the table settings. The waitresses all had miniskirts on unlike anything I had ever seen. Once or twice the producer even took me to a topless restaurant for a treat, which left me impressively scandalized.

I had become more sophisticated by the time I returned to the United States a year later. The 1982 trip was organized by the Edgar Snow Memorial Fund at UMKC, which invites one Chinese faculty member to campus each year to teach as a visiting professor in a particular department (usually in the sciences or social sciences). For my appointment as a humanities professor in the theatre department, I taught acting and directing, and at the end of the term, I translated and directed a Chinese play called *Family*.[25] Cao Yu had originally adapted the novel for the stage, but his version was too long for present-day audiences, so I asked Cao Yu and Ba Jin if I could basically "murder" one of the characters by cutting him out of the play, and they agreed. I eliminated Second Brother, because one minute he was agreeing with First Brother and the next he was agreeing with Third Brother, so it really didn't hurt the play to lose him. Cao Yu's stage adaptation of *Family* is not really a great play, but the influence of both the play and the original novel on the literary scene in China during the revolutionary years was significant. In my director's notes in the playbill for the 1982 UMKC production, I described the play as a reflection of Chinese life in the 1920s—specifically the disintegration of the age-old patriarchal family system in the face of China's traumatic encounters with the outside world. To this explanation, I added, "As understanding is the basis of true friendship among peoples of the world, it is my fervent hope that our endeavors here may contribute to a better understanding and development of the friendship between the peoples of China and the United States." The production was videotaped at UMKC and later aired on television in China.[26]

Shiliang lived with me in Kansas City, and we traveled around the United States together for the entire month of November while I made appearances at places like the University of Pennsylvania, Yale, Wellesley, Oklahoma State University, and Washington University in St. Louis.[27]

I came back to UMKC as a visiting professor again in 1984, teaching courses for students at the university and directing *Fifteen Strings of Cash* with professional actors at the Missouri Repertory Theater.[28] There were some very funny incidents during that experience. One of my students, a very pretty girl, often asked questions in class, much like everybody else—but I noticed she had a rather low voice. Much, much later I discovered that she was actually male. She told me she was trying to save enough money for an operation. Once I knew she was male, I gave her some tips on female impersonation, which had been a common performance practice in China for centuries, because we didn't really have female actresses onstage until the 1920s. Beijing opera master Mei Lanfang was the top actor who trained and performed those roles, but even our beloved former prime minister Zhou Enlai had been the star "actress" in his middle school, playing female roles in early spoken dramas.

American acting students were much more outspoken than their Chinese counterparts. When we were rehearsing *Family* in 1982, we came to the crucial scene of the wedding night of the two main characters. I had to teach the two student actors how to be shy, and they found it very funny.

"What's there to be shy about?" they asked. They were ready to embrace at any moment.

"You can't do that," I said. "You're not supposed to."

I still had to make the students play their roles according to the aesthetic of Stanislavskian realism. If the groom and the bride felt shy about things, they needed to feel that from the inside of their hearts and not just pretend to be shy. So, in order for these American students in the 1980s to be able to approach their roles in a realist mode, I had to give them lessons about the social conditioning of girls in early twentieth-century China.

When I returned to Kansas City for a third time, it was not as Edgar Snow Visiting Professor, nor was it to direct a production for the university or for the repertory theatre, but to play the title role in Missouri Rep's production of *King Lear*, directed by the theatre's artistic director, George Keathley.

We had been in rehearsal for about a week when the director asked me, "Will you stay on for a few minutes? I have something to say to you."

He was rather high-handed about it, speaking quite loudly.

"You know, unfortunately, I underestimated—there's a lot of work that has to go into the preparation of a Shakespeare part, and now I've come to the conclusion that it's not fair to make you act this part. You are young for Lear. We can hardly expect you to outshine the other actors. Of course, I'm sure with some effort, we could pull this off. But I don't think we have enough time."

"If that's what's worrying you," I said, "I don't think I should trouble you anymore with this. It wasn't my idea to begin with."

He never told me specifically what I was doing that he didn't like and never offered any specific reason why it wasn't working. In fact, he didn't give me much direction at all during those first five rehearsals.

At the end of our brief talk, he said, "We will pay you the money we agreed to in the contract."

"That won't be necessary," I replied.

I felt cheated. At sixty-two, I was not too young to play Lear, though I was not as tall as some of the other actors and the timbre of my voice was not yet that of an old man. The director had chosen the other actors himself—I alone was assigned to him as a guest artist. From the very beginning, he treated me differently and did not seem to feel comfortable with me, and because of this, I never felt entirely at ease with him or the rest of the cast.

But I tried to be diplomatic.

"I'm afraid I can't see this project through," I said. "I have other commitments in the United States I must fulfill."

Ying Da was at the rehearsal when all this happened, so I discussed it with him afterward, and we agreed that George Keathley was being a jerk.

The next morning, I was supposed to attend a class I would be teaching, but I felt too humiliated. I wrote a note explaining that I was leaving and ran off.

As far as I knew, no one else was aware of what had happened except the director. I certainly did not tell anybody. But Felicia Londré got wind of it before we left town and came to find us. She was extremely upset about what George had done. She got in her car and took us with her to her office.

"This is by no means the end of this episode," she said. She wanted to raise hell, I suppose. I think a part of me wanted to as well.

But instead I said to her, "I understand this. The director does have the authority to make cast changes. And I am quite busy after this."

I did my best to handle it with dignity. I tried to sound somewhat relieved not to have to play the role—it was a demanding task in addition to my other commitments, after all—but truthfully, I was terribly disappointed.

The authorities at the theatre in Beijing were disappointed too. They had been very excited about one of our actors going to America to play a golden part from Shakespeare. And people in Kansas City were excited as well, especially people like Felicia Londré and John Ezell.[29] After that incident, the Beijing People's Art Theatre avoided collaborations with the United States for quite a while.

When the news was reported publicly, we made it sound like it was my decision to leave. Since I had been hospitalized briefly before leaving Beijing to come to Kansas City, the official story was that I returned to China for the sake of my health.[30]

I would not want to work with George Keathley again. And I don't think he really saw my true strengths and weaknesses as an actor playing the part of King Lear. I do believe I brought something genuine to the role.

Looking back on my experiences at UMKC and Missouri Rep, however, I remain very positive. I feel I owe UMKC for all it has done for me. My residencies there as a visiting professor and director helped me linguistically a great deal. The most important thing in creating theatre exchange, in spite of everything else it entails, really is the study of language.

I am especially grateful to Felicia Londré and John Ezell. I'd love to have them and a few of my other UMKC colleagues in China right now. China is going through a very interesting period, and talented people like Felicia and John would make their presence felt.[31]

The ill-fated *King Lear* project would prove to be a lost opportunity to take the stage professionally in an English-language theatre production—an opportunity that would never come along again. But I would soon return to the United States to direct two plays—*Death of a Salesman* at the College of William and Mary in April 1993, and my own translation of Jin Yun's *Uncle Doggie's Nirvana* at Virginia Commonwealth University that same year. As in my visiting professorships at UMKC, I taught an undergraduate acting course in addition to directing the play. I must admit that when I was directing *Salesman*, it felt rather odd at times to be explaining to American actors how Americans behave.

In 1993, I received an honorary degree of doctor of humane letters from Bowdoin College. This came about as a result of the visit of Marvin Green, chairman of the board of trustees, to China a few years earlier. I was ready to step down from the cultural ministry at that point and was eager to take on as many trips as possible that would keep me away from the office and its usual operations. When this delegation from the United States arrived, I was only too happy to take them off for a sight-seeing excursion. The group was called the Young Presidents Club, comprised of businessmen from various companies. To join the club, one had to be below age forty-five, employ at least a thousand people, and have a certain sum of capital. The group I hosted had some fifty people, but it seemed to include their most esteemed members.[32] I took them on a tourist cruise of the Yangtze River gorges. The boat was like a four-star hotel, and I was still drinking pretty heavily at the time, so by the end of the trip, the young presidents knew their guide was fond of whiskey and cognac.

Final Farewell

I had always hoped to visit the cemetery in Taiwan where my father is buried in order to sweep his tomb, as filial children in China should. Because of the strained political relations between China and Taiwan, it was impossible for me to travel to Taiwan during the twenty years he lived there (from 1949 until his death in 1969) or for more than twenty years after he died—particularly once I became a Communist government official in the 1980s. Fortunately, Ma Yingjiu, one of my father's former students at Taiwan University, was influential in the KMT-led government and was able to pull some strings so that I could visit in 1993.[33] One of the purposes of that visit was to promote the film *Little Buddha*, and the other was the Beijing People's Art Theatre performance of *Top Restaurant* (*Tianxia diyilou*)—the first tour of a mainland spoken drama to Taiwan. There were no direct flights between the mainland and Taiwan, so we flew to Hong Kong first (which was still in British hands) and then to Taipei.[34]

Because my father had been such a prominent figure in Taiwan—and I suppose because I had just served as the vice minister of culture in Beijing—my sweeping of my father's grave became a major news event. There were at least five television cameras taping, and the footage was shown all over Taiwan.

I visited the Qinghua University campus in Taiwan, and of course I spent time at Fu Jen (Furen) Catholic University, the school my grandfather had founded in Beijing in 1925, which had closed in 1952 and was reestablished in Taiwan in 1960.

They invited me to give some lectures at Furen while I was there, and I also met with Zhang Xueliang, the famous Young Marshal of China's warlord era, who was ninety-two years old.[35] Ma Yingjiu held a special party for me, too. I was quite honored by the whole experience, and of course very moved when I visited my father's gravesite. In the photograph on his tomb, he is much older than I remembered him. As soon as I returned to Beijing, I became seriously ill, so I was never able to visit Taiwan again. The "reunion" with my father at his grave in 1993 proved to be our final farewell.

That trip prompted me to reflect on my father's legacy, and becoming ill shortly afterward prompted me to reflect on my own legacy as well. I have been thinking a lot about my family legacy—and my responsibility to it—during my illness. I don't want to go out with a bad smell. What I mean by that is that I don't want my departure from this world—from history—to be just an unpleasant puff of air. I want to go out with a rather powerful noise. There are so many people throughout history who accomplished little, and I don't want to be like them. I hope to be remembered as a man of his times who, with all his greatness and weakness, represented his era and lived up to the family legacy that was passed down to him.

Of all my experiences, the one I would never give up is the chance to have learned a foreign language. I inherited that—and so much more—from my father and my grandfather. They spread their mantel over my small shoulders, with momentous results for this one intellectual family. My siblings, too, contributed in economics, architecture, and other aspects of modernizing China. We all felt the obligation to carry a heavy load as intellectuals in New China and as responsible bearers of our family legacy.

I'm beginning to feel, at the end of my life, that all of this did not happen as a fluke or by chance. And I must say I am not sorry that history turned out this way. It's not that I have any conceit about what I did—it's not that—but I hope that more comrades will join our ranks, so to speak. China is now headed in the right direction, and we need people who are willing to go forward. It's not easy, and I always knew I would have to pay a rather high price for urging China toward modernity, toward learning from the West.

For millennia, China remained self-contained and considered itself the center of the world. Attempts to open the country by force failed, leaving regrettable casualties and bad feelings. Most Chinese, especially the more articulate, have always rallied around a political force that defies foreign manipulation, real or imagined. The latent patriotism of China's people can thus be harnessed during times of political crisis. One of the most important factors in present-day international relations is that isolation for nearly one quarter of humankind has ended. China's doors are now open, and they were opened by a consensus that extended from the highest leaders to the man in the street. There is no going back.[36]

We in China must learn from the West. It's as simple as that. I believe that—and it has always been a credo with me—because I am aware that the great danger is always that China can go backward. In China we could so easily sink into a kind of sleepiness, then be weakened, and comfort each other by saying, "We discovered the circulation of the earth before those foolish priests" or some other phrase to placate ourselves.

I wish the leaders would see this and be more supportive of innovative ideas and people. During my lifetime, I certainly tried to reach as high as I could. In my mind, the new ideas all came from the West, and I looked at them truly as pointers to the future. From them, I always sought inspiration of a kind that would urge China on toward new horizons.

Epilogue
Claire Conceison

A Dream of the Forbidden City

When I called Ying Ruocheng in his Beijing hospital room from my parents' home in Massachusetts on December 24, 2003, to wish him a merry Christmas, neither he nor his nurse answered the telephone. This had never happened before, so I sensed something was wrong. Three days later, my father came to me in the early morning bearing a grim expression on his face and the *Boston Globe* opened to Ying Ruocheng's photograph and obituary. Ying had already been moved to the intensive care unit by Christmas Day and had died there on December 27, 2003. He was seventy-four years old when he took his last breath at Peking Union Medical College Hospital. He was surrounded by loved ones: his daughter, Xiaole, had flown in from Chicago with her husband; Ying Da was there with his wife, Liang Huan, and her brother Liang Tian; and Ying's nephews Ying Zhuang and Ying Ning were also among those gathered at his bedside.

As Ying Da stood by his father during his final moments, he flashed back to his mother's death in 1987. It was the same scene of unstoppable internal bleeding that lasted for several days, prompting a hospital vigil by family members staring helplessly at bloody sheets. Like Wu Shiliang, Ying was going in and out of consciousness during his final days, but was lucid for moments on the afternoon he died. He knew where he was, and he recognized his daughter, Xiaole, and his youngest grandson, Bayan (Rudi).

187

Ying Da sensed that, to his father, that day was just like the day before. Ying Ruocheng did not know he was about to die. He didn't talk about the family's future or other topics that would indicate he knew the end was near, and Ying Da says that his father experienced a sense of shock when he realized it was over. Xiaole's husband, John King (Jin Yijian), would say later that he read fear in Ying Ruocheng's eyes during his final moments. When the doctor approached Ying Da and said, "*Ying Lao buxing le*" (meaning that things were not good), Ying Da rushed to his bedside with his other relatives, knowing that the moment he had prepared for for more than a decade was coming. He even recalls feeling surprised that his father had held on for so long through such a difficult illness, while many colleagues and friends had succumbed to various ailments.[1]

Ying Ruocheng's cirrhosis of the liver was not diagnosed until 1994, although he had experienced a serious nosebleed episode in 1991 (during the opening night of *Major Barbara*) that kept him hospitalized for two weeks. From 1994 to 2003, Ying would fluctuate between being gravely ill and responding to medical treatment, moving into and out of the hospital. He spent several of his final years (particularly 1996–1999 and 2002–2003) in a room at Peking Union Medical College, where he would often speak of his prison experience, a period thirty years earlier that paralleled the frustrating lack of freedom and mobility he was feeling.

But even during the most trying stages of his illness, Ying Ruocheng remained cheerful, engaged, and productive—graciously receiving visitors from near and far, voraciously reading, and even translating Shakespeare's *Coriolanus* during his last months for a new production to be directed by his good friend Lin Zhaohua.[2] For hours upon end during the summers of 2001, 2002, and 2003, I sat with him while he narrated and reflected on his life experiences so that his story could be told and his voice—and legacy—could carry on. We both hoped to finish the project before he died, but that was not to be.

During the years we collaborated on his autobiography, Ying Ruocheng never ceased to amaze me with his vivid memory and powerful ability to recall in detail events and people that, for most of us, would have long since retreated far into the recesses of our minds, never to be retrieved. Ying was well known for this gift, and we are its beneficiaries.

Still, there were days toward the end when illness gripped him—or a strong dose of medication overwhelmed him—and he confused dream with reality, addressing an intravenous pole as a visitor, conversing with his deceased wife as if she were seated right beside him, or, in one case, delivering speeches to the People's Congress as a nurse listened in amazement. On this particular occasion, Ying Da says that his father told the nurse to clap after his speech, which she did—but he insisted the applause sound like thunder, so the nurse gathered her colleagues from other patients' rooms and all the nurses assembled around Ying's bed and clapped together. Ying would sometimes mistake his doctors for foreign spies, and then exclaim to his son when he entered the room, "Oh, you are here to save me. Help me—they are all spies. I cannot run away to escape because they took my pants!" Even in these confused moments, Ying Ruocheng's sense of humor was intact and irresistible.

On May 31, 2002, Ying Ruocheng told me about a dream he had had during a critical point in his illness six years earlier, in which his subconscious grappled with his impending death. The Forbidden City represents passage into the afterlife, and literally perched atop the gate's limen is a threshold space symbolically representing the journey from one world to the next and physically resembling both his prison cell from 1968 and his hospital room. A nurse from PUMC functions as a guide, while a man spouting political history over a loudspeaker symbolizes years of government campaigns throughout Ying's life. His battle to survive is mirrored in the process of the Manchus setting off to fight the Russian army. Far from being about Manchus and Russians and Americans and Chinese, the dream is about Ying Ruocheng and his own confrontation with death at the height of his illness: it is about having the choice at that moment to either pass over into the other world or remain living in this one.

This book would not exist had Ying Ruocheng died that day. Thankfully, he stayed behind a little longer.

Here is how he recounted the dream:

It was during the early part of my stay in the hospital, when the doctors had more or less given me up as a hopeless case, that I had a very strange dream.

In the dream, I was told that for reasons that the state said must remain top secret, I was going to be moved outside the Peking Union Medical College for a few days. I was moved to an area of the Forbidden City called the Meridian Gate, where they used to chop people's heads off. They told me all prominent Manchus were being brought to the Forbidden City for a series of meetings, and that I would be sleeping there at least through the weekend.

As we were all led up to the main gate in the south, I noticed that the streets had been swept clean and looked distinctly different from how I remembered them. There was a crowd of us, but I only recognized a few other people, and I think I was the only one from the hospital. When we went in, I discovered that the space on top of the gate was quite large and had been fixed up as a kind of communal dormitory. I was led to one of the rooms, which was tastefully decorated in the classical style, and shown a bed with a sort of mosquito curtain. I noticed the bed next to mine was empty. Just then, a nurse came over and I recognized her—she was from the hospital, and was dressed in her PUMC uniform.

"Ah! There you are!" she said. "I'm afraid our neighbor is too old and was unable to come, so you'll have to enjoy this little space yourself."

"But what is all this about?" I asked.

"You'll know all about it soon," she replied.

I was put in the bed and the nurse continued talking to me, until there was a sudden hush and a man appeared with a loudspeaker. He looked like some kind of leader.

Using the loudspeaker, he announced, "Some of you may be a little too young to understand the context for this meeting, so I'll explain the background. In 1948, an agreement was reached between Lin Biao, the commander of the Fourth Field Army, and the leaders of the Manchu minority. Today you are all gathered here as part of the agreement that a meeting should be held every five years."

He continued, "We want everyone present to know that we take historical agreements seriously. And we want all of you to know about the situation in the northeast. Chairman Mao said on more than one occasion that we needn't be mincing words about the Russians—they're still after our territory and they've amassed a huge army on the border of Manchuria and Siberia. As we agreed at the time when the papers were signed between the Manchus and Marshall Lin Biao, we expect every Chinese national to stand up and defend the Motherland against our neighbors to the north."

Then he proceeded to list the Chinese army and detail what the numbers were, including divisions and regiments, and they were all battle-ready. "And we're no longer the victim of Russian chauvinism which bullied us in the 1950s, when we were forced to fight the Americans in Korea. So now we'll take it seriously against the Russians and defend our land. We are certain of victory because this land is still full of able-bodied Manchus, minorities who have always been the best soldiers in China—and they've had adequate training, so tonight we'll show you their military maneuvers."

After he made his speech there was a lot of applause, and then we could hear tanks rolling toward us—the tanks were huge, so the inspection of the armed forces took quite some time. I was just standing there, looking at it, and very complicated thoughts started going through my mind.

"Is this wise?" I wondered. Apparently I was still inside this game of strategy and tactics and military—every Chinese was during that period. But by the time the infantry marched past us, even I couldn't help feeling my blood surge. There was a lot of shouting and cheering. And then the order was given that we should all get a good night's rest—the meetings would begin the next morning. The leader said that

since we Manchus have always been very familiar with the land, we should contribute our wisdom to the battle strategy. There were also some lectures on past history, how the Russians had bullied us with their forceful occupation of Dalian and Port Arthur and the Siberian railway—and we were shown huge tunnels with military trucks pulling cannons and tanks.

After that, we were taken back to the top of the gate of the Forbidden City. Everyone was very excited. We were told that each of us should get a good night's sleep, so that we would be in good shape the next morning to proceed with the conference. We obeyed these orders, of course. I remember the beds—they were the same adjustable beds we had at PUMC.

In the dream, I woke up a short while later and it was daylight again. We were led down to a new place. There seemed to be some logic in its arrangement, but not everything made sense. We were taken to a field, somewhere between Beijing and Tianjin, where the army was at the training grounds. For some reason we had been taken away from the Forbidden City area to this place, where we were divided into groups and embarked on intense discussions. Some people were talking about the topography of the land in Manchuria and how best to defend it.

I forget now how the dream ended, but it seemed to end logically, in the sense that I was simply awakened in my bed in one of the PUMC patient rooms. And when I woke up there were nurses surrounding me as I lay there, and someone exclaimed, "He's woken up!"

They asked me whether I could go on with my account. But I felt very tired.

Then in came the head nurse, whom I recognized from my dream, and she instructed the other nurses, "No, no, no. Let him rest. He needs rest."

All but one of the nurses reluctantly departed from the room.

I couldn't make up my mind whether this whole trip to the Forbidden City was real or just a fantasy, so I turned to the nurse who remained.

"Did you hear anything I said?" I asked her.

"Sure I did," she replied. "We all did. You were talking for three hours."

Timeline

1866	Birth of Hesheli Yinghua (Ying Lianzhi, 1866–1926).
1874	Birth of Aixin Jueluo Shuzhong (1874–1925).
1898	Ying Lianzhi flees Beijing for Hong Kong, then Vietnam.
1900	Ying Lianzhi moves from Yunnan to Tianjin via Shanghai.
1900	Birth of Ying Qianli (1900–1969).
1901	Birth of Cai Baozhen (1901–1989).
1902	Founding of *Dagongbao* in Tianjin by Ying Lianzhi.
1911	End of Qing dynasty (Manchu), and founding of Republic (Yuan Shikai becomes president).
1912	Ying Lianzhi retires from editorship of *Dagongbao*, leaves Tianjin, and returns to Beijing.
1912	Ying Lianzhi and Ma Xiangbo write letter to Pope Pius X.
1912	Ying Qianli sent to Europe (returns 1920).
1913	Furen Learned Society (*Furenshe*) established by Ying Lianzhi in Beijing (1913–1918).
1916	Ying Lianzhi sells *Dagongbao*.
1920	Ying Qianli returns from Europe (Belgium, France, Ireland, England).
1920	Marriage of Ying Qianli and Cai Baozhen. Ying Qianli returns to England and remains there until 1926, with occasional visits to Beijing.
1921	Birth of Ying Ruoya (Mengzhao) (1921–1943).
1923	Death of Cai Rukai (c. 1867–1923) (father of Cai Baozhen).
1925	Founding of Furen University in Beijing.
1925	Birth of Ying Ruoqin (1925–2001).

1925   Death of Aixin Jueluo Shuzhong.

1926   Death of Ying Lianzhi. Ying Qianli returns from England.

1926   Ying Lianzhi knighted posthumously by Pope Pius XI (Sir Vincentius Ying).

1927   Birth of Ying Ruojing (1927–1941).

1928   Birth of Wu Shiliang (August 21, 1928–January 11, 1987).

1929   Birth of Ying Ruocheng (June 21, 1929–December 27, 2003).

1931   Birth of Ying Ruocong (1931–   ).

1933   Birth of Ying Ruocai (1933–   ).

1935   Births of twins Ying Ruoshi and Ying Ruozhi (1935–   ).

1937   Japanese occupation of China begins (until 1945).

1941   First imprisonment of Ying Qianli by Japanese.

1943   Second imprisonment of Ying Qianli by Japanese (until 1945).

1944   Birth of Ying Ruoxian (1944–   ).

1945   Ying Qianli knighted by Pope Pius XII (Sir Ignatius Ying).

1948   Ying Qianli taken to Taiwan (via Chongqing, arrival in Taiwan either 1948 or 1949).

1949   Founding of People's Republic of China.

1950   Ying Ruocheng and Wu Shiliang graduate from Qinghua University; marry on July 17; join founding group of Beijing People's Art Theatre (officially established 1952).

1951   Birth of Ying Xiaole on June 7.

1951   Ying Ruocheng plays Liu Zhanggui in Lao She's *Dragon Beard Ditch* (*Longxu gou*).

1956   Ying Ruocheng plays Fr. Pavlin in Gorky's *Bulichov and Others*.

1957   Ying Ruocheng plays Liu Siye in Lao She's *Camel Xiangzi* (*Luotuo Xiangzi*).

1958   Ying Ruocheng plays Daoist Ding He in *Taking Tiger Mountain by Strategy* (*Zhiqu Weihushan*).

1958   Ying Ruocheng plays Liu Mazi (Pockmark Liu) and Liu Mazi Jr. in Lao She's *Teahouse* (*Chaguan*).

1960   Birth of Ying Da on July 7.

1960   Furen University reestablished in Taiwan as Fu Jen University.

1965   Ying Ruocheng plays Interpreter Tong in film *Doctor Bethune* (*Bai Qiu'en*).

1966   Cultural Revolution begins (ends 1976).

1969   Death of Ying Qianli in Taiwan.

1975   Ying Ruocheng leaves the Beijing People's Art Theatre and joins the Foreign Languages Press, working for *China Reconstructs* magazine.

1979   Ying Ruocheng returns to the Beijing People's Art Theatre.

1979   Ying Ruocheng and Wu Shiliang join the Chinese Communist Party.

1979   Ying Ruocheng plays Liu Mazi (Pockmark Liu) and Liu Mazi Jr. in revival of Lao She's *Teahouse*.

1980   Ying Ruocheng plays Yuan Shikai in film *Soulmates* (*Zhiyin*).

1982   Ying Ruocheng plays Kublai Khan in television miniseries *Marco Polo*.

1982   Ying Ruocheng directs Cao Yu's *Family* (*Jia*), adapted from Ba Jin's novel, at University of Missouri in Kansas City.

1982   Ying Ruocheng codirects *Measure for Measure* with Toby Robertson (UK) at Beijing People's Art Theatre.

1983   Ying Ruocheng plays Willy Loman and collaborates with Arthur Miller when Miller directs *Death of a Salesman* at Beijing People's Art Theatre.

1984   Ying Ruocheng directs *Fifteen Strings of Cash* (*Shiwu guan*) at Missouri Repertory Theatre.

1985   Ying Ruocheng directs *Amadeus* at Beijing People's Art Theatre.

1986   Ying Ruocheng appointed vice minister of culture (until 1990).

1987   Ying Ruocheng plays governor of prison in film *The Last Emperor*.

1987   Death of Wu Shiliang on January 11.

1989   Death of Cai Baozhen on August 10.

1991   Ying Ruocheng directs *Major Barbara* at Beijing People's Art Theatre.

1993   Ying Ruocheng directs *Uncle Doggie's Nirvana* (*Gou'er ye niepan*) at Virginia Commonwealth University.

1993   Ying Ruocheng directs *Death of a Salesman* at William and Mary.

1993   Ying Ruocheng plays Lama Norbu in film *Little Buddha*.

1993   Ying Ruocheng visits his father's, Ying Qianli, grave in Taiwan.

1994   Ying Ruocheng diagnosed with cirrhosis of the liver.

2003   Death of Ying Ruocheng on December 27.

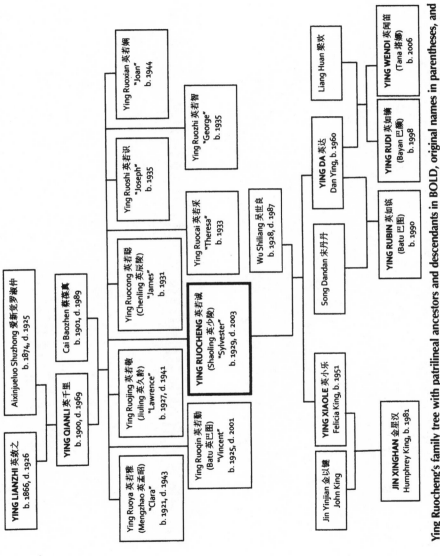

Ying Ruocheng's family tree with patrilineal ancestors and descendants in BOLD, original names in parentheses, and Catholic names in quotes. The original names of his first five siblings were changed after the birth of the twins, Ruoshi and Ruozi (see chapter 3, note 10). Ying Da's first wife was Ge Xin, but they did not have any children.

Notes

Introduction

1. "Ying Ruocheng," http://groups.google.to/group/alt.obituaries.

2. These descriptions of Ying Ruocheng are translated from the remarks of his colleagues at a posthumous memorial (*zhuisi hui*) conducted at the Beijing People's Art Theatre on January 9, 2004, two weeks after his death. Among those quoted and paraphrased are Pu Cunxin, Su Min, Zhu Xu, Mi Tiezeng, Hu Zongwen, Lin Zhao-hua, Qin Zanyao, Yang Lixin, Xu Fan, and Xie Yanning. See "Huainian pian" (Cherished Memory Essays), 29–37.

3. Personal diary of Felicia Londré, unpublished document. September 2, 1991.

4. Carolyn Wakeman, "*Measure for Measure* on the Chinese Stage," *Shakespeare Quarterly* (Winter 1982): 499.

5. All quotations are from Miller, *"Salesman" in Beijing*, 181, 247–48, 49, 20, 15, 65, 239–40.

6. Charlton Heston, *Beijing Diary*, 19. *The Caine Mutiny Court-martial* opened in Beijing on October 18, 1988, toured in Shanghai on December 1 and 2, and was revived in Beijing in both January and February 1989, with two more performances on May 2 and 3. (The next day was the anniversary of the May Fourth Movement, which fell during the height of the 1989 prodemocracy demonstrations in nearby Tiananmen Square, leading to a military response on June 4 and subsequent crackdown on literature, arts, and media—the theatre did not stage any plays after the May 3 performance of *Caine Mutiny* until a revival of *Top Restaurant* at the end of July.)

7. Following Hu's death in April 1989, and leading up to Russian president Gorbachev's state visit to Beijing, students (later joined by ordinary citizens) demonstrated publicly in Tiananmen Square, calling for political and social reforms and "democracy." At the movement's height, the square held more than one million people. In the wee hours of June 4, 1989, soldiers and tanks were deployed to clear the square (estimates of loss of life generally range from 300 to 3,000, but an official toll has never been determined). For more information about June Fourth, as well as the reform era during which Ying served as vice minister of culture, see Schell and Shambaugh, eds., *The China Reader* (especially 50–245).

8. The May Fourth Movement is named for the date in 1919 when a general strike was held in an outraged response to the Treaty of Versailles, which ceded German interests in Shandong to Japan, furthering China's national humiliation at the hands of foreign powers. May Fourth subsequently became the term for the entire era, during which intellectuals lived abroad (in Japan, Europe, and the United States) and, upon their return, endeavored to implement Western ideas (such as science and democracy, as exemplified by the New Culture Movement) to reform Chinese society and "catch up" to the West.

9. This was not an uncommon practice in China; the function of a "spy" (*tewu* or *jiandie*) in China is broader than in the United States and thus not equivalent to the kind of espionage an American secret agent would conduct. Simply put, numerous Chinese citizens informed on foreigners (and fellow Chinese) throughout various political movements during the twentieth century. However, Ying and Wu's service as informants was somewhat more substantial than their peers: Wu was actually assigned to the work unit of the Public Security Bureau (see notes 12–16), and both had exceptional access to prominent foreigners (through their command of English and their social status). These facts, plus the longevity of their efforts, prompts those who knew about their work to categorize it as "spying." American readers should note that the Public Security Bureau in China (at both national and municipal levels) is a quite visible branch of the government, in some aspects similar to police in the United States while also including intelligence work—there is no direct equivalent of this kind of organization in the United States.

10. Ying said this on May 16, 2002, in his room at Peking Union Medical College Hospital (2002 Audiotape 1).

11. Li Ke and Li You'an, *Liang ge Meiguo jiandie de zishu* (Beijing, 1958). The title of the 1978 Hong Kong edition is *The Truth about Life in a Chinese Prison* and the title of the 1957 original English version is *Prisoners of Liberation: Four Years in a Chinese Communist Prison*. In their book, Allyn and Adele Rickett refer to themselves as "informants" and "spies," admitting that they were conducting espionage for Naval Intelligence, the American Consulate, and the British Negotiation Mission (see note

2 in chapter 5 for more information). The work they describe—gathering information from Chinese contacts and reporting it to authorities—is parallel to the efforts Ying and Wu made as informants. In a new preface to the 1973 edition, the Ricketts stand by their original account, denying charges that they had been brainwashed in prison into believing they were spies. The agents who approached Ying and Wu were from the *Beijingshi gong'anju* (Beijing Public Security Bureau) that some thirty years later became the *Guojia anquanju* (State Security Bureau), which Ying Da calls the "Chinese equivalent of the CIA." He surmises that the Ricketts never knew his parents collaborated with Chinese authorities to facilitate their arrest, and he witnessed a reunion of the two couples in 1979.

12. The document prepared by the Beijing State Security Bureau upon the occasion of Wu's death in 1987 says she joined the party on March 17, 1984, but her son and other relatives maintain that both Wu and Ying joined in 1979.

13. Wu Shiliang's name is 吴世良, Ying Ruocheng's name is 英若诚. The code name they used to sign their reports was 武英. Ying Ruocheng likely retrieved the original reports from government files while he was serving in the ministry of culture 1986–1990.

14. Information about Ying Ruocheng and Wu Shiliang's work for "Section Two" comes from reports written by Wu and Ying between 1964 and 1978, and an internal document dated January 15, 1987, prepared by the Beijing State Security Bureau that was read aloud at Wu's funeral (attended only by immediate family members and fellow employees of the organization who already knew of her secret intelligence work), as well as conversations with Ying Da in 2007.

15. According to Ying Da, his mother was formally transferred from the Beijing People's Art Theatre to the *Beijingshi gong'anju* (Beijing Public Security Bureau) in 1958 but began intelligence work in 1950; the document read at Wu Shiliang's funeral specifies that her affiliation with the organization began in 1951. The following is my translation of part of that document: "Comrade Wu Shiliang's participation in secret service intelligence (*mimi zhencha*) since 1951 displayed high revolutionary responsibility and diligence toward the cause of defending the party. Under long-term practice of struggle, she remained true to her duty to defend from start to finish without any thought of fame or benefit, diligent and conscientious, obeying leaders, diligently making a careful study of and improving her own artistic combat (*douzheng yishu*). Standing throughout on the front line in an intense, complex covert battlefront, giving all her energy for her entire life to the cause of defending the party, she was an outstanding soldier of our covert battlefront. For the past thirty years, under organization leadership, comrade Wu Shiliang made an important contribution through her counterespionage efforts and intelligence work. She was never satisfied, and never claimed credit for herself, ever forging ahead positively. She is our capital's unsung heroine on the covert battlefront. During the decade of chaos [1966–1976], due to the Gang of Four's plan to totally smash the police, prosecution, and legal

systems, Wu Shiliang was framed and persecuted by the Gang of Four's evil hench-
man Liu Chuanxin, and in April 1968 was arrested and put in prison, incarcerated
for three years and not released until June 1971. While in prison, comrade Wu Shiliang withstood rigorous interrogation; after being released, in spite of the devastation
to her health, and also the implication of her family members, she persevered, for the
sake of the party cause, despite the danger to herself, in the positive cause of defending the party. . . . Eternal glory to comrade Wu Shiliang!"

16. Ying Ruocong's wife, Zhao Ziqiang, told me in 2007 that she had urged Ying
Ruocheng to write an autobiography, but he said it was not easily written (*buhaoxie*) because there were so many sensitive (*minggan*) matters he could not write about, referring
specifically to the government and activities with foreigners. Ying Ruocong explained to
me that their older brother Ruoqin went through official intelligence training but did
not become a spy, though he later joined the CCP. Ruocong maintains that Ruocheng
did not undergo any official training, but was utilized due to his English fluency and access to foreigners.

17. Jill Kerr Conway, "Points of Departure," and Annie Dillard, "To Fashion a
Text," in Zinsser, *Inventing the Truth*, 50, 154–55.

18. Kathleen Mullen Sands speaks of similar characteristics of her collaboration
with Native American elder Ted Rios in *Telling a Good One: The Process of a Native
American Collaborative Biography*, xi, 68, 147, 155–57. She also speaks of their process
as collaborative autobiography, though this is not the term used in the book's title.
The major difference between Rios/Sands and Ying/Conceison is that Sands describes their relationship as "cordially formal," whereas my relationship with Ying was
informal and close, since I had been periodically integrated into aspects of his world
(the professional theatre community in Beijing) for a decade when we began our collaboration on his autobiography, and we had met and spoken at length on previous
occasions and knew many people in common.

19. These are some of the salient characteristics of autobiography, as distinguished from biography, identified by James Goodwin, Sidonie Smith, Philippe Le-
Jeune, William Zinsser, and others (see bibliography). In addition to the material he
narrated directly to me on audiotape and videotape, Ying also gave me permission to
incorporate into his autobiography any previously published or documented material
he had authored in English, or interviews he had given in English; such sources are
noted when used.

20. See James Goodwin, *Autobiography: The Self Made Text*, 6; and Zinsser, *Inventing the Truth*, 15.

21. See Hoopes, *Oral History*, 3, 12.

Chapter One

1. This poem is one of those Ying transcribed in his prison notebook. It is a *ci* to
the tune of "Bu Suan Zi," written by Mao in December 1961 as a response to his reading of Lu You's "Ode to the Plum Blossom." For Chinese and English versions of the

poem, see Guo Baoqin and Hu Kaimin, eds., *Mao Zedong Poems* (Mao Zedong shici), bilingual edition (Beijing: Foreign Languages Press, 2003): 84–85.

2. "Big character posters" (*dazibao*) were large hand-written wall-mounted posters used to express protest and propaganda. The most famous example from the Cultural Revolution, posted by Nie Yuanzi on May 25, 1966, at Peking University, was subsequently published in the *People's Daily* at Mao's urging. Big character posters then spread, and their effects on those denounced in them were severe. For more on *dazibao*, see Lee, *The Politics of the Chinese Cultural Revolution*, 27, 34; see also Hua, "Big Character Posters in China."

3. In contrast to the rebels and the loyalists, Ying's group was regarded as neutral.

4. The Four Cleanups or Four Cleans (*Siqing*) campaign was a measure included in the "First Ten Points" of May 1963, which was the nationwide launch of the Socialist Education Movement that Mao started in late 1962. The campaign was intended to mobilize the masses (especially ordinary peasants) to expose corruption among party cadres and their collusion with rich peasants. The four practices to be scrutinized were how cadres tallied work points, kept records, distributed supplies, and supervised granaries and warehouses. The resolution stressed "self-education" and the need for cadres and officials to labor alongside peasants in the fields. Targets of the Four Cleanups were removed from their posts, assigned to manual labor or otherwise detained, and forced to undergo political "remolding."

5. At this point and several others, Ying Ruocheng named Number One Model Prison (*diyi mofang jianyu*) as the first location of his incarceration (and the entire incarceration of his wife, Wu Shiliang). However, Ying Da is certain that they were held not in Number One Model Prison (called *Zixin lu* in Chinese, meaning "road to self-renewal"), but rather at *Banbuqiao juliusuo* (Half-Step Bridge Detention Center), which was located next to Beijing Number One Model Prison. According to Ying Da, Banbuqiao held political prisoners, whereas the Model Prison held criminals convicted of violent crimes. He specifies his mother was held in K-Building (K-*zi lou*) at Banbuqiao throughout her imprisonment, but he does not know the specific building his father was detained in before being transferred after one year to the prison at Jixian.

Chapter Two

1. *On the Docks* (*Haigang*) was a "model" revolutionary opera (*yangban xi*). A revised version of it was published in 1972. The Cultural Revolution (or Great Proletarian Cultural Revolution) in China lasted from 1966 to 1976, during which time the only sanctioned stage performances were of eight revolutionary model operas (in modified *jingju* form) and ballets, per order of Mao's wife, Jiang Qing.

2. The poem is "Reply to Li Shuyi" (*Da Li Shuyi*):

> I lost my proud Poplar and you your Willow
> Poplar and Willow soar to the Ninth Heaven
> Wu Kang, asked what he can give,

> Serves them a laurel brew.
> The lonely moon goddess spreads her ample sleeves
> To dance for these loyal souls in infinite space.
> Earth suddenly reports the tiger subdued,
> Tears of joy pour forth falling as mighty rain.

English translation cited here is taken from Guo and Hu, eds., *Mao Zedong Poems*, 65; the original poem in Chinese accompanies it.

3. It was Mao's second wife, Yang Kaihui, who was executed by the KMT in 1930 and who inspired the poem. Mao was already espoused in an arranged marriage when he met her, but Ying's identification of Yang as Mao's first wife is consistent with Mao's own representation of his marriages. Mao was married to Luo Yixiu 1907–1910, Yang Kaihui 1921–1927, He Zizhen 1928–1939, and Jiang Qing from 1939 until his death in 1976.

4. For an account of another rural Hebei prison that confirms many of Ying's observations, particularly in comparison with Beijing prisons, see Edward Friedman, Paul Pickowicz, and Mark Selden, eds., *Revolution, Resistance and Reform in Village China* (New Haven, CT: Yale University Press, 2005). For a brief account of Cultural Revolution imprisonment from a philosophical standpoint similar to that of Ying Ruocheng, see Zhang Zhiyang's "Walls" in Schoenhals, ed., *China's Cultural Revolution, 1966–1969*, 338–354.

5. Cigarettes were not available in Jixian prison, but butts were sometimes left on the ground (presumably by guards) and prisoners collected them, emptied the remaining tobacco, and rolled new cigarettes using paper provided to write letters home twice a year. Ying recovered tobacco that had been confiscated from arrested prisoners from a drawer during one of his volunteer projects and distributed this tobacco stash evenly among the cells, trying to prioritize prisoners who were already heavy smokers, though all claimed this status once the luxury became available. Ying had been taught by a prisoner at the previous Beijing prison three methods to light cigarettes without matches, but was never able to try the techniques until Jixian. The device he used there consisted of a small tin lid about the size of a quarter (such as one on a mentholatum container), two dime-sized porcelain buttons with four holes (somewhat common on clothing at the time), and a piece of thread. Holding the thread between his teeth on one end and between his fingers on the other, he spun the threaded buttons very fast, bringing the tin lid into contact with the spinning porcelain to create sparks. He taught this method to older prisoners because it was the least taxing (2002 Audiotape 12: June 1, 2002, PUMC).

6. Peng Zhen (1902–1997) joined the CCP in 1923 and was one of its founding members in Shanxi Province; he was imprisoned by the KMT from 1929 to 1935. Peng held various posts in the CCP Central Committee, and became mayor of Beijing in 1951. He fell out of favor with Mao in 1966 and was sent to the countryside, making him the first high-ranking official targeted in the Cultural Revolution; he returned more than a decade later after Mao's death and was rehabilitated by Deng Xiaoping, returning to prominence in the CCP as chairman of the Standing Commit-

tee of the Sixth National People's Congress (1983). A conservative hard-liner (particularly during the reform era of the late 1980s and during the prodemocracy events of spring 1989), he died in 1997.

7. Yao Wenyuan, propagandist for the Gang of Four, penned the November 1965 essay igniting the campaign against Wu Han's historical drama *Hai Rui Dismissed from Office* (*Hai Rui baguan*) that triggered the Cultural Revolution of 1966–1976. Yao called the play an "anti-party poisonous weed" for its allegorical critique of Mao's dismissal of Peng Dehuai. The Gang of Four, reportedly given its name by Mao Zedong, directed the purge of moderate party officials and intellectuals throughout that period. The three other members were Wang Hongwen, Zhang Qunqiao, and Mao's wife, Jiang Qing. Receiving most of the official blame for the decade of political violence, the Gang of Four was condemned and imprisoned after Mao's death in 1976, bringing an end to the Cultural Revolution. Wang, Zhang, and Jiang all died in prison (the last from suicide in 1991). Yao, the last surviving member, served a twenty-year prison sentence from 1976 to 1996 and died in December 2005.

8. For a thorough yet concise discussion of the campaign against Wu Han and the subsequent campaign against Peng Zhen, see Lee, *The Politics of the Chinese Cultural Revolution*, 11–15.

9. On May 16, 1966, the CCP Politburo formally dismissed Luo Ruiqing from his post (Chief of the General Staff) in the PLA. The event is referred to as "5-1-6" (*wu yao liu*) in Chinese, and later an ultraleftist group was dubbed the May 16 Group, which was struggled against in 1971 along with Chen Boda and other Lin Biao supporters.

10. By some accounts, Peng was purged individually, while by others, he was purged along with the three others Ying mentions here as part of the Peng-Luo-Lu-Yang Clique. See Schoenhals, ed., *China's Cultural Revolution, 1966–1969*, 380.

11. In Chinese, addressing someone by their surname with the prefix Old is a form of polite familiarity; if the person addressed is younger than the speaker, the prefix Young or Little (Xiao) is used. Ying Ruocheng was often called Teacher Ying (Ying Laoshi) by colleagues, out of respect for his knowledge and status. The form of address by which he was most commonly known by acquaintances was an abbreviated version: Ying Lao.

12. Quemoy and Matsu, two Taiwan-controlled islands off the coast of China, were a source of tension in four heated presidential debates between John Kennedy and Richard Nixon in 1960, with the two disagreeing about where the line of defense against Communism in the Far East should be drawn.

13. The Anti-Rightist Movement, launched by Mao in June 1957, purged intellectuals, "capping" (*dai maozi*) them as "Rightists" and displacing an estimated 520,000 city dwellers to the countryside for rustication or "reform through labor," partially as a response to the criticism of the CCP that emerged during the Hundred Flowers Movement initiated two months earlier. The Great Leap Forward (1958–1961) was Mao's ill-fated attempt to jump-start China's industrialization

and modernization through collectivization and "backyard" steel production. The shift away from agriculture triggered grain shortages—the 1959 grain harvest quota fell short by two hundred million tons—but reports were falsified in efforts to cover up the disaster, resulting in widespread famine and a catastrophic thirty million rural deaths from starvation by the end of 1960. Both campaigns occurred during the period when Ying was "spying" for Peng Zhen. Ying was being contacted by Peng's associates from the early 1950s up until 1965 when Peng was disgraced. The Quemoy incident and Ying reading about the Great Leap Forward in *The Economist* happened in the late 1950s. Peng Dehuai's criticism of Mao's policies amid the Great Leap, and his subsequent purge, were in 1959; he was recalled to Beijing from Sichuan in 1966, arrested, and died in prison in 1974, then posthumously rehabilitated in 1978. For Ying's memory of the Great Leap Forward and Anti-Rightist Movement, see chapter 5.

14. According to Ying Da, his parents were approached by the Security Bureau (*gong'an ju*) during their senior year at Qinghua University, and their spy activities began at that point, lasting virtually up until their deaths. Similar to Ying Ruocheng's account here, Ying Da describes his father's involvement as focused on deliberate interactions with foreigners, after which he was required to report findings to authorities. However, the nature and extent of the activity as described to me by Ying Da (and others) is far more extensive than Ying Ruocheng chose to reveal here (see introduction). One would think that therefore Ying Ruocheng was fully aware that his imprisonment was related to his intelligence work for the government, though it is understandable that Ying would expect to be spared from prison because of his covert government activity and the desire of powerful officials to benefit from his language skills and contact with foreigners. Since Ying and his wife were the only members of the theatre company imprisoned, and both were incarcerated from 1968 to 1971, it is clear that their backgrounds, contacts with foreigners, and intelligence activities (as well as knowledge gained from such activities) were considered more of a liability than an asset to those in power at the time.

15. Peng Zhengyuan was the theatre's army representative (*jun daibiao*) Ying speaks of here. See note 35 in chapter 5.

16. Lin Zhaohua, about eight years Ying's junior, was part of the younger contingent at the theatre when Ying was arrested. He is currently Beijing People's Art Theatre's most esteemed director, best known in the West for his collaborations with playwright Gao Xingjian (2000 Nobel Laureate for Literature) during the early to mid-1980s. Lin supervised the revival of Jiao Juyin's production of *Teahouse* that toured the United States in 2005. During his lifetime, Ying strove to arrange a U.S. tour for *Teahouse*, but unfortunately he did not live long enough to see this goal fulfilled. (See chapter 5 for more on *Teahouse*.)

17. Ying Da recalls that his parents were arrested at the end of the month, when only a few yuan remained of the household spending money. "The next week, we starved," he said. "So we started selling everything in the house—even furniture from the Ming dynasty. But that income didn't last long, so the next year, while my sister

was in Inner Mongolia, I was on the street begging for food." (Taped interview at Wenquan, August 19, 2007.)

18. According to Ying Da, Ying Ruocheng and Wu Shiliang spent their first hours together after being reunited comparing notes on their interrogations (which revolved around espionage case reports they had written and submitted together before their imprisonment, to which he attributes their incarceration): "When my mother and father both got out of the jail and met, I still remember that. They didn't go to sleep for three nights. They were just talking and talking. Talking about what—about their love? No. They went through every case, every report they ever reported for the past twenty years. They were saying, 'What did you say about that case? Oh, you explained like that—okay, I did too . . . ' Something like that. They had been separated for more than three years and went through a trial [interrogation] almost every week [in prison]. Sometimes [when they were talking at home] they would just go through one case over and over again. They felt that they had won if they didn't tell [the guards] something and they both made it up the same way without talking to each other." (Taped interview at Wenquan, August 19, 2007.)

Chapter Three

1. The following is a brief history of the *Dagongbao* from its founding by Ying Ruocheng's grandfather to the beginning of the Japanese occupation, excerpted from Wang Ke-wen, "*Dagongbao* and the *Guomindang*,": "The original *Dagongbao* was founded by Ying Lianzhi, a reform-minded Catholic intellectual, in June 1902. In the wake of the 1911 Revolution Ying retired from its editorship and in 1916 sold the newspaper to a financier with connections to the Anfu Clique in the Beiyang Government. From 1916 till 1925, when the newspaper folded following the fall of the Anfu Clique from power, it served essentially as a mouthpiece of the Clique. In September 1926 the *Dagongbao* was revived under the triumvirate of Wu Dingchang, Hu Zhengzhi, and Zhang Jiluan. Hu had managed the old *Dagongbao* and its weekly, the *Guowen Zhoubao* (founded in 1924), and brought in many of its original staff. Wu, a banker, provided most of the funding, and Zhang, an experienced journalist, assumed the chief editorship. It was arguably the most influential private-owned newspaper in the Nanjing Decade. Known for its pledge of 'four nots'—not associating itself with any political party or faction, not receiving any funding from political groups, not serving the personal interest of any of its owners or workers, and not blindly following any prevailing opinion in its positions—the newspaper was widely regarded as a major forum for liberal views in KMT China. From 1927 to 1937 it competed successfully with KMT propaganda on the one hand, and urban mass movements on the other, for the expression of China's public opinion. Despite increasing party control of the press, it managed to survive and grow, all the while maintaining a cordial relationship with the rulers in Nanjing."

2. Ying Ruocheng recalled that the plane his father boarded went to Chongqing, but his brother Ying Ruocong says his father was flown to Nanjing before proceeding

to Taiwan. It was he who accompanied his father to the makeshift runway near Dong-dan. He recalls that everything was rushed and confirms Ying Ruocheng's claim that mobility had been restricted and that Ying Qianli's flight was the last (or one of the last) to get out of China. (Taped interview, November 20, 2006.)

3. Ying Qianli died in Taiwan in 1969 while Ying Ruocheng was in prison on the mainland during the Cultural Revolution. Ying Ruocheng did not learn of his father's death until much later.

4. Ying Ruocheng's brothers Ruocong and Ruoshi tell slightly different versions of the circumstances of their father's relocation to Taiwan. They concur that it was too dangerous for Ying Qianli to remain in Beijing and that he had no choice but to go to Taiwan, and also on the fact that neither he nor the family expected the separation to last long. Their accounts differ in that Ruoshi maintains that his father was able to contact the family when he first arrived in Taiwan, inviting his wife to move the children there, whereas Ruocong claims there was no such communication. (Taped interview with Ying Ruoshi, November 18, 2006.)

5. According to another account, Cai Baozhen prepared tasty food and drink and offered it to the Japanese keeping watch outside, while Ying Ruocheng retrieved the list from a book called *Huayixue zhi* (*Studies of Overseas Chinese Citizens*) and disposed of it in the stove. See Chang, "Yingshi jiazu de jiwei jiechu renwu," 351.

6. Ying Ruocheng's mother's name was Cai Baozhen (蔡葆真). Originally the third character was 贞 (zhen) meaning chastity or virginity, but, according to Ying, it was likely changed by her father to the character 真 (zhen) meaning truth because the former term was considered by the family to be somewhat vulgar or too common-place. Cai Baozhen (1901–1989) was the daughter of Cai Rukai 蔡儒楷 (1870–1923) and Chen Woling 陈握灵 (1884–1969), also known as Chen Zhi. Some in the family believe Chen was Cai's concubine (*qie*), not first wife.

7. See note 1 in this chapter for information about the *Dagongbao* from its origins through 1937. For more on the newspaper during the Japanese occupation (1937–1945), see Wang Ke-wen, "The *Dagongbao* and Wartime Chinese Politics, 1937–45." As Wang points out, very little scholarship exists in Western languages about the *Dagongbao* or the history of the wartime press in China. Available sources include L. Sophia Wang, "The Independent Press and Authoritarian Regimes: The Case of the Dagongbao in Republican China," *Pacific Affairs*, Vol. 67, no. 2 (1994): 216–241; and Chang-tai Hung, *War and Popular Culture: Resistance in Modern China, 1937–1945* (Berkeley: University of California Press, 1994). The *Dagongbao* still exists, but has been based in Hong Kong since 1938.

8. According to a sign posted outside the original site of Furen University on Dingfu Street in Beijing, "The Vatican appointed the Order of St. Benedict of America to establish a Catholic university in Beijing in 1925." The Taiwan-based Fu Jen University website specifies that Furen Catholic University was founded in 1925 in Beijing by the Benedictines of St. Vincent Archabbey in Latrobe, Pennsylvania, at the request of the Holy See, was originally opened as a single college under the name of Fu Jen Academy, and was officially recognized as a university by the Ministry of Education in 1929. In

1952, Fu Jen officially closed, becoming annexed to Beijing Normal University. In 1959, the Chinese Diocesan Clergy, the Society of Jesus, and the Society of the Divine Word collaborated on the reestablishment of the university, and in 1960, the Ministry of Education granted permission to restore Fu Jen in Taiwan (www.fju.edu.tw). The effort to create the university began with Ma Xiangbo and Ying Lianzhi's letter to Pope Pius X in 1912, continued with Ying Lianzhi's founding of Furen Xueshe (Furen Academy, which closed in 1918), and resulted in discussions between Ying and Father George Barry O'-Toole of the Latrobe Benedictine Abbey in 1922 that eventually culminated in the founding of the university in 1925—the year O'Toole was named the first president of Beijing Catholic University and that Ying Lianzhi reopened Furen Academy. Ying Lianzhi died in 1926 and that same year O'Toole returned to the United States, returning to China in 1927 when the Nationalist government sanctioned the establishment of Beijing Furen University (a result of the efforts of both Ying and O'Toole). The stock market crash of 1929 forced the Benedictines to transfer administration of the university to the German order Society of the Divine Word in 1933. Due to its German-allied administration, Furen was the only university that continued to operate freely in Beijing during the Japanese occupation. See Barry, "Fujen Catholic University Celebrates 80 Years of Its Foundation," 15–24. Another excellent (and more thorough) source on the history of Furen University from 1925 to 1952 is Chen's *The Rise and Fall of Fu Ren University, Beijing.*

9. The surname Ying using the character 应 is a relatively common name, however. (It was the surname of Ying Ruocheng's mother-in-law, Ying Lingyan.)

10. The Chinese characters used to represent the original Manchu surname of Ying Ruocheng's paternal grandfather are 赫舍里 (Hesheli) and for his given name are 英华 (Ying Hua); his *zi* (self-given name) was 英敛之 (Ying Lianzhi—this is the Romanized spelling using contemporary mainland pinyin romanization; in his own lifetime, it was spelled Ying Lien-chi). See note 24 in this chapter for more information about his chosen *hao*. Ying Lianzhi's son (Ying Ruocheng's father) was 英千里 (Ying Qianli). Ying Ruocheng's name was 英若诚 (*cheng* meaning honest or sincere). As a child, Ying Ruocheng's family nickname was 小毛 (Xiao Mao or Little Mao) or 毛三爷 (Mao Sanye or Third Master Mao because he was the third son in the birth order). Ying Ruocheng's original name, given by his father, was Shaoling (少陵); his Christian name, also given by his father, was Sylvester. When twin brothers were born to the family in 1935, the names of the existing children were Qixiang (Mengzhao), Batu, Jiuling, Shaoling, and Chenling; the youngest was a two-year-old sister who remained unnamed until after the birth of the twins (she was simply referred to as Xiaomei or Little Sister). When the twins were born, Ying Qianli asked Chen Yuan to rename all the children in the family, and the character *Ruo* 若 was incorporated into the names for all the siblings; it was then that the unnamed sister and twins were named (see family tree for names). The last child was born nine years later. Ying Qianli gave all his children Catholic names as well (see family tree). Ruoqin was the only sibling given a Manchu name (Batu). Ying Ruocheng's son, Ying Da (英达), who goes by Dan Ying in English, does not have a Manchu name, but he

has given his sons and daughter Manchu names: Batu (巴图 ; from his marriage to Song Dandan), and Bayan (巴颜) and Tana (塔娜 ; from his marriage to Liang Huan); their English names are Rubin, Rudi, and Wendi (correlating to the pinyin spellings of their Chinese names). Ying Ruocheng's daughter is Ying Xiaole (英小乐). Combining Ying Da's and Ying Xiaole's given names in the combination *daguan* (达观) and *leguan* (乐观) means to approach life philosophically and optimistically, a fitting reflection of Ying Ruocheng's personality.

11. None of the Ying family members were able to provide any genealogy going back further than Ying Ruocheng's paternal and maternal grandparents. It is only known that the surname of Ying Lianzhi's father was Yu (玉) and he died sometime in the 1920s, and that the surname of Ying Lianzhi's mother was Hu (胡) and she died after Yu (Ying Ruocheng's siblings remember their great-grandmother, whom they called Lao Zu, being a frequent presence during their youth, even after the death of her son and daughter-in-law). The land at Wenquan was passed down through Ying Lianzhi's mother—Wenquan was originally a village comprised of residents with the surname Hu.

12. The Manchu imperial name of the rulers of China's Qing dynasty (1644–1911) was 爱新觉罗, Romanized in standard pinyin as Aixin Jueluo, and elsewhere as Ai-hs'in Goro and Aisin Gioro, among other spellings. Ying Ruocheng's preferred spelling was Aixin Jiero, but I have employed standard pinyin here, making his grandmother's full name Aixin Jueluo Shuzhong.

13. The Catholic (saint's) name that Ying Lianzhi adopted was Vincent (Vincentius in Latin, the form Ying Ruocheng preferred). John Shujie Chen cites Donald Paragon's article in providing background on Ying Lianzhi's conversion, indicating "Vincent Ying was the first [in his family] to convert. Later his wife became a Catholic, then his mother, brothers, and sisters. His father was the last one to convert." See Chen, *The Rise and Fall of Fu Ren University, Beijing*, 218.

14. It is generally accepted that Ying Qianli's birth in 1900 was in Vietnam, though Ying Ruocheng once said that his father told him he was conceived in Yunnan (where the family went after Vietnam) and born in Shanghai, which would have placed Ying Lianzhi and his wife in Shanghai by November 1900. Surviving family members confirmed to me in 2007 and 2008 that Ying Qianli was born in Hanoi, Vietnam.

15. The Empress Dowager Cixi placed her nephew, Emperor Guangxu, under arrest on September 21, 1898, and annulled his edicts, upon which Kang Youwei and Liang Qichao fled abroad (other reformers also fled, and many who did not flee were imprisoned or executed). On August 15, 1900, the Empress Dowager and Emperor fled Beijing; on October 26 they arrived in Xi'an; and on January 7, 1902, they returned to Beijing.

16. According to Ying Da, the Han surname of the Hesheli clan was Yu (玉), thus making the Han version of Ying Lianzhi's original name Yu Yinghua. His name was among a list kept by Empress Dowager Cixi of names of wanted persons who were in danger of being executed (it is for this reason that he fled to Vietnam temporarily).

When Cixi granted amnesty, Yu Yinghua's name was inadvertently left on the list, and when this was brought to the Empress Dowager's attention, she allegedly approved the removal of "Ying Hua" but neglected to mention his surname, Yu, and thus effectively transformed his surname to Ying. Ying thereby became a *cixing* (賜姓) or "name bestowed by royalty" and required that all family members (including those still living from previous generations) change their surname to Ying (both because the family name was recorded that way by the Empress Dowager and because it was unsafe to continue using the surname of Yu, which remained on the danger list). Whichever account is accurate, it resulted in a Chinese character (英) that previously only appeared in names as a given name becoming a surname, and explains why it is so rare.

17. The former conventional spelling of Beijing is Peking, but I have chosen to use the currently accepted pinyin spelling of Beijing wherever Ying Ruocheng mentioned the city's name, except where he specifically referred to "old Peking." The university *Beijing daxue*, however, uses the name Peking University in English, so I have retained this spelling. Its abbreviated name is *Beida*.

18. This educational institution founded by Ying Lianzhi in 1912 is usually referred to as Furen She (辅仁社) and in English as Furen Academy. See (in Chinese) Chang, "Yingshi jiazu de jiwei jiechu renwu" and (in English) Barry, "Fujen Catholic University," 15–24. Chen (42–46) adds that when Furen She was revived after it closed in 1918, it was also called MacManus Academy of Chinese Studies.

19. The full text of this letter is published as an appendix in Chen's book, *The Rise and Fall of Fu Ren University*, 195–197. The letter is signed only by Ying Lianzhi (Ying Lien Chih) and dated July 1912.

20. It was Pope Pius XI who answered the letter, twelve years later. Barry, "Fujen Catholic University" (15–24), maintains that Rome's delay was "due to disruptions caused by the First World War" and "not waiting for a papal response, Ying Lianzhi started a small school in Beijing's Xiangshan area, called 'Fujen She.'" Chen, *The Rise and Fall of Fu Ren University* (42–51), offers a far more detailed explanation for the delay, citing the war in Europe as a main reason, but also the passing of both Pope Pius X in 1914 and of Pope Benedict XV in 1922, and other factors. See note 8 for more information on the founding of Furen University.

21. Ying Lianzhi was knighted (*fengjue*) posthumously shortly after his death by Pope Pius XI, and Ying Qianli was likewise honored by Pope Pius XII in 1945 (while he was still living). The papal citation of March 2, 1926, bestowing on Ying Lianzhi (Ying Lien-chih) the Knighthood of St. Gregory the Great praises him as "a man illustrious for the upbuilding of the Catholic University of studies at Beijing; and moreover, that learnedly perform[s] in that University . . . the office of a Professor, [and] strives also to assist in every way the work of the Fathers [of the Abbot of the Monastery of St. Vincent, of the American Cassinese Congregation of the Order of St. Benedict]." An excerpt of the citation is quoted in Paragon, "Ying Lien-chih (1866–1926)," 214–215. Another important contribution of Ying Lianzhi was his influential 1917 "Exhortation to Study," which called for propagation of the Catholic

faith in China through intellectual instruction (it is an appendix in Chen, *The Rise and Fall of Fu Ren University*, 199–208).

22. John Paul II was still pope when Ying Ruocheng said this, and when he died in 2003. Pope John Paul II died in April 2005 and was followed by Pope Benedict XVI.

23. At a family gathering on August 19, 2007, Ying Ruocheng's brothers Ying Ruocong and Ying Ruozhi held an extensive discussion upon my inquiry regarding the dates of Ma Xiangbo's birth and death. Published sources in both Chinese and English record Ma's dates as either 1839–1939 or 1840–1940, and I was seeking the more accurate of the two. However, after a lengthy conversation among the two brothers and their spouses and children, the definitive dates of Ma's life (as determined by the living members of the Ying family) were reported as 1841–1937. The brothers remembered clearly that Ma Xiangbo personally told their mother, Cai Baozhen, that he was exactly sixty years her senior, and she was born in 1901. They also recall the specific instance of his death. Upon hearing of the victory at the battle of Tai'erzhuang (one of the Chinese army's few victories over the Japanese), Ma Xiangbo laughed, and died. The Yings confirm that the Tai'erzhuang battle was in 1937 and that by the time Japanese troops attacked Shanghai a few months later, Ma Xiangbo had already died there. If the Yings are correct and Ma Xiangbo lived from 1841 to 1937, his century-long life span is indeed legend rather than fact.

24. Ma Xiangbo's original name was Ma Zhide (马志德), but his various other names included Siqiang (斯戕), Qinshan (钦善), and Jianchang (钦善) before he changed it to Ma Liang (马良) with the chosen *zi* of Ma Xiangbo (马相伯, meaning "Ma who resembles his uncle"), the last of which also has various versions in Chinese characters (including 马湘伯 and 马湘伯). See Fang Hao, *Zhongguo tianzhushi renwuzhuan* (Zhonghua shuju, 1988), 292. This source also gives alternative nicknames such as Qiuzai Wozhe (求在我者) and Huafeng Laoren (华封老人). For Ying Hua (Ying Lianzhi), the source offers alternative nicknames of Anjian Zhaizhu (安蹇斋主人, meaning "one who dwells in a study room") and Wansong Yeren (万松野, meaning "free man of the ten thousand pines"), 305. The latter is a reference to his years of residence in Fragrant Hills (Xiangshan), and in particular his publication of "Wansong Yeren yanshan lu" (万松野人言善录). See Chang, "Ying Lianzhi," 165–166. On the sign posted outside the former site of Furen University on Dingfujie in Beijing, Ma Xiangbo's name is written using the Chinese characters 马相柏.

25. According to Ying Ruocheng, playwright Cao Yu based the central female character of Chen Bailu in his play *Sunrise* (*Richu*) on Ying Yin. Ruan Lingyu (1910–1935), a Chinese silent film starlet of the 1930s, became an icon of Chinese cinema due to her tragic suicide, which was instigated by immense tabloid coverage of Ruan's private life, particularly her lawsuit against her first husband.

26. Ying Ruocheng was well known for his stage and film portrayal of the character Pockmark Liu (Liu Mazi) in Lao She's 1958 play *Teahouse*. See chapter 5 for more information.

27. Lao She's 1937 novel *Luotuo xiangzi* (known in English as *Camel Xiangzi* or *Rickshaw Boy*) was adapted for the stage and produced by the Beijing People's Art Theatre in 1957.

28. In February 1913, at the age of forty-seven, Ying Lianzhi climbed Xianlong Mountain (显龙山) near the family's summer home in Wenquan while there with his wife and son. Upon viewing the scene from the hilltop (the flowing spring waters and white cloudy mist), he was moved to recite a poem by Du Fu:

坦腹 江亭暖, 长吟野望时。

水流心不竞, 云在意俱迟

Tan fu jiang ting nuan, chang yin ye wang shi.

Shui liu xin bu jing, yun zai yi ju chi.

[Baring my belly in the river pavilion's warmth, I hum a long tune while gazing at the wilderness. The water flows by, calming my mind. Like the clouds above, I long to linger.]

The next day, Ying Lianzhi carved the four-character phrase, "The water flows by, but the cloudy mist remains," 水流云在 (*shui liu yun zai*), excerpted from the poem, into the north surface of a huge rock on the west side of the hilltop. Beneath it he wrote: 英敛之偕内子小儿千 里游此偶取杜句寄意时宣统退位之次年正月也 ("In the second year after the abdication of Xuantong [1913], I, Ying Lianzhi, accompanied by my wife and son, having traveled a great distance to arrive here, by happenstance chose a line from Du Fu to convey my sentiments.") See Chang, "Yingshi jiazu de jiwei jiechu renwu," 345.

29. The new family compound at Wenquan was built during the three years that Ying Ruocheng lived in the hospital (2001–2003). In 2002, he brought me to see the progress of the construction, and also the enormous rock with his grandfather's calligraphy. In 2003 just before Chinese New Year, construction was completed, and on occasion Ying Ruocheng was able to leave the hospital to stay overnight there. During his reminiscences in 2001 about the 1987 death of his wife, Wu Shiliang, and her subsequent cremation, I asked Ying whether he intended to be cremated or buried after his death, and he replied, "We're restoring Wenquan and will designate a plot of land there for family graves." After he died in December 2003, Ying Ruocheng was cremated; his son, Ying Da, had his ashes stored with those of Wu Shiliang and of Ying's mother, Cai Baozhen, and hopes to move them to Wenquan in the future. Ying Da sculpted a bronze bust as a memorial to his father, which he first displayed on the campus of *Shoudu jingji maoyi daxue* (Capital Economic and Trade University), where he had established Yings' Film & TV Institute (*Yingshi yingshi xueyuan*); in 2007 the sculpture was moved to Jili (Geely) University, an educational institution in Beijing established in 2000.

30. Mengzhao is called Ruoya throughout this book because Ying Ruocheng used that name in speaking of her (and for consistency in referring to Ying siblings, who all share the second character *ruo*, 若), but the reader should note that she was addressed while living—and is referred to by her surviving family members—as Mengzhao, not Ruoya. Her siblings also noted her original name, Qixiang.

31. Feng Yuxiang (1882–1948) joined Yuan Shikai's Beiyang army and became a powerful warlord after the fall of Yuan's government in 1916. Having converted to Christianity in 1914, he was known as the Christian General. He was a member of the Zhili Clique along with Zhang Zuolin and his son Zhang Xueliang (the Young Marshal—see note 35 in chapter 6), and he was in and out of favor with the KMT, serving as a regional commander-in-chief during the Anti-Japanese War (1937–1945).

32. Homosexual behavior was condemned and punished in China beginning in 1949 and served as grounds for persecution during the political upheavals of the 1950s and 1970s. For more on the history of homosexuality in China, see Jin Wu Ma, "'Long Yang' and 'Dui Shi' to Tongzhi: Homosexuality in China," *Journal of Gay and Lesbian Psychotherapy* 7, no. 1–2 (2003). See note 13 in chapter 2 for more information on the Anti-Rightist Movement.

33. Lugou Bridge, located in the Fengtai suburb south of Beijing, is also known as the Marco Polo Bridge because it is believed to have been described in the explorer's *Travels*. Linking Beijing to one of the KMT-controlled areas, capture of the bridge meant capture of the city. The initial incident at Marco Polo Bridge occurred late in the evening on July 7, 1937.

Chapter Four

1. What Ying Ruocheng refers to as the prince's palace is usually referred to as prince's mansion in English vernacular by the Chinese government and tourism industry. The term translated as "mansion" is *wangfu*, and collectively the princes' palaces or mansions of the Qing dynasty era are known as *qingwangfu* (清王府). Numerous princes' mansions were erected in Beijing from the era of Ming dynasty Emperor Yongle. The most prominent were those of the eight great families of the early Qing, as well as four additional mansions built after the reign of Emperor Tongzhi (1862–1874). Among these, the largest and best maintained are the mansions of Prince Chun and Prince Gong. Nearby on Dingfu Dajie is Qingwangfu (庆王府), the former residence of Prince Qing (Qing Qinwang, 庆亲王) which was bestowed upon Prince Yi Kuang in 1908 and became the residence of the Ying family during Ying Ruocheng's childhood (from 1932 to 1940). It is not open to the public, but now houses government offices—including some military administration, according to the guard on duty at the front gate in November 2006. It became a designated protected cultural relic in 1984 but is in a severe state of decay. Located nearby on Hugousi Street is the former residence of renowned Beijing opera star Mei Lanfang, a site that was originally part of Prince Qing's compound.

2. He Shen (1750–1799) is a common stock villain role in Chinese arts and popular culture. His massive wealth was accumulated during two decades as the most powerful official in the Qing imperial government. In 1799, he was prosecuted for corruption and ordered by Emperor Jiaqing (son of Emperor Qianlong) to hang himself. When He Shen's residence was searched, his possessions were valued at 800 mil-

lion taels of silver, the equivalent of ten years of Qing government revenue. Emperor Jiaqing confiscated He Shen's residence, giving half of it to his younger brother, Prince Qing Xi, whereupon the residence became known as Prince Qing's Mansion; it was later ceded to Prince Gong. Therefore, the site of He Shen's residence was actually not the palace of Prince Qing where Ying Ruocheng lived as a child, but rather the larger, more elaborate palace of Prince Gong nearby.

3. Here again, Ying's reference differs from the conventional belief that the site described is the neighboring compound. As one Chinese government website details: "According to research by literary scholars, it was at Prince Gong's Mansion that Cao Xueqin, author of *Hongloumeng*, lived the life he was to write about in his famous novel. Researchers believe that the mansion and large garden resemble the Rongguo Mansion and Daguan (Great View) Garden, since certain features described by Cao, including the layout of the buildings, tally with their layout. There is much controversy over the question, but as former Premier Zhou Enlai pointed out, the problem will not be easily resolved and whatever the outcome, the garden should be preserved as a memorial to Cao Xueqin" (www.china.org.cn).

4. PUMC Hospital, or Peking (formerly Peiping) Union Medical College Hospital, is located on the former site of Prince Yu's Mansion in the Third Western Lane at Dongdan. This is the hospital where Ying Ruocheng received his medical treatment for cirrhosis, living there off and on throughout his illness; he died there on December 27, 2003.

5. It was Prince Qing Zai Zhen (1876–1948) who lent his residence to the Ying family and other Furen faculty. He was the son of Prince Qing Yi Kuang (former minister for foreign affairs and prime minister), to whom the mansion was given in 1908. After the Qing dynasty fell in 1911, father and son retreated to Tianjin, where Yi Kuang died in 1917. Zai Zhen purchased the Tianjin residence of a former imperial eunuch in 1925 and made his livelihood investing in industrial corporations in Tianjin, where he died in 1948.

6. There is some discrepancy about when the family moved out of the prince's palace. In certain instances, Ying Ruocheng recalled the family moving out in 1941, before the Japanese attack on Pearl Harbor; in other instances, he recalled returning to the palace from St. Louis boarding school in Tianjin for Christmas holidays that year. Ying Ruocheng's brother, Ying Ruocong, recalled in 2006 that the family moved out in 1940 or 1941. In 2001, Ying Ruocheng said that he lived in the palace until age eleven, with the family leaving the palace just before he left for boarding school. At an August 19, 2007, family gathering, the matter of the precise date of the evacuation from the prince's palace was discussed at length and it was decided that the family moved from the palace to the family compound at Zhenrujing in 1940.

7. Mao Zedong died in 1976. Ying Ruocheng recalls the first family visit to Qing qinwangfu was in 1980 and the second just before his mother's death, which occurred in 1989.

8. Adjacent to the sites of the original Furen University (now a satellite campus of Beijing Normal University) and Furen Middle School (now No. 13 Middle School), the

Qing qinwangfu compound is closed to the public, so I followed Ying's lead and "gate-crashed the place" in November 2006. Although there is nothing posted at the main gate identifying the work units contained within, a sign warns "People and Vehicles not Belonging to this Compound are PROHIBITED FROM ENTERING." A gentleman who can enter informed me that it houses several offices and dormitories, some of which belong to divisions of the military. He invited me to the cafeteria for lunch, but the guard posted at the gate did not permit me to enter. Upon explaining the reason for my interest in seeing the site, I was again denied entry. When leaving the neighborhood on my bicycle, I saw a side gate ajar on Deshengmen neidajie and entered it. I was able to view a small section of the compound (which is indeed in a rather dilapidated state, as Ying Ruocheng described) and take some photographs before being seen and ordered to leave. Located just down the street, Prince Gong's Mansion is open to the public and a popular tourist destination, as are the former residences of Guo Moruo and Mei Lanfang, which are just steps away from Qing qinwangfu.

9. From Verdi's *Rigoletto* (Ying specified this was not a holy song, meaning not a usual church hymn).

10. Ying Ruocong echoed his brother's sentiments that Ruoya and Ruojing were both very devout Catholics from a young age and that Ruoya had intended to become a nun after college. He believes their ascetic practices (Ruojing rising before daylight to attend Mass every morning and Ruoya denying herself nutritious food and refusing to spend money despite the family's wealth) led to their illness and death. When someone told his heartbroken mother that God took Ruoya and Ruojing to heaven because he loved them so much and they were so pure, she loosened her strict rules for the remaining children, afraid that God would take them if they were too devout. (Taped interview with Ying Ruocong, November 20, 2006.)

11. According to Ying Da, Ying Ruocheng did not attend his mother's funeral. (Perhaps this was because he was serving as vice minister of culture and attendance at a Catholic ceremony would have been awkward for a high-ranking government official, particularly in August 1989, just after the events at Tiananmen Square.)

12. The gospel story that Ying is recalling here is commonly known in English as "the loaves and the fishes" and is told in Matthew 15:32–39; Mark 6:34–44; Luke 9:12–17; and John 6:1–14. It actually does not coincide with the Sermon on the Mount, but in John's version (which is the most commonly recounted), Jesus takes his disciples "up the mountain" and thus an image of a mountaintop setting is evoked (whereas Matthew, Mark, and Luke place the event in a "desert-place"). Ying's numbers, though reversing the foods and exaggerating the crowd, also seem to come from John's version (in which "five barley loaves and two fishes [feed] a very great crowd . . . of about five thousand," *New Catholic Edition of the Holy Bible*, Catholic Book Publishing Company, 1957).

13. The attack on Pearl Harbor in Hawaii by the Japanese forces began on December 7, 1941, at approximately 8 a.m. local time, which would have been midnight December 8 in the Japanese and Chinese capital cities of Tokyo and Beijing.

Thus, the scene Ying describes is indeed on December 8, the feast of the Immaculate Conception.

14. According to Ying Ruocheng's brothers and son, Ying Lianzhi purchased the residence for his mother sometime between 1912 (when he left Tianjin and settled in Beijing after his tenure at the *Dagongbao*) and 1919, since Cai Baozhen and Ying Qianli were wed there in 1920. Zhenrujing is named for its *hutong*, and Ying Lianzhi purchased two full courtyard dwellings (*siheyuan*) with eighteen or nineteen rooms each. He never lived there himself, but stayed at Jingyiyuan (Jingyi Imperial Garden) at Fragrant Hills. In addition to his mother, Ying Lianzhi's siblings and their families also moved in, so it was fully inhabited by the extended Ying clan when Ying Ruocheng's parents and siblings moved back there from the prince's palace in 1940.

15. Previous to serving as vice minister of culture (under Minister Wang Meng) from 1986–1990, Ying Ruocheng was elected to the People's Congress (*Renmin daibiao dahui* or *Renda* for short) at the district (*qu*) level (*Qu renda daibiao*) for the East Beijing District (*Beijing dongcheng qu*). Before leaving the Ministry of Culture, he was appointed chairman of the China Arts Festival Foundation (*Zhongguo yishujie jijinhui huizhang*), a post he held until the year preceding his death. According to Ying Da, his father's position as vice minister raised his status to deputy in the National People's Congress, to which he was elected as a member of the Standing Committee (*quanguo changwei*), bypassing the interim municipal (*shi*) level, and thus his subsequent reelections to the Congress remained at the *changwei* level. He retained several ministry benefits for life, including a private secretary and driver.

16. Ying Ruocheng told me about his Gang of Four in 2002. He provided me with the full name of the "helicopter man" but requested that it not be published. His other two comembers were identified for me by a family member after his death. At the request of both Ying himself and this family member, the three men's names are not being published here in order to protect their anonymity.

17. Ying Ruocheng made this comment on May 16, 2002. Indeed, Ding Guangen left his post shortly after this.

Chapter Five

1. "Liberation" (*jiefang*) is the common term used in contemporary China in reference to the founding of the People's Republic in 1949.

2. For a vivid description of the atmosphere at Qinghua University from 1948 to 1950 (the latter half of Ying Ruocheng's enrollment and precisely the time that Wu Shiliang was there), see Rickett and Rickett, *Prisoners of Liberation*, 1–60.

3. See note 13 in chapter 2 for information on the Anti-Rightist Movement.

4. See note 19 for information on the founding of the Beijing People's Art Theatre.

5. Konstantin Stanislavsky, *Stanislavsky Produces Othello*, trans. Helen Nowak (London: Geoffrey Bles, 1948). Ying Ruocheng translated Nowak's English transla-

tion into Chinese while at Qinghua, and it was published while he was an actor at the Beijing People's Art Theatre.

6. Sergei Eisenstein, *The Film Sense*, trans. and ed. Jay Leyda (New York: Harcourt Brace, 1947).

7. In Shaw's 1905 play, the character of Undershaft is a philanthropist who made his fortune from a munitions factory, causing an ethical dilemma for his daughter (the title role) when he makes a donation to the Salvation Army, where she works. Though many interpret the play as a critique of religion and hypocrisy, Shaw was defending the integrity of charitable donations regardless of their source, a view Ying seems to favor here. Ying would go on to translate both plays and stage them thirty-three and forty years later, respectively.

8. *The Corn Is Green* is an autobiographical play by Emlyn Williams about an ambitious Welsh schoolteacher working in a destitute mining town; at the center of the story is her relationship with an illiterate student who eventually graduates with honors. *The Corn Is Green* was produced on Broadway in 1940. A film version was made in 1945 with Bette Davis in the role of Moffat.

9. George Pierce Baker (1866–1935) graduated from Harvard in 1887 and was on the faculty of the English Department from 1888 to 1924, where he started his Forty-seven Workshop playwriting course in 1906 and mentored luminaries in early Chinese drama and film such as Hong Shen (1894–1955). He left Harvard in 1925 and helped to found the Yale School of Drama.

10. Ying Xiaole and Ying Da spoke of their late parents' relationship in a 2004 interview on Ying Da's televised marriage talk show, *Marriage Theatre* (*fuqi juchang*). Usually, Ying Da is the host and interviews celebrity couples directly, but in this instance, Jiang Naiming hosted the interview. The edited transcript was published in a collection from the show and includes the following information related to Ying's reminiscences: that Wu played a character that shot Ying's character dead in *The 41st*, that their mother's fashionable hairdo prompted Ying to call her Lion Head (*shizitou*), and that the meal teams they each supervised were part of a communal food system at Qinghua organized and paid for by the students (with up to a thousand on each team, and Ying's called the Cold Poor Meal Team, *qinghan shantuan*). They also elaborated on the cabbage patch story and shared their mother's recollection that Ying courted her by saying he couldn't promise fame or riches but would make her happy and never let her be lonely—and that he kept her laughing every day of their marriage. See "Smiling at Life (*xiao dui rensheng*)—Ying Ruocheng and Wu Shiliang," in *Fuqi juchang* (2004): 79–112.

11. The rape Ying Ruocheng refers to was of nineteen-year-old university student Shen Chong by U.S. Marine William Pierson (assisted by Warren Pritchard) and occurred in Beijing on Christmas Eve 1946. The following commentary from Robert Shaffer confirms Ying's recollection: "Students at the city's three main universities declared a three-day strike in protest, and 10,000 students participated in a seven-mile march on December 30. The protestors demanded not only punishment of the rapists and compensation for the young woman but also the withdrawal of all U.S.

troops from China." Protests spread to Shanghai, Suzhou, Nanjing, Kunming, and Guangzhou as well. See Robert Shaffer, "A Rape in Beijing, December 1946: GIs, Nationalist Protests, and U.S. Foreign Policy," *The Pacific Historical Review*, Vol. 69, no. 1 (2000): 31–64. See also James Cook, "Penetration and Neocolonialism: The Shen Chong Rape Case and the Anti-American Student Movement of 1946–47," *Republican China*, Vol. 22, no. 1 (1996): 65–97.

12. For information on anti-U.S. and anti-KMT Shanghai protests of the civil war era, some of which were triggered by the 1946 Beijing rape case and related events (including incidents involving American servicemen in jeeps hitting Chinese civilians), see Jeffrey N. Wasserstrom, *Student Protests in Twentieth-Century China: The View from Shanghai* (Stanford, CA: Stanford University Press, 1991).

13. Wu Shiliang (吴世良) was originally named Lu Xing (卢星). Her mother, Ying Lingyan, was first married to a man with the surname Lu; they divorced in 1932, when Wu Shiliang was four years old. Ying Lingyan later married Wu Baofeng, who came to the marriage with three children. Together they had one child, Wu Shirang. The five children's names in the combined family were each given the surname Wu (吴), the character Shi (世), and one of the five Confucian virtues (by birth order from oldest to youngest): *wen, liang, gong, jian,* and *rang* (温，良，恭，俭，让).

14. Wu Baofeng (1899–1963) served as president of Jiaotong University from its temporary location in Chongqing in 1942 until he was forced to resign in July 1947 (he was acting president from 1941, formally appointed in 1944, and retained in 1946 when the campus moved back to Shanghai). During the anti–Chiang Kai-shek Patriotic Movement, he protected progressive students, and is remembered for rescuing an underground CCP member in his car.

15. Ying and Wu's son, Ying Da, indicated in August 2007 that a possible factor in Wu's finally leaving the city of Shanghai and opting for a university in Beijing was that she and her cousin were in love and the families disapproved of the relationship and insisted on their separation.

16. Here, Ying uses the term "long march" as a humorous metaphor for Wu Shiliang's journey through several universities (and, possibly, potential suitors) before meeting him at Qinghua. The Long March to which he alludes began in October 1935 when Communist troops, led by Zhu De, fled KMT forces. Altogether, approximately 100,000 people participated in the march, which covered 6,000 miles and ended a year later with only 7,000 survivors arriving in Sha'anxi to set up a new soviet. Mao Zedong assumed leadership of the Chinese Communist Party during the Long March, at Zunyi in January 1936.

17. Cao Yu (1910–1996) and Ouyang Yuqian (1889–1962) were two pioneers in the development of *huaju* (spoken drama). Cao Yu (originally named Wan Jiabao) served as president of the Beijing People's Art Theatre for nearly a half-century (from its founding until his death), and as a junior at Qinghua University wrote his most famous play, *Thunderstorm* (1934), followed by *Sunrise* (1936), *Wilderness* (1937), *Metamorphosis* (1940), and *Peking Man* (1940). Wu Shiliang was his creative secretary (*chuangzuo mishu*) at the theatre when he wrote his final play, *Wang Zhaojun,* in

1978 (see note 41). According to its official brochure, the Central Academy of Drama was established in Beijing in 1950—it was a merger of the Lu Xun Art College in Yan'an, the arts faculty of North China University, and the Nanjing National Academy of Drama.

18. According to Ying Da, his parents were assigned to the newly formed *Duiwai youhui* (Foreign Friendship Association) along with two other Qinghua classmates, and were in the process of going when they suddenly heard about the establishment of the Beijing People's Art Theatre and decided to apply there instead. (See Ying Da, *Fuqi juchang*, 90.)

19. The archive of the Beijing People's Art Theatre records the stage premiere of *Dragon Beard Ditch* as 1953, but the play was indeed staged in 1951, as Ying Ruocheng recalls. The official date, time, and place of the establishment of the Beijing People's Art Theatre (*Beijing renmin yishu juyuan*, or Renyi for short) is June 12, 1952, at 7 p.m. at 56 Shijia hutong, and the recorded chronology of public staged productions begins with that date. However, Renyi was preceded by (and emerged from) the Amalgamated Beijing People's Art Theatre (*Zonghexing de Beijing renmin yishu juyuan*)—more commonly referred to as Old Renyi (Lao Renyi)—which included performing troupes and training for spoken drama, Western opera, dance, and music. It was decided that these various forms would be separated from spoken drama and remain under the auspices of the Ministry of Culture, while the Municipal Bureau (Beijing) would retain its own spoken drama troupe composed of the spoken drama section of Old Renyi and the professional spoken drama troupe of the Central Academy of Drama. Cao Yu was installed as president (*yuanzhang*), with Jiao Juyin appointed to oversee the process (as *jianyuan sheji xiaozu*), and the plan was approved by Zhou Enlai. The course of action was decided at a meeting of high-ranking cadres (*zhuyao ganbu hui*) of both Old Renyi and the Central Academy of Drama that was held on April 4, 1952. Thus, *Dragon Beard Ditch* was produced by Old Renyi in 1951, and again by "New Renyi" in 1953. Ying Ruocheng played the role of Liu Zhanggui (Old Liu) in both productions. (See Huang and Zhou, *Huihuang de yishu diantang*, 4–10.)

20. Ying Da elaborates that his father arrived at Beijing People's Art Theatre overconfident from his success at Qinghua and was actually not as talented an actor as his mother. Theatre leaders were disappointed and transferred him to the archives. "Today everyone has heard of the actor Ying Ruocheng, but my father almost did not succeed in becoming an artist at all," he says. (See Ying Da, *Fuqi juchang*, 94.)

21. According to Ying Ruocheng, this play was never staged (at Lao She's request). Indeed, it is not included in the official production chronology published by the Beijing People's Art Theatre, and Liu Zhangchun (head of the marketing and publications section of the theatre company) confirmed to me in August 2007 that the play was never produced.

22. During the 1950s the Soviet Union sent numerous advisors to China to aid development of socialist agriculture and industry. Some say their influence was superficial due to China's vast size and radically different culture, but their impact on the newly formed spoken drama institutions was significant and lasting.

23. Ying Ruocheng said that Boris Kulinev was head of the acting school at Vak-tangov Theatre, but my research has not located his precise name or affiliation. Ma-terials of the Beijing People's Art Theatre translate his name from Russian into Chinese as 库里涅夫 (Keliniefu) and into English Romanization as Kurinev. His pho-tograph can be seen at the Beijing People's Art Theatre Museum (an impressive per-manent exhibit, constructed largely from theatre archives, that opened at the Capi-tal Theatre in 2007).

24. In the published chronology produced by the archives of the Beijing People's Art Theatre, Xia Chun and Mei Qian are listed as the production's directors, not Ku-linev. But in publications by scholars who have researched the theatre's history, Kulinev is credited with taking charge of "artistic direction" (*yishu zhidao*) for the production. (See Wu, *Naren nayi*, 178–179.)

25. There were about fifty performances of *Teahouse* when it premiered in 1958 and another fifty when it was revived in April–September 1963. It was restaged twelve times during 1979–1981. See note 32 for later international touring infor-mation.

26. Ying's recollection of the Anti-Rightist Movement and Great Leap Forward come from his article "China's Wild Ride" in *Time International*. See note 13 in chap-ter 2 for more on both campaigns.

27. Archival statistics of the Beijing People's Art Theatre illustrate the startling accuracy of Ying Ruocheng's recollections: in 1957, audiences for plays (as deter-mined by the length of the run of each play) increased from a previous average of less than or about one or two dozen performances to at least thirty and often upwards of fifty, sixty, or even seventy performances. Audience numbers peaked with 120 per-formances of Guo Moruo's *Cai Wenji* in May–December 1959, then began to fall again in 1960 and remained low until an increase in mid to late 1962. (See *Beijing renmin yishu juyuan 1952–2002*, 138–153.)

28. During the six years from June 1966 until September 1973, there were no spo-ken dramas created or performed publicly by the Beijing People's Art Theatre. There were, in fact, performances of a very limited number of political plays at the Beijing People's Art Theatre during the later years of the Cultural Revolution, but they were relatively few. From September to December 1973, three plays were performed there. In 1974, five plays were performed, three of them the same as in 1973. In 1975, the same group of plays was performed (with one addition) but with increased frequency. Then, 1976 began with the same kind of repertoire, but activity picked up by midyear. All propaganda plays staged during the Cultural Revolution were collec-tively scripted works resembling *huobaoju* (living newspaper plays). For precise list-ings with full production information, see *Beijing renmin yishu juyuan 1952–2002*, 153–160.

29. Ying Ruocheng's reminiscences about *Teahouse* (both the 1958 original pro-duction and the 1979 revival) are drawn from two sources: our taped interview on July 1, 2000, and an article he wrote in English in 1979 ("Lao She and His *Teahouse*," 3–11).

30. Lao She (Shu Qingchun, 1898–1966) drowned himself after being interrogated by Red Guards at the beginning of the Cultural Revolution. The revival of *Teahouse* in February 1979 with the original cast was ostensibly to commemorate the eightieth anniversary of his birth.

31. The current Beijing People's Art Theatre's official founding date is 1952, though its establishment (Old Renyi), as detailed in note 19, dates to 1950—which is when then-president Li Bozhao commissioned Lao She to write the play that would become *Dragon Beard Ditch* (*Longxu gou*). The play is listed in the theatre's official documents as premiering in 1953, though Ying Ruocheng correctly recollects that it was first staged in 1951, the year after Lao She wrote it. Plays Lao She wrote for the Beijing People's Art Theatre between 1950 and 1958 were *Longxu gou* (*Dragon Beard Ditch*, written 1950, staged 1951 and 1953), *Yijia daibiao* (*A Family of Delegates*, written 1952, not staged), *Chunhua qiushi* (*Spring Flowers, Autumn Fruits*, 1953), *Qingnian tuji dui* (*Young Assault Troop*, 1956), *Luotuo Xiangzi* (*Camel Xiangzi*, original novel 1937, stage adaptation 1957), *Chaguan* (*Teahouse*, 1958), and *Hong dayuan* (*Red Courtyard*, 1958). Ying Ruocheng recalls *Nüdianyuan* (*Saleswomen*, or as Ying translates, "Girl Shop Assistants") as being produced before the premiere of *Teahouse*, but according to Beijing People's Art Theatre records, it was staged afterward, in March–May 1959. (See "Lao She and His *Teahouse*," p. 7, for Ying's recollection; see *Beijing renmin yishu juyuan, 1952–2002*, p. 145, for theatre archive listing.)

32. *Teahouse* toured Europe between September and November 1980; visited Japan in 1983; played in Hong Kong, Singapore, and Canada in 1986; went to Taiwan in July 2004; and toured Washington, DC, Berkeley, Pasadena, Houston, and New York in October–December 2005, marking the first time a professional spoken drama from China was ever performed in the United States. Ying Ruocheng's English translation was used for the supertitles during performances.

33. Jiao Juyin (1905–1975) founded the school in 1930 and served as its president. In 1935, he enrolled at the Sorbonne in Paris, France, where he earned a doctorate in 1938. He spent 1942–1946 in the wartime capital of Chongqing, then returned to Beijing and became the dean of the Humanities College/Western Languages Department at Peking Normal University. In 1952, he was appointed vice president of the Beijing People's Art Theatre (as one of its founding members). During the Cultural Revolution, he was sent to Heavenly River (*Tiantanghe*) cadre school for labor reform. He returned to Beijing and died of lung cancer in 1975, during the final year of the Cultural Revolution. (See Zhang, *Huashuo Beijing Renyi*; and Liu, *Zhongguo shi da ziju daoyan dashi.*)

34. Richard Nixon's historic trip to China in 1972 reestablished diplomatic ties between the two nations. In a series of articles remembering Ying Ruocheng shortly after his death, Mi Tiezeng mentions that Ying was sent down to Heavenly River because of the government's desire to make Beijing politically secure by removing all reactionaries and counterrevolutionaries during Nixon's visit. Mi names some of the more esteemed colleagues among the dozen or so members of the theatre company who were sent to that location, including himself, Ying, Jiao Juyin, Mei Qian,

ZhaoYunru, Li Daqian, and Wang Zhi'an. He also describes in greater detail than Ying the process by which Ying organized the production of fertilizer at the cadre school. See Mi Tiezeng excerpted in "Ying Ruocheng zhuisihui fayan zhaiyao" ("Summary of speeches at Ying Ruocheng memorial symposium") in "Huainian pian," 32.

35. Peng Zhengyuan ran the Beijing People's Art Theatre as general secretary (or *yibashou*) during most of the period the army assumed control of the theatre (from late 1968 until after the end of the Cultural Revolution). Installed there just before Ying Ruocheng was released from prison, it was he who sent Ying to Heavenly River and dispatched Little Wang (Wang Weimin) to keep an eye on Ying and Yu when they were sent on the road by Zhao Qiyang.

36. *Sui* (岁) is a compound combining *shan* (山) and *xi* (夕). The upper half was blown away by the wind, leaving only *xi* (夕), which means evening. The familiar slogan *Mao zhuxi wansui* means "Long Live Chairman Mao" (literally, "May Chairman Mao Live for Ten Thousand Years"), so the new slogan could be interpreted to mean that Mao would live for only ten thousand more evenings rather than ten thousand years, or even that his last evening was at hand.

37. More precisely, the title of the play means "workers and peasants are one" or "workers and peasants are one family."

38. See chapter 1, note 2 for more information on *dazibao*.

39. Two years after, in 1976, the Gang of Four fell and Zhao Qiyang (1918–1996) was appointed to the Art Bureau of the Ministry of Culture (1978), then became China's vice minister of culture (1981), the post Ying Ruocheng would hold from 1986 to 1990.

40. The play Ying refers to here as *Taoyuan* may have been *Going up Peach Peak Three Times* (*Sanshang Taofeng*), a Jinju (Shanxi opera) performed at the North China Theatrical Festival in 1974. It was heavily criticized on ideological grounds, primarily for defending the Peach Garden Experience (*Taoyuan jingyan*), as Liu Shaoqi's pre–Cultural Revolution agricultural model was called. Taoyuan was a brigade in Funing County, Hebei Province, with a style of agriculture contradicting Mao's Dazhai model. See Colin Mackerras, "Opera and the Campaign to Criticize Lin Piao and Confucius," *Papers on Far Eastern History*, no. 11 (March 1975): 169–198.

41. According to Ying Da, Wu Shiliang's position as Cao Yu 's creative secretary was primarily a cover for her spy activities; her official *danwei* (work unit) was actually the Beijing Public Security Bureau (the Beijing State Security Bureau after 1983), not the Beijing People's Art Theatre, whereas her husband's work unit remained the theatre throughout his intelligence work.

42. The awarding of the Nobel Prize to Gao Xingjian in October 2000 triggered controversy, with mainland China criticizing the choice and disclaiming Gao's status as a Chinese writer due to the fact that he had been living in France since 1987. Gao had been the target of criticism by the government in 1983 when his play *Chezhan* (*Bus Stop*) was produced at the Beijing People's Art Theatre, and became a political exile after writing the play *Taowang* (*Escape*) in 1989 following

the military suppression of prodemocracy demonstrations in Tiananmen Square. His works have not been published or produced in China (beyond Hong Kong) for nearly twenty years.

43. Three of Gao Xingjian's plays were produced by the Beijing People's Art Theatre before Gao became an exile in France, all directed by Lin Zhaohua: *Juedui xinghao (Alarm Signal)* in 1982; *Chezhan (Bus Stop)* in 1983; and *Yeren (Wild Man)* in 1985. Gao does not concur with Ying's version of how he came to be employed at the theatre—he maintains that he approached Yu Shizhi on his own and that it was Yu and Cao Yu who facilitated his transfer, though he notes that he had a close relationship with Ying Ruocheng as well. (Interview with Gao Xingjian in Paris on June 11, 2006.)

44. Richard Thwaites, in *Real Life China 1978–1983*, recalls being an audience member that night: "I had witnessed [Ying Ruocheng] perform a remarkable feat, unscripted, as the on-stage translator for a Bob Hope stand-up routine before a live Beijing audience. Hope's jokes were appalling, occasionally insulting to China, and aimed, anyway, over the heads of the politely bewildered Chinese to American TV cameras. But Ying Ruocheng managed to put the whole thing across, instantly, even mimicking Bob Hope's laboured inflections." Richard Thwaites, *Real Life China 1978–1983* (Sydney, Australia: William Collins Pty Ltd, 1986). Republished electronically in 2004 by Rich Communications, Canberra, Australia. Available at: http://www.thwaites.com.au/rlc/index.htm, January 13, 2008. Ying Ruocheng's colleague Qin Zanyao was also at the Bob Hope performance at the Capital Theatre that night. According to Qin's recollection, Hope began telling his jokes using prepared Surtitles for Chinese translation and there was no reaction, but the audience burst into laughter when Ying Ruocheng subsequently took the stage and began interpreting for him, prompting Hope to embrace Ying with delight. The American reporter seated beside Qin told him that Ying's English was better than his own. (See Qin Zanyao excerpted in "Huainian pian," 31.)

45. Su Shi (1036–1101), also known as Su Dongpo, was a master writer, painter, and calligrapher. He and three others were known as the Four Greatest Calligraphers of the Song Dynasty and Su was considered the best. His interests also included cooking, wine making, and tea tasting. Wang Anshi (1021–1086) was a poet and writer known for his government reforms, particularly his implementation of the New Laws or New Policies of 1069–76. Academic debates sparked by his reforms endured for centuries.

46. Zhang Yongqiang was visiting Ying Ruocheng in the hospital the day we taped our conversation about *Amadeus*. Zhang had this to say about working with Ying as a director: "I read the script as it had been translated by someone in Shanghai, and I was disappointed [but] when I read Ying's translation, I had a totally different feeling. It was so good. . . . I was very lucky to be chosen to play this role. I've worked with lots of directors who have different methods and styles, but I feel Ying is an excellent director. He helps actors develop techniques to create character. I learned how to create a character—how to act—through *Amadeus*. . . . At the time, I was a student

5. At the time that Ying met Miller in 1978 in Beijing, Ying had never traveled outside of China (Miller was incorrect when he claimed in his preface to *"Salesman" in Beijing* that Ying had "some personal experience in the United States" when they first met). The touring production of *Teahouse* that Cao and Ying tried to promote on their visit to the United States in 1980 never materialized. The play did tour to Europe, Japan, and Taiwan during Ying's lifetime (with him in the role of Pockmark Liu), but never reached the United States. It was not until 2005 that *Teahouse* finally toured the United States (with a younger cast than its original version), two years after Ying Ruocheng had died. Ying's translation of *Teahouse* has been published by China Translation and Publishing Corporation (1999, 2005) and is included, in a version revised by Claire Conceison, in a forthcoming anthology of modern Chinese drama edited by Xiaomei Chen.

6. A piece titled "Scar" by Lu Xinhua was published in Shanghai's *Wenhuibao* on August 11, 1978. After its publication, a flood of similar works lamenting directly or indirectly the evils of the Gang of Four were published, collectively categorized as scar or wounded literature.

7. Spoken drama (*huaju*) was imported to mainland China during the first decade of the twentieth century by Chinese who were exposed to Japanese stagings of Western drama while studying abroad in Tokyo. An adaptation of *Uncle Tom's Cabin* led the way, followed by productions of plays by Ibsen, Wilde, Shakespeare, and others. Native playwrights also began to write in the new form, using vernacular rather than classical Chinese. For further discussion of the depiction of foreigners in modern Chinese plays, including the use of "realistic makeup" (*xianshi huazhuang*) to simulate racial difference, see Conceison, *Significant Other*, and William Sun, "Power and Problems of Performance across Ethnic Lines," *The Drama Review* (Winter 2000): 86–95.

8. Ying Ruocheng's reflections about his translation strategy and about foreigner makeup practices in contemporary Chinese theatre (as well as in the 1983 production of *Death of a Salesman*) were drawn from the following sources: "The 'Salesman' Cast Speak for Themselves," *China Reconstructs*, Vol. 32, no. 8 (1983): 26; the transcript of Ying's introduction of Arthur Miller at the 1983 Kennedy Center Honors awards ceremony: 91–93; and the following transcripts of interviews: 2002 Videotape 2 (May 27, 2002), 2001 Audiotape 5 (July 24, 2001), and 1994 Audiotape 1 (June 28, 1994).

9. Miller's wife, Inge Morath, also joined him onstage. For Arthur Miller's complete account of his collaboration with Ying Ruocheng and the staging of *Death of a Salesman* in China (including the makeup dilemma, costume parade, and the audience's reaction opening night), see Miller, *"Salesman" in Beijing*.

10. At the age of fifteen, Ying Xiaole became the second student (of approximately twenty) at her school to be "struggled against"—in the form of public criticism, big character poster displays, and assignment of demeaning janitorial duties—from August to October 1966, at which point she fled Beijing. She accompanied her aunt Ying Ruoxian (Ying Ruocheng's youngest sibling, eight years older than his

daughter) to participate in the "great link-up revolution" (*geming dachuanlian*), which allowed students to travel throughout the nation in the name of revolution. Hoping to arrive in Sichuan, they boarded a chaotic, crowded train and ended up instead in Fuzhou, where Ying Xiaole drew illustrations for the weekly Red Guard newspaper *Dahan dajiao*. In 1968, she was sent to Inner Mongolia for four years (1968–1971). From her labor alongside the peasants, she now possesses skills ranging from making rugs to digging wells to building houses. From 1973 to 1975, she studied painting in the home of master artist Huang Yongyu in Beijing, though her residence permit (*hukou*) was still for Inner Mongolia (making it technically illegal for her to live elsewhere). In 1975, she was officially permitted to return to Beijing. In 1984, she moved to the United States, following her husband Ji Yijian (John King), who had gone in 1982. (Interviews with Ying Xiaole [Felicia King] on September 14–15, 2007, in Batavia and Naperville, IL.)

11. *Marco Polo* was a ten-hour, four-part television miniseries featuring Ken Marshall as the title character. Other cast members included John Gielgud, Anne Bancroft, Leonard Nimoy, and Burt Lancaster. The first Western production filmed on location in China since World War II, the shoot lasted over one year and cost an estimated twenty-five million dollars. Press materials introduced the project as a coproduction of Radiotelevisione Italiana and the Procter and Gamble Company; Ying Ruocheng referred to it as a Sino-Italian coproduction; another source (Hal Erickson, *All Movie Guide*) called it an "American-Italian-Austrian-French-British co-production." *Marco Polo* was broadcast on NBC in the United States May 16–19, 1982.

12. *The Romance of the Three Kingdoms* is a compilation of material from a variety of forms and time periods (including oral tradition, historical records, Tang dynasty poetry, and Yuan dynasty dramas) written by Luo Guanzhong between 1330 and 1400. Luo's twenty-four-volume work was condensed to 120 chapters by Mao Zonggang during the Qing dynasty, and that is now the standard version. Chronicling battles, rulers, and intrigues from the Yellow Turban Rebellion in 184 C.E. to the unification of the three kingdoms during the Jin dynasty in 280 C.E., it is considered one of four great classical novels of China and has been adapted in various literary and cinematic forms.

13. *The Last Emperor* was released in 1987. The film recounts Pu Yi's childhood— and mentorship by a British tutor—against the backdrop of the maneuvers of the Empress Dowager Ci Xi and the fall of the Qing dynasty in 1911, as well as Pu Yi's retention by the Japanese as a puppet ruler of Manchuria during the 1930s and 1940s. These sequences are juxtaposed with the present, depicting Pu Yi's prison life, his experience during the Cultural Revolution after his release, and his visit as a tourist to the Forbidden City near the end of his life.

14. *Little Buddha* was released in 1993. Ying Ruocheng played Lama Norbu, who travels to Seattle searching for the reincarnation of his late teacher, Lama Dorje. He brings three child candidates (from the United States, India, and Kathmandu) to Bhutan to find out which is the true reincarnation. Lama Norbu also recounts the story of Buddha's journey to enlightenment, with Keanu Reeves playing Siddhartha in the historical flashback sequences.

15. Ying Ruocheng's reflections about his experiences as vice minister of culture come from a taped interview on May 20, 2002 (Audiotape 4) as well as four letters Ying wrote to Stella Shen between January 1988 and December 1989. Two of the letters were written after June Fourth, one of which was "hastily scribbled" and given to a Canadian acquaintance to take on his person out of China to mail from North America. In total, the four correspondences are: a typed letter dated January 24, 1988, on University of Missouri–Kansas City Department of Theatre stationery with personalized letterhead; a typed letter dated January 23, 1989, on *Marco Polo* stationery; an undated letter typed on *Marco Polo* stationery (the second page is missing, but the content of the letter suggests it was written in August 1989); and a handwritten letter dated December 14, 1989, on UMKC theatre department memo stationery with personalized letterhead.

16. In his January 24, 1988, letter to Stella Shen, Ying writes: "I am a busy but lonely man. Pray for me." This is a rare instance of Ying referring to his faith and religion in a spiritual way during his adult years.

17. In the 2004 interview on her brother's talk show, Ying Xiaole said her father often called out Wu Shiliang's name and spoke with her during the final years of his illness. Ying Da added, "He would address anyone around him as if they were my mother. This was because he had this habit his whole life: whatever he encountered in life—regardless of whether or not it was important or noteworthy—his first thought would be that he had to tell my mother about it. Even though their marriage technically only lasted thirty-seven years, in reality it lasted fifty-four years, because my father never left the marriage." (Ying Da, *Fuqi juchang*, 112 [translation mine].)

18. As far as family members can ascertain, Wu Shiliang died of complications of acute aplastic anemia. She died twenty-nine days after being diagnosed, and during her treatment it was also discovered that she had cancer.

19. Ying Da was married to his first wife, Ge Xin, at the time; her father was a doctor.

20. Ying refers to the play as *Weihushan* (*Tiger Mountain*), but the full title of the play was *Zhiqu Weihushan* (*Taking Tiger Mountain by Strategy*). This title is best known as one of the eight model operas (*yangbanxi*) of the Cultural Revolution, the form to which the play was later adapted. The spoken drama version (itself an adaptation) premiered at the Beijing People's Art Theatre on May 10, 1958, and played through July 26 (for seventy-five performances). It was revived in September–October of the same year, again in November, and then in January–February 1960, and once more in July 1964. Since the event occurred before Wu Shiliang's pregnancy with Ying Da and Ying Ruocheng recalls it being extremely hot and "August," it likely took place in late July, at the end of the initial run of the play. This is also consistent with Ying Da's claim that the event happened in 1958, during the Great Leap Forward, when all citizens were exerting themselves and his mother continued working up until the final days of her pregnancy (to which he attributes the tragic outcome).

21. Here, Ying Ruocheng suggests that Wu Shiliang consumed quinine late in her pregnancy, either to alleviate recurring symptoms from her previous malaria or to

expedite the birth of the baby (on the advice of a fellow actress at the theatre who told her that she had learned from a Western doctor that drinking quinine would induce labor). This would explain Wu's feelings of remorse, but I have been unable to verify from other sources that she ever drank quinine during the pregnancy, or that the baby's death in her womb at term was triggered by such an act. Ying Da does not believe that this was the case, but Ying Ruocheng's claim is plausible, since quinine was used to induce labor in pregnant women in the West several decades previous to Wu's experience, and sometimes led to miscarriages. See Sadler, Dilling, and Gemmell, "Further Investigations into the Death of the Child following the Induction of Labour by means of Quinine," BJOG: An International Journal of Obstetrics and Gynaecology, Vol. 37, no. 3 (1930): 529–546. See also Guy I. Benrubi, "Labor Induction: Historic Perspectives," Clinical Obstetrics and Gynecology, Vol. 43, no. 3 (2000): 429–432.

22. Ying Da's version of his abandonment by his maternal grandmother after his parents were taken to prison is even sadder than Ying Ruocheng's recollection. According to Ying Da, she sent him to his uncle (Ying Ruocong) for a visit on a Sunday afternoon, and when he returned that evening, she had already left. Entering the courtyard, he noticed that their home was dark and all of their possessions that were normally stored outside had been cleared away. The door was locked and there was an envelope addressed to "the Ying family" (Ying jia), which Ying Da took back to his uncle's house. He slept there that night, and remained with Ying Ruocong and Zhao Ziqiang until his paternal grandmother assumed care for him. (Taped interview at Wenquan, August 19, 2007.)

23. Ying Da was unaware of this abortion twelve years after his birth, but he does recall that his parents approached him around that time and asked him if he would like to have a brother or sister. He replied that he would not, because he had been without his parents for the past three years and did not now want to share them with a younger sibling. He believes that they likely consulted him while making the decision and that his opinion entered into their decision.

24. According to his own account in Travels, Marco Polo (1254–1324) spent seventeen years in the service of the great Mongol ruler Kublai Khan (1215–1294), grandson of Genghis Khan, during China's Yuan dynasty. Ying Ruocheng identified with the Khan character in particular because the Mongols were great horsemen, hunters, and warriors from the north, a trait shared with the Manchus from which Ying's clan hailed.

25. The UMKC production of The Family was Ying Ruocheng's English translation and revision of Cao Yu's 1942 stage adaptation of the 1931 novel Jia (Family) by Ba Jin. Written in Shanghai after Ba Jin's return from Paris, the semiautobiographical work depicts the disintegration of a large feudal family at the turn of the century. Sometimes called the "bible of modern Chinese youth," it portrays the young intelligentsia of the May Fourth generation in rebellion against feudal society through the figures of the three Gao brothers and the plight of the elder brother's wife. The first in a trilogy, Family was followed by the novels Spring (1938) and Autumn (1940). Author Li Yaotang

(1904–2005) chose his penname Ba Jin from the Chinese transliteration of the first and last syllables of the surnames of Russian anarchists Bakunin and Kropotkin.

26. The following excerpt is taken from "A Brief History of the UMKC Department of Theatre" by Felicia Hardison Londré on the university's website: "The academic production with the greatest international resonance in the history of the department came in 1982 when the renowned Chinese actor-director and vice-minister of culture Ying Ruocheng served as visiting professor and directed *The Family* by Cao Yu. Professor Ying gave the students a crash course in Chinese culture and worked with them on ritual gestures like kowtowing and calligraphy brush-handling. The result was a superbly nuanced production that was seen by millions when shown on Chinese television. Overnight the names of UMKC student actors were known to taxi drivers and food vendors from Beijing to small villages; many Chinese spoke of their appreciation for the care taken by the 'big-nose actors' in their recreation of Chinese manners. Ying returned to UMKC in 1984 to direct *Fifteen Strings of Cash* for MRT. His son, Ying Da (Dan Ying), earned his MFA in acting/directing at UMKC in 1987 and is now a prominent film actor (*Farewell My Concubine*) and television director" (http://cas.umkc.edu/theatre/about.html). Ying Ruocheng directed *The Family* for UMKC in October 1982 and *Fifteen Strings of Cash* for MRT (Missouri Repertory Theatre) in September 1984. For a review of the latter production, see Robert W. Butler, "'15 Strings of Cash' Pays Off Quite Nicely," *Kansas City Star*, September 7, 1984.

27. This list represents a partial itinerary of Ying's travels to lecture at various universities November 3–30, 1982. Of particular note is the fact that they were greeted in Philadelphia on November 3, 1982, by Allyn and Adele Rickett, who accompanied them on their travels in Pennsylvania, New Jersey, Washington, DC, and Maryland until November 9, including hosting them at their home over the weekend of November 6–7 ("Lecture Schedule," unpublished document, UMKC).

28. *Fifteen Strings of Cash* was performed September 6–16, 1984, at MRT. Titled *Shiwuguan* in Chinese, it was adapted by the Zhejiang Kunju Opera Troupe in 1955, based on the story by Qing dynasty scholar Zhu Sucheng. In the seventeenth-century tale of corruption that nearly ruins the lives of innocent young lovers, the main character Kuang Zhong (a version of the upright official Bao Zheng character in Chinese literature and opera) is told in a dream about a miscarriage of justice; he investigates carefully to right the wrong, explaining that the victim has been misled by superstitious ideology and feudal doctrines. Tao Jin directed an operatic film adaptation in 1956.

29. John Ezell was Hall Family Foundation Professor of Scenic Design at UMKC and Felicia Londré was Curators' Professor of Theatre. They visited Ying in China from December 27, 1991, to January 8, 1992 (with Londré arriving a few days before Ezell and his partner Gene Friedman), continuing a collaboration on a book project begun when Ying was in Kansas City (which was never completed).

30. In a riveting account in her personal diary, Felicia Londré details all events and conversations that took place between July 22 and September 2, 1991, related to

the aborted *King Lear* project. Described in vivid detail is a complex web that involves most centrally concerns about Ying Ruocheng's health and "stamina" along with Keathley's feelings of intimidation working with an actor of Ying's intellectual caliber and international renown.

The meet-and-greet for cast members and production staff—along with design presentations, script cuts, and read-through—took place from 1 p.m. to 5:45 p.m. on August 6, 1991, and continued in the evening after a two-hour break. Londré went to Seattle from August 7 to 11 while rehearsals got underway, and was struck the day after her return with an unexpected "bombshell of international proportions"—the news that Ying and Keathley had "agreed that Ying should give up the role of Lear, because he doesn't have the stamina." Two days later, an article in the local press reported that "internationally known Chinese actor Ying Ruocheng . . . has dropped out of the production [after] decid[ing] he should withdraw from the role because of health reasons, [according to] Keathley," indicating that Ying had been replaced by fellow cast member Richard Bowden. (Robert Trussell, "Actor Leaves Rep's 'Lear,'" *Kansas City Star*, August 14, 1991: G-8.)

Keathley's was an assessment with which others vehemently disagreed, but by the time they were consulted, it was too late. The situation caused a great loss of face for Ying Ruocheng (and, by extension, Ying Da, who had recently completed his master's degree in directing at UMKC). Londré describes her devastation at the turn of events, particularly Keathley's denying himself "an opportunity most directors would die for" to work with a "world-class talent and a brilliant mind," thereby ruining "the best thing that had ever happened to the Rep." Londré and others quoted in her diary lament the fact that Ying was treated so poorly, and they express admiration for the dignity with which he handled the situation.

In spite of the fact that the bleeding incident on opening night of *Major Barbara* on June 1, 1991, was the first sign of Ying's illness, he was in generally good health for three years between that incident and a serious attack during which he vomited blood on September 24, 1994 (after which his cirrhosis was finally diagnosed). When he arrived in Kansas City in August 1991, Ying did not display quite the zest he had possessed while at UMKC and MRT a decade earlier, but Londré, Ying Da, and others remain certain that Ying was healthy enough to play the role of Lear, and indeed capable. Londré was present at the read-through and remarks in her journal on Ying's superior command of the language compared to the other actors; in a subsequent entry, she relays that Ying Da had attended all five rehearsals, during which Keathley had offered no specific direction to (nor expressed any apparent dissatisfaction with) Ying regarding his role or its depiction.

Londré's final two diary entries (August 28 and September 2, 1991) indicate that complications had arisen regarding payment that was due to Ying by UMKC and MRT, and also that Ying Da would return to China on September 5 to begin his role in a film (*Farewell My Concubine*), while Ying Da's wife, Song Dandan, would remain with Ying Ruocheng while he went to Virginia. Londré and Ying agreed to meet at Yale the weekend of September 13, and Ying had plans to meet Arthur Miller in New

York City on September 17. He also expressed hopes of returning to Beijing via Taiwan in order to negotiate a tour of *Death of a Salesman* and *Major Barbara*, and to visit his father's gravesite for the first time; however, this visit would not occur until 1993.

31. These remarks were made by Ying Ruocheng on August 21, 2003 (Audiotape 5).

32. Marvin H. Green Jr. (Bowdoin College '57, H'99, P'80) is currently a trustee emeritus of Bowdoin College. When he traveled to China, he was still serving as president of the Bowdoin College Board of Overseers (a body that dissolved and became the Board of Trustees in 1996). Ying was slightly older than Green, so Green was certainly not under forty-five years old when he met Ying in China, but he was a distinguished businessman (his corporate directorships include the international consulting firm Polaris Corporation and the Bermuda-based mutual fund LePercq/Ameur). Green himself received an honorary doctorate from his alma mater in 1999, and was cited on that occasion for his generosity to the college, including his endowment of a professorship in film studies and a gift to renovate an auditorium used for film screenings and live performances.

33. Ma Yingjiu (Ma Ying-jeou) earned law degrees from Taiwan University (1972), New York University, and Harvard University, and became a personal translator for President Jiang Jingguo (Chiang Ching-kuo) upon his return to Taiwan. Ma was deputy secretary-general of the KMT from 1984 to 1988, and President Li Denghui (Lee Teng-hui) appointed him minister of justice in 1993, a post he held until 1996. He was mayor of Taibei (Taipei) from 1998 to 2006 and chairman of the Kuomintang from 2005 to 2007. In 2008 he became president of Taiwan.

34. *Top Restaurant* (*Tianxia diyilou*), about a famous Peking duck restaurant, was written by female playwright He Jiping and opened at the Capital Theatre in Beijing on June 12, 1988. When performed in Taipei May 17–June 5, 1993, it was indeed the first mainland drama staged there since 1949 and was thus a very significant cultural and political event. Among the group from Beijing participating in the tour (in addition to the play's large cast and crew) were Ying Ruocheng, Yu Shizhi, and composer Wu Zuqiang—famous for his score for the model revolutionary ballet *The Red Detachment of Women*. (E-mail from Yang Lixin, February 1, 2008.) Direct flights to Taiwan did not begin until 2008.

35. Zhang Xueliang (1901–2001), nicknamed the Young Marshal, was son of warlord Zhang Zuolin and ruled Manchuria and much of north China after his father was assassinated by the Japanese in 1928. He instigated the Xi'an Incident of December 12, 1936 (capturing Chiang Kai-shek and holding him by force until he agreed to a United Front with the Communists on December 25), for which he spent over fifty years under house arrest, both before and after the KMT evacuation from China in 1949. Zhang was not released from house arrest until 1990, after the death of Chiang Kai-shek's son and successor Chiang Ching-kuo, making him perhaps the world's longest-serving political prisoner. He immigrated to Hawaii in 1993, sometime after Ying Ruocheng's visit to Taiwan. He was often invited to visit mainland China, where he is considered a patriotic hero, but he

claimed political neutrality between the KMT and CCP and declined. He is buried in Hawaii, where he died of pneumonia in 2001.

36. Ying Ruocheng's final thoughts about his family's legacy and China's present condition are drawn from interviews on four different days in 2003 (August 14, 16, 21, and 24—Audiotapes 2, 5, and 6), as well as two additional sources: his September 27, 1999, article in *Time* magazine titled "China's Wild Ride," and his acceptance speech for the Ramon Magsaysay Award in the Philippines on August 31, 1998. Ying received the 1998 Ramon Magsaysay Award in the field of Journalism, Literature and Creative Communication Arts—one of six categories of the award given annually in memory of the young president of the Philippines who was killed in a tragic plane crash on March 17, 1957. In 1998, Filipina Corazon Aquino received the award in the category of Peace and International Understanding. Other recipients were from Pakistan, Cambodia, and Thailand. The citation for Ying Ruocheng "recognizes his enhancing China's cultural dialogue with the world-at-large and with its own rich heritage through a brilliant and persevering life in the theater" (http://www.rmaf.org.ph/Awardees/Citation/CitationYingRuo.htm). Ying's trip to receive the award was his last travel overseas before his death in 2003.

Epilogue

1. Ying Da's recollections come from two taped interviews, on June 15, 2004, and August 18, 2007.

2. Lin Zhaohua's production of *Coriolanus*, translated by Ying Ruocheng, opened at the Beijing People's Art Theatre on November 27, 2007, with Pu Cunxin in the title role.

Bibliography

English Sources

Barry, Peter, MM. "Fujen Catholic University Celebrates 80 Years of Its Foundation." *Tripod*, Vol. 26, no. 142 (2006): 15–24.

Chen, John Shujie. *The Rise and Fall of Fu Ren University, Beijing: Catholic Higher Education in China*. New York: RoutledgeFalmer, 2004.

Conceison, Claire. *Significant Other: Staging the American in China*. University of Hawaii Press, 2004.

Conceison, Claire. "In Memoriam: Ying Ruocheng 1929–2003." *American Theatre*, (January 2005): 26–27.

Goodwin, James. *Autobiography: The Self Made Text*. NY: Twayne Publishers, 1993.

Guo Baoqin and Hu Kaimin, eds. *Mao Zedong Poems* (*Mao Zedong Shici*), bilingual edition. Beijing: Foreign Languages Press, 2003.

Heston, Charlton. *Beijing Diary*. New York: Simon and Schuster, 1990.

Hua Sheng. "Big Character Posters in China: A Historical Survey." *Journal of Asian Law*, Vol. 4, no. 2 (1991).

Lao She. *Teahouse* (trans. Ying Ruocheng). China Translation and Publishing Corporation and Theater Museum of Beijing People's Art Theater, 2005.

Lee, Hong Yung. *The Politics of the Chinese Cultural Revolution*. Berkeley: University of California Press, 1978.

MacFarquhar, Roderick. *The Origins of the Cultural Revolution* (Volumes 1, 2, and 3). Royal Institute of International Affairs (Oxford University Press and Columbia University Press): 1974, 1983, 1997.

Mackerras, Colin. *Modern China: A Chronology from 1842 to the Present*. London: Thames and Hudson, 1982.

Mackerras, Colin. *The New Cambridge Handbook of Contemporary China*. Cambridge, UK: Cambridge University Press, 2001.

Meisner, Maurice. *Mao's China and After: A History of the People's Republic*, third edition. New York: Free Press, 1999.

Miller, Arthur. *"Salesman" in Beijing*. New York: Viking Press, 1983.

Morath, Inge, and Arthur Miller. *Chinese Encounters*. New York: Farrar, Straus and Giroux, 1979.

Paragon, Donald. "Ying Lien-chih (1866–1926) and the Rise of Fu Jen, the Catholic University of Peking." *Monumenta Serica*, Vol. 20 (1961).

Rickett, Allyn, and Adele Rickett. *Prisoners of Liberation: Four Years in a Chinese Communist Prison*. New York: Doubleday Anchor Books, 1973 (originally published by Cameron Associates, 1957).

Roberts, J. A. G. *A Concise History of China*. Cambridge, MA: Harvard University Press, 1999.

Schell, Orville, and David Shambaugh, eds. *The China Reader: The Reform Era*. New York: Vintage Books, 1999.

Schoenhals, Michael, ed. *China's Cultural Revolution, 1966–1969: Not a Dinner Party*. Armonk, NY: M.E. Sharpe, 1996.

Sheridan, James E. *China in Disintegration*. New York: Free Press, 1975.

Tian Benxiang, ed. *Modern Chinese Drama* (trans. Yang Liping). Beijing: Culture and Art Publishing House, 1999.

Wang Ke-wen. "*Dagongbao* and the *Guomindang*: Public Opinion in Nationalist China, 1927–37." Unpublished paper, 2004.

Wang Ke-wen. "The *Dagongbao* and Wartime Chinese Politics, 1937–45." Unpublished paper, 2006.

Wintle, Justin. *The Timeline History of China*. New York: Barnes & Noble, 2002, 2005.

Chinese Sources

Beijing renmin yishu juyuan 1952–2002 (Beijing People's Art Theatre 1952–2002). Beijing: Renmin wenxue chubanshe, 2002.

Chang Hua. "Yingshi jiazu de jiwei jiechu renwu" (Several Outstanding Members of the Ying Clan) in *Xinhai geming hou de Beijing Manzu* (Manchu Beijingers after the Xinhai Revolution). Beijing chubanshe, 2002.

Chang Hua. "Ying Lianzhi" in *Mingren yu lao fangzi* (Famous People and Old Dwellings). Beijing chubanshe, 2004.

Hou Jie. "*Dagong bao*" *yu jindai Zhongguo shehui* (The *Dagong bao* and Contemporary Chinese Society). Nankai daxue chubanshe, 2006.

"Huainian pian" (Cherished Memory Essays). *Beijing People's Art Theatre Journal*, no. 1 (2004): 29–52 [five remembrances of Ying Ruocheng, including transcript of speakers at official posthumous memorial].

Huang Weidiao and Zhou Ruixiang. "*Huihuang de yishu diantang*"—*Beijing renmin yishu juyuan wushi nian* ("Splendid Art Palace"—Fifty Years of the Beijing People's Art Theatre). Beijing: Jinghua bolan congshu, 2002.

Liang Yuansheng. "Sanzhong wenhua shenfen de ronghe: Zhongguo xiandai lishi xingcheng de Yingjian sandai" (The Fusion of Three Cultural Positions) in *RuYe duihua xinlicheng* (New Developments in Confucian-Christian Dialogue). Chung Chi College, Chinese University of Hong Kong, Religion and Chinese Society Research Center, 2001.

Li Ke and Li You'an. *Liang ge Meiguo jiandie de zishu* (Confessions of Two American Spies). Beijing: Qunzhong chubanshe, 1958.

Li Ke and Li You'an. *Zhonggong jianyu shenghuo zhenxiang* (The Truth about Life in a Chinese Prison). Hong Kong: Tiandi tushu youxian gongsi, 1978.

Liu Liexiong, ed. *Zhongguo shi da ziju daoyan dashi* (Ten Great Chinese Directors). Beijing: Zhongguo Renmin Daxue chubanshe, 2005.

Wu Tong. *Naren nayi* (Those People, That Art). Beijing: Jinghua chubanshe, 2004.

Ying Da. *Fuqi juchang—mingren qinggan shilu* (Couples Theatre—A True Record of Celebrity Feelings). Zhongguo wenlian chubanshe, 2004.

Zhang Fan. *Huashuo Beijing Renyi* (Tales of Beijing People's Art Theatre). Beijing: Baihua wenyi chubanshe, 2004.

Selected Sources by and about Ying Ruocheng

"Biography of Ying Ruocheng." The 1998 Ramon Magsaysay Award for Journalism, Literature and Creative Communication Arts. http://www.rmaf.org.ph/Awardees/Biography/BiographyYingRuo.htm.

Ke Wenhui, ed. *Ying Ruocheng*. Beijing People's Art Theatre Artist Series. Beijing October Literature and Art Press, 1992.

Mufson, Steven. "Changing Channels: From Red Guard to Avant-Garde." *Washington Post*, June 15, 1998: A1.

Pao, Angela C. "Changing Faces: Recasting National Identity in All-Asian(-)American Dramas." *Theatre Journal*, Vol. 53, no. 3 (2001): 389–410.

Wang Jing. "You Ying Ruocheng xiansheng de yizuo shuoqi" (A Discussion of Mr. Ying Ruocheng's Translation Work). *Journal of the Beijing People's Art Theatre*, no. 2 (2000): 43–44.

Wilson, Patricia. " . . . A Real Interpreter Who Can Also Act." *Chinese Literature*, no. 3 (1982): 55–75.

"Xiju rensheng" (Theatre and Human Life). *Beijing Youth Daily*, December 24, 1999: 3.

Ying Ruocheng. Prison notebooks and notes (1968–1971, unpublished).

Ying Ruocheng. "Lao She and His *Teahouse*." *Chinese Literature*, no. 12 (1979): 3–11.

Ying Ruocheng. Audiotaped and videotaped interviews with Claire Conceison. June 1994, July 2000, June–July 2001, May 2002, August 2003.

Ying Ruocheng. "China's Wild Ride" (cover story). *Time International*, September 27, 1999: 28–34.

Ying Ruocheng, trans. *Ying Ruocheng mingju yisi* (Ying Ruocheng Famous Play Translation Collection [8 vols.], includes *Teahouse* by Lao She, *Family* by Ba Jin, *Uncle Doggie's Nirvana* by Jin Yun, *Measure for Measure* by William Shakespeare, *Death of a Salesman* by Arthur Miller, *Major Barbara* by George Bernard Shaw, *Caine Mutiny Court Martial* by Herman Wouk, *Amadeus* by Peter Shaffer). Beijing: China Foreign Translation Publishing Corporation, 1999.

Ying Ruocheng. *Ying Ruocheng yi mingju wuzhong* (Ying Ruocheng's Translations of Five Famous Plays). Liaoning Education Press, 2001.

Selected Sources on Autobiography and Oral History

Bjorklund, Diane. *Interpreting the Self*. Chicago: University of Chicago Press, 1998.

Chamberlain, Mary, and Paul Thompson, eds. *Narrative and Genre*. London: Routledge, 1998.

Charlton, Thomas L., Lois E. Myers, and Rebecca Sharpless. *Handbook of Oral History*. Lanham, MD: Altamira Press, 2006.

Clifford, James, and George E. Marcus, eds. *Writing Culture: The Poetics and Politics of Ethnography*. Berkeley: University of California Press, 1986.

Derrida, Jacques. *The Ear of the Other: Otobiography, Transference, Translation*. New York: Schocken Books, 1985.

Dunaway, David K., and Willa K. Baum, eds. *Oral History: An Interdisciplinary Anthology* (second edition). Lanham, MD: Altamira Press, 1996.

Eakin, Paul John. *How Our Lives Become Stories: Making Selves*. Ithaca, NY: Cornell University Press, 1999.

Gunn, Janet Varner. *Autobiography: Towards a Poetics of Experience*. Philadelphia: University of Pennsylvania Press, 1982.

Hoopes, James. *Oral History: An Introduction for Students*. University of North Carolina Press, 1979.

LeJeune, Philippe. *Je est un Autre*. Paris: Editions du Seuil, 1980.

LeJeune, Philippe. *On Autobiography* (trans. Katherine Leary, ed. Paul John Eakin). Minneapolis: University of Minnesota Press, 1989.

Olney, James, ed. *Autobiography: Essays Theoretical and Critical*. Princeton, NJ: Princeton University Press, 1980.

Olney, James. *Memory and Narrative*. Chicago: University of Chicago Press, 1998.

Perks, Robert, and Alistair Thomson, eds. *The Oral History Reader*. London: Routledge, 1998.

Rios, Theodore, and Kathleen Mullen Sands. *Telling a Good One: The Process of a Native American Collaborative Biography*. Lincoln: University of Nebraska Press, 2000.

Smith, Sidonie, and Julia Watson. *Reading Autobiography: A Guide for Interpreting Life Narratives*. Minneapolis: University of Minnesota Press, 2002.

Zinsser, William, ed. *Inventing the Truth: The Art and Craft of Memoir*. Mariner, 1998.

Index

239

About the Authors

Ying Ruocheng (1929–2003) graduated from Qinghua University in 1950 and became a founding member of the Beijing People's Art Theatre, where he performed as an actor and served as an archivist, literary supervisor, and director. He is the translator of numerous plays from English into Chinese and vice versa, including works by William Shakespeare, Arthur Miller, and Lao She. Between 1982 and 1993, he was a visiting professor and guest director at several universities in the United States, and received an honorary doctorate from Bowdoin College in 1993. He was appointed China's vice minister of culture 1986–1990, and remained a member of the National Congress until shortly before his death. A featured actor in Bernardo Bertolucci's films *The Last Emperor* (1987) and *Little Buddha* (1993), he also starred as Kublai Khan in the 1982 Italian-Sino-American joint production *Marco Polo*. He was the grandson of Ying Lianzhi (1866–1926, founder of the *Dagongbao* newspaper and Furen Catholic University), son of Ying Qianli (1900–1969, a prominent scholar and educator in Taiwan), and father of actor, director, and television host Ying Da.

Claire Conceison is associate professor in the Department of Drama and Dance at Tufts University, where she is also on the faculties of the Asian Studies and International Relations programs. She earned her PhD in theatre studies from Cornell University in 2000, her master's degree in regional studies–East Asia from Harvard University in 1992, and her bachelor's degree in theatre and East Asian studies from Wesleyan University in 1987.

Her publications include *Significant Other: Staging the American in China* (2004, University of Hawai'i Press) and numerous articles in academic journals in performance and Asian studies. She has conducted research in the Beijing and Shanghai theatre communities since 1990 and is the translator of several contemporary Chinese plays, as well as being an active director. She is an associate in research at the Fairbank Center for Chinese Studies at Harvard University.

Made in the USA
San Bernardino, CA
07 September 2016